Our Maryland Heritage

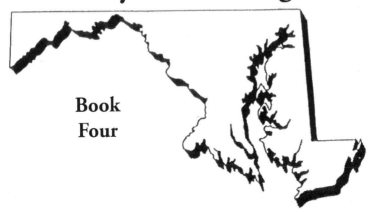

**Book
Four**

The
Watkins
Families

William N. Hurley, Jr.

HERITAGE BOOKS
2009

HERITAGE BOOKS

AN IMPRINT OF HERITAGE BOOKS, INC.

Books, CDs, and more—Worldwide

For our listing of thousands of titles see our website
at
www.HeritageBooks.com

Published 2009 by
HERITAGE BOOKS, INC.
Publishing Division
100 Railroad Ave. #104
Westminster, Maryland 21157

International Standard Book Numbers
Paperbound: 978-0-7884-0752-9
Clothbound: 978-0-7884-8260-1

ALSO BY W. N. HURLEY, JR.

Available from the publisher: Heritage Books, Inc.

Neikirk-Newkirk-Nikirk, Volume 1

Neikirk-Newkirk-Nikirk, Volume 2

Hurley Families in America, Volume 1

Hurley Families in America, Volume 2

John William Hines 1600, And His Descendants

Maddox, A Southern Maryland Family

Pratt Families of Virginia

Lowder Families in America

Our Maryland Heritage Series:

    Book One: The Fry Families

    Book Two: The Walker Families

    Book Three: The Fulks Families

INTRODUCTION

The fourth in a series of studies of Maryland families and their descendants, this volume presents an introductory look at the descendants of the Watkins families in Montgomery County, and other counties of Maryland.

As some indication of the prevalence of the Watkins clan in Montgomery County, reference is made to the 1879 *Atlas of Fifteen Miles Around Washington, Including the County of Montgomery, Maryland*, compiled from actual surveys by C. M. Hopkins, CE. In the index of that study, there are no less than sixteen references to Watkins families, including: Ed Watkins in the Bethesda District; G. Watkins in Clarksburg; Joseph S. Watkins heirs in Clarksburg; L. L. Watkins in the city of Rockville; L. M. Watkins in Damascus (adjoining the store of R. A. Hurley, a family member of the author); Lorenzo Watkins in Clarksburg and the village of Hyattstown; Noah Watkins in Clarksburg; O. P. Watkins in Cracklin and Mechanicsville Districts; Oliver T. Watkins at Cedar Grove; Perry Watkins, R. G. Watkins and Richard Watkins, all in Clarksburg District; Rudolph Watkins in Rockville District; Samuel B. Watkins at Browningsville; Spencer Watkins in Bethesda District; and William Watkins in Clarksburg.

I am grateful for the information furnished to me by various members of the family, and allied families, still living in and around Gaithersburg, Montgomery County, Maryland, and for their patience in working with me on this study.

I would like particularly to thank Jane Sween at the library of the Montgomery County Historical Society in Rockville, Maryland, for her encouragement and generous assistance; without her, much of this report would not have been possible.

ORDER OF PRESENTATION

The study concerns itself primarily with the descendants of John Watkins, 3rd, who died c.1696 in Anne Arundel County, Maryland. He appears as the principal subject of Chapter 2. Chapters 3, 4 and 5 follow his numerous descendants in accordance with the following chart of lineal descent (Thomas, born 1774, is discussed in the chapter with his father, Jeremiah):

John Watkins, 3rd	Chapter 2
died c.1696	
*	
*	
Nicholas Watkins, Sr.	Chapter 3
1691-	
*	
*	
Jeremiah Watkins	Chapter 4
1747-	
*	
*	
Thomas Watkins	
1774-	
*	
*	
Alpha Watkins	Chapter 5
1803-	

Chapter 6 is devoted to the descendants of Samuel B. Watkins, born 1807; Chapter 7 to the descendants of Denton Watkins, born 1795; both in Montgomery County, Maryland. Neither has been identified in the main body of the study, but both are believed to be related. Finally, Chapters 8 and 9 will discuss a number of other individuals, bearing the Watkins surname, found in the same geographic areas as the others discussed, and perhaps related. Further study is required.

CONTENTS

*To be ignorant of what occurred before you
were born is to remain always a child.
For what is the worth of human life unless
it is woven into the lives of our ancestors.*

- *Cicero*

CHAPTER 1

Early Watkins Families
Primarily of Anne Arundel County

We began our initial research into the Watkins genealogy at the library of the Montgomery County Historical Society, located in Rockville, Maryland. There, in a family folder file, we found a number of papers dealing with various members of the family. One packet, with no name of the submitter, but apparently a descendant of Robert Ellsworth Dubel, contained information indicating that one of the earliest known ancestors of the Watkins family was one Watkins Watkins, born about 1410 in Wales. The papers then follow his descendants in a single male line for several generations, tracing their arrival in Virginia in the company of Captain John Smith, and finally to Maryland. Although we find some problems with certain dates appearing in the document, and have not personally verified the information presented, we have followed the lineage here in order to establish a background.

Watkins Watkins
1410-

This individual is said to have been born in Wales, and probably had several children, among them:
1. William Watkins, who died c.1539 at Shotten, England, having had at least two children:
   a. William Watkins, 2nd.
   b. Francis Watkins, who married Elizabeth Lee of the Virginia families associated with General Robert E. Lee. They had children, including:
      (1) James Watkins, of whom more.

1

James Watkins

This individual is said to be a son of Francis Watkins and Elizabeth Lee, probably born in England. He reportedly sailed with Captain John Smith during the "Three Voyages of Discovery" and Captain Smith named Watkins Point in his honor. He was married, and had at least three children:

1. John Watkins, 1st, died after 1665 at South Pond, Nansemond County, Virginia. He reportedly arrived in Virginia about 1638, when he received a grant of land for 150 acres in James City County, for having transported three persons to settle. In 1644, he received 200 acres on the Elizabeth River, and later lived in Nansemond, where he died. He was married to Frances, who was born before 1650 and died before 1680. After the death of John, Frances was married second to Edward Lloyd, who was commander of the Puritans on the Severn River in Maryland. At the time of her marriage, she released her dower rights in the lands of her first husband, with the stipulation that her son, John Watkins, 2nd, was to be compensated by Lloyd. This is perhaps the same Colonel Edward Lloyd who held the estate of *Linton*, on the Wye River, in Talbot County, Maryland. According to local history, Colonel Lloyd came to the area from Virginia, was named to the Governor's Council, and acquired more than five thousand acres in Talbot County. He was a skilled surveyor, a politician, fur trader, planter, merchant, shipper, tobacco buyer, agent for immigrants, and a land speculator. John Watkins, 1st had children, including:

   a. Sarah Watkins.

   b. John Watkins, 2nd. In 1658, Edward Lloyd surveyed out 100 acres of land, whereupon John Watkins, 2nd, demanded more land as his right. In 1663, he received title to *Watkins Hope*, containing 100 acres on the north side of the West River, in Anne Arundel County, and in 1675 was living on the Severn River near Annapolis. Under the will of Edward Lloyd, he is described as a son-in-law, but is actually the step-son of Lloyd, as discussed above. He was married to Alice Lloyd, daughter of Edward Lloyd and Alice Crouch, and died about February 26, 1696/97. They had children, including:

    (1)   Ann Watkins, who married first to John Watkins Lord. She married second August 13, 1697 to William Burgess, Jr., the son of Colonel William Burgess and his wife, Ursula. The will of William Burgess, Jr. left one thousand acres of land in Baltimore County to the children of his wife by her first marriage to Lord.

    (2)   John Watkins, 3rd, of whom more in Chapter 2.

2.   Edward Watkins.

3.   Francis Watkins.

Ann Watkins
1737-

This individual is included here, although we have not yet established a direct connection with the family groups just discussed above. It most surely exists, however, in recognition of the fact that she lived in Anne Arundel County, as did the others first discussed; she married a member of the Harwood family, as did several of the others, and some of her descendants can be shown to have married members of these same families. She could be the Ann Watkins who was born 1737 and married Richard Harwood, and had nine sons and two daughters, who were twins, including:

1.   Richard Harwood, born December 1, 1738, lieutenant colonel, West River Battalion, commissioned March 2, 1778. Married Margaret Hall, born December 17, 1746 in Anne Arundel County, Maryland, daughter of Major Henry Hall and his second wife, Elizabeth Lansdale. Children, born Anne Arundel County:

    a.   Ann Elizabeth Harwood, born December 11, 1769, and married Jonathan Sellman, Jr.; license May 22, 1794.

    b.   Elizabeth Ann Harwood, born February 11, 1770, and married Osborn Harwood; license October 31, 1791.

    c.   Richard Hall Harwood, born October 23, 1771. Married Anne C. Green; license October 23, 1798.

d. Henry Hall Harwood, born April 2, 1773, and married to Elizabeth Lloyd; license February 14, 1805.
e. Joseph Harwood, born April 17, 1775. Married to Anne Chapman; license September 22, 1802.
f. Thomas Harwood, born February 22, 1777.
g. Mary Harwood, born November 23, 1778
h. Henrietta Harwood, born September 14, 1780. Married Thomas Cowman; license November 15, 1798
i. Benjamin Harwood, born January 6, 1783. Married to Henrietta Batte; license October 5, 1811.
j. Priscilla Harwood, born November 14, 1785
k. William Harwood, born March 7, 1788
l. Edward Harwood, born November 23, 1790
2. Thomas Harwood, first treasurer of the Western Shore of Maryland about 1776. Children:
   a. Richard Harwood, married Callahan, and had a son:
      (1) William Harwood married Hester Ann Lockerman. Descendants held *Harwood House* of Annapolis.
3. John Harwood, married Mary Hall, daughter of Major Henry Hall.
4. Samuel Harwood, married Mary Elizabeth Stockett, the daughter of Thomas Stockett, III (1691) and Elizabeth Noble. They moved to Montgomery County, Maryland, and their daughter married Alexander Warfield, of Seneca.
5. Nicholas Harwood, who married and had children:
   a. Sarah Harwood, married Duvall.
6. Mary Harwood, who reportedly married William S. Green. However, *Anne Arundel Gentry*, Volume 2, by Harry Wright Newman, reports the marriage of Mary Harwood, daughter of Richard Harwood and Ann Watkins, on November 13, 1770, to Dr. Thomas Noble Stockett, born July 12, 1747 at *The Obligation* in Anne Arundel County, died May 16, 1802, son of Thomas Stockett, III (1691) and his second wife, Elizabeth Noble of Prince George's County. As reported in *Mareen Duvall of Middle Plantation,* Mary was married to Thomas Noble Harwood, which appears to be an error in printing. Dr. Stockett served as an assistant surgeon during the Revolution, and was a well-read, substantial citizen of his community. At

his death, his personal estate included a violin, books, medical instruments and books, 37 negro slaves, and 37 ounces of silver plate. Ten children were born to the marriage of Mary Harwood and Thomas Noble Stockett:

a.   Mary Harwood Stockett, born December 4, 1771; died July 26, 1827. She married May 14, 1799 William Alexander, a merchant of Annapolis. Children:
   (1)   Thomas Alexander.
   (2)   William Alexander, Jr.
   (3)   Mary Alexander.
   (4)   Anne E. Alexander.
   (5)   June Alexander.
   (6)   John H. Alexander.

b.   Richard Galen Stockett, born February 7, 1776 at the family estate called *The Obligation*. He studied medicine in Philadelphia, and became a doctor like his father. Married March 28, 1799 to Margaret Hall, born April 11, 1781, daughter of Henry Hall and Margaret Howard (1752). Richard Galen settled in what later became Howard County, where he died February 27, 1861. His will, dated 1858, was probated in Howard March 19, 1861, in which he requested burial between his wife and daughter in the orchard near their home. One son, and the deceased daughter, unknown:
   (1)   George Lee Stockett, born August 15, 1800, and died c.1875 at *Stockwood*. Marriage license dated December 4, 1821 in Anne Arundel County, for marriage to Christiana Walton Thompson. They had children:
      (a)   Margaret Ann Stockett, married November 30, 1847 to Rinaldi W. Dorsey.
      (b)   Maria R. Stockett, born c.1826.
      (c)   Georgette Stockett, born c.1828, married November 11, 1856 to John Shaaff Stockett.
      (d)   Galena Stockett, born c.1830.
      (e)   John Thomas Stockett, born about 1832, an engineer, married to his cousin, Mary Sophia Stockett, born November 16, 1831, daughter

of Joseph Noble Stockett and Sophia Watkins (1799), and widow of Dr. Richard Harwood Cowman. License dated February 10, 1859, Anne Arundel County.

    (f)   Frances E. Stockett, born c.1845

c.   Thomas Mifflin Stockett, born December 4, 1777; died at sea in 1799 in an engagement with French privateers, single.

d.   Joseph Noble Stockett, born November 11, 1779 at *The Obligation* in Anne Arundel County, and died December 21, 1854. Married November 19, 1812 to Ann Caroline Batte, born June 3, 1797, and died December 22, 1814, with no surviving issue. She was the daughter of Captain John Batte, and his wife, Lucy Batte. Joseph Noble was married second June 25, 1816 to Ann Sellman, born July 1, 1795, and died July 19, 1824, daughter of General Jonathan Sellman. They had several children, most of whom died young. Only one of them is listed here below, as his first child. He married third November 17, 1825 to Sophia Watkins, born November 8, 1799, and died April 11, 1839, daughter of Colonel Joseph Watkins (1776) and his wife, Ann Gray. Nine children, and Sophia died the day after the birth of the last one. Joseph Noble married for the fourth time May 30, 1841 Anne Watkins, the sister of his third wife, born October 14, 1795, and died childless May 2, 1846. The nine children born to the marriage to Sophia Watkins are included in the section devoted to her family, which see. The one surviving child born to the second marriage of Joseph Noble Stockett was:

    (1)   Francis Henry Stockett, born May 1, 1821, and married November 19, 1846 Mary Priscilla Hall, daughter of William Hall and Margaret Harwood.

e.   Helen Stockett, born June 27, 1782; married to Robert McGill and settled in Kentucky. License dated June 4, 1804 in Anne Arundel County, Maryland.

f.   Margaret Rutha Stockett, born July 17, 1784, single.

g. William Shippen Stockett, born November 4, 1786, and married Margaret Rutter of Baltimore. He was a captain in the merchant marine and died at sea of yellow fever on April 16, 1818. Marriage license April 18, 1812 in Anne Arundel County.

h. John Shaaf Stockett, born November 27, 1788. Married Ann Matilda Grason, of Queen Anne's County; license dated April 18, 1812, Anne Arundel County.

i. Ann Stockett, born June 10, 1792, and married to Roderick Warfield.

j. Eleanor Stockett, born April 15, 1797. Married Turenne Watkins, son of Colonel Gassaway Watkins (1752), and moved to Kentucky.

7. Matilda Harwood, married John Nicholas Watkins. However, notice the discussion relative to her sister, immediately above, relative to reports that Mary had married William S. Green, which is apparently incorrect. Marriage records report that John Nicholas Watkins was married at Annapolis, January, 1836, to Matilda Green, which could be Matilda Harwood Green, from a prior marriage.

8. Nicholas Harwood, married his cousin, Mary Augustus Harwood.

9. Benjamin Harwood, single, succeeded his brother as Treasurer of the Western Shore of Maryland.

CHAPTER 2

John Watkins, 3rd
died 1696

This son of John Watkins, 2nd, and Alice Lloyd, was married in 1688 to Ann Gassaway, daughter of Colonel Thomas Gassaway and Hester Besson. After the death of John Watkins, 3rd, who was buried February 27, 1696, his widow married second Captain Richard Jones. The children of John Watkins, 3rd will be first listed following in order, and then each child will be discussed in detail following:

1. John Watkins, 4th, born August 15, 1689, of whom more as Child 1.
2. Nicholas Watkins, Sr., born March 3, 1691 and died 1757 or 1770, of whom more as Child 2, and in Chapter 3, which see
3. Elizabeth Watkins, born April 11, 1693; married January 27, 1714 to Samuel Smith, of whom more as Child 3.
4. Gassaway Watkins, born March 31, 1695, of whom more as Child 4.
5. Ann M. Watkins, of whom more as Child 5.

CHILD 1

John Watkins, 4th
1689-1743

This son of John Watkins, 3rd (died 1696) and Ann Gassaway was born in Anne Arundel County, Maryland, August 15, 1689 and died in 1743, leaving three sons and four daughters. Married in All Hallows Parish about 1715 to Mary Warman of Prince George's County, Maryland, daughter of Stephen Warman, who was descended from Colonel Ninian Beall, commander of the Maryland Rangers, and held an estate in Prince George's County, Maryland. In 1715, he conveyed land in Kent County, on Swan Creek, which he had inherited from his father, to his brother, Nicholas Watkins, Sr. Children, including at least:

1. Elizabeth Watkins, born March 8, 1715 and died March 3, 1733.

2. Sarah Watkins, born July 3, 1718; married first to Keene, and second Thomas Gassaway, son of Colonel Nicholas Gassaway and Catharine Worthington. In her mother's will, Sarah is called Sarah Keene. She was the second wife of Thomas Gassaway, who had first been married to Sarah Dorsey, widow of C. Geist. Thomas left his entire estate to Sarah, including the tract called *Uplands* near Triadelphia; originally held by Sarah Geist from her first marriage; which she sold to Joseph Dick. Thomas Gassaway was the father of several children, although we are not quite sure from which of his marriages. For the record, his family included:

   a. Nicholas Gassaway, married Amelia Berry, and held lands near Glenelg, including the tracts called: *Dorsey's Addition to Thomas' Lot*, and *Morehouses Generosity*. He had children:
      (1) Hanson Gassaway.
      (2) John Gassaway, who was married to Eliza Dorsey, daughter of Caleb Dorsey and Mary Gassaway.
      (3) Berry Gassaway.

3. Ann Watkins, born January 4, 1720.

4. Frances Watkins, born May 1, 1723; married February 16, 1742 to John Hammond Dorsey of *Success*, born 1718 and died February 12, 1774, the son of John Dorsey and Comfort Stinson. Children:

   a. John Hammond Dorsey, Jr., born 1744; died 1748
   b. Stephen Dorsey, born 1747; died 1749
   c. Mary Hammond Dorsey, born March 21, 1749. Married John Hammond Cromwell, born 1745, died 1819, son of Thomas Cromwell of Huntingdon, England, and Venetia Wooguist, of Wales. Ten children.
   d. Rebecca Dorsey, born March 22, 1752; married in 1768 to John Lane.

e. John Hammond Dorsey, Jr., second use of the name, born 1754, and married twice: first to Anne Maxwell, and second to Zilfew.

f. Frances Dorsey, born April 18, 1756

g. Stephen Dorsey, a second use of the name, born March 7, 1758, and married to Rachel Ewing.

h. Anne Maxwell Dorsey, perhaps.

i. James Maxwell Dorsey, married in 1789 Martha McComas, and moved to Ohio.

5. Mary Watkins, born May 10, 1725; died about age 18

6. John Watkins, 5th, born September 7, 1727, of whom more

7. Hester Watkins, born January 26, 1729; married Lane.

8. Jane Watkins, born June 22, 1732, and married Anthony Smith. At least one daughter, named in her grandmother's will:

a. Mary Smith.

9. Stephen Watkins, born June 27, 1735, married February 1, 1757 Eleanor Boyd, who died in Monongalia County, Virginia (now West Virginia), the daughter of Benjamin Boyd. They had children, including:

a. Nicholas Watkins, born March 9, 1758; married to Elizabeth.

b. Benjamin Watkins, born August 2, 1759; married April 16, 1780 to Elizabeth Sheckles.

c. Mary Watkins, born March 17, 1761, and married May 18, 1783 to Gassaway Pindel.

d. Stephen Watkins, born February 3, 1763

e. John Watkins, born November 23, 1764, died February 14, 1815; married December 5, 1797 to Elizabeth Hall, the daughter of William Hall and Margaret Harwood. Children, including:

(1) William Watkins.

(2) Henry Hall Howard Middleton Watkins, born August 14, 1799.

(3) Eleanor Watkins, born September 18, 1800. Married Richard Sellman.

(4) Rachel Sprigg Watkins, born c.1802, and died November 10, 1849; buried at All Hallows, in Anne Arundel County. Married Dr. Thomas Blake Hall,

who died c.1840, the son of Dr. Richard Thomas Hall (1777) and Sarah Bond Blake. They had children, including:

    (a)   Elizabeth Watkins Hall.

    (b)   Thomas Blake Hall.

   (5)   John Edward Watkins, born c.1805

   (6)   Elizabeth Sellman Watkins; April 23, 1808

f.   Thomas Watkins, born February 11, 1767

g.   Eleanor Elizabeth Watkins, born October 10, 1769

h.   Sarah Harwood Watkins, born July 20, 1771

i.   Rachel Watkins, born July 3, 1773

10. Nicholas Watkins, born c.1737, and married January 12, 1764 to Peggy Boyd, daughter of Benjamin Boyd.

John Watkins, 5th
1727-1781

This son of John Watkins, 4th, (1689) and Mary Warman, was born September 7, 1727, and died 1781; married to Esther Belt, daughter of Benjamin Belt, and father of, at least:

1.   John Watkins, 6th, born November 6, 1753.

2.   Leonard Watkins, born 1754, enlisted January 20, 1776, under Captain Barton Lucas and Colonel William Smallwood, served as sergeant in the 6th Maryland Regiment during the Revolution, and later became a member of the House of Delegates from the Medley District of Montgomery County. He died October 10, 1828 at Barnesville, Maryland, where he was a saddler and wheelwright, and a teacher. He was married December, 1781 in Montgomery County, Maryland, to Mary Eleanor Higdon, and was father of at least the following children:

a.   Ann Elizabeth Watkins.

b.   Townsend Watkins.

c.   Benjamin B. Watkins, born September 24, 1788 and died September 12, 1823. Buried at Piketown, Ohio. Married twice; second being to Louisa Red.

d.   William Watkins, born November 2, 1792, died January 26, 1870, and buried at Prospect Cemetery, in Mt. Airy,

Maryland. Married January 24, 1829 in Montgomery County to Henrietta Maria Purdum, born January 17, 1809, died June 23, 1888, daughter of John Purdum and Eleanor M. Riggs. William and Henrietta are buried at Prospect Cemetery, Mt. Airy, Maryland, as are their first two children listed. Children three and five are buried at Providence Cemetery, Kemptown, and child four is buried at Unionville Methodist Cemetery. The five children were born in Frederick County, Maryland:

- (1) Mary Ellen Watkins, born December 5, 1829, and died December 19, 1898. Married to John Penn.
- (2) Martha L. Watkins, born May 9, 1832 and died May 15, 1905. Married to Henry B. Wilson.
- (3) John L. Watkins, born January, 1840; died May, 1920. Married to Margaret J. Flood. The couple are listed in the 1900 census for New Market, in Frederick County, Maryland, with seven of their children:
  - (a) Laura G. Watkins, born c.1877
  - (b) William F. Watkins, born c.1879
  - (c) John L. Watkins, born c.1881
  - (d) Howard H. Watkins, born c.1884
  - (e) Clifford Harris Watkins, born May 23, 1887
  - (f) Winni Voers Watkins, born January 14, 1891
  - (g) Raburn Leonard, born c.1895; christened December 8, 1907.
- (4) Lydia Isabella Watkins, born 1843, died March 13, 1904. Married March 22, 1862 to William G. Wilson.
- (5) Laura Victoria Watkins, born September 5, 1848; died July 4, 1930. Married to Jesse Lemuel Baker.

e. Thomas Watkins, born October 18, 1798, died July 22, 1887. Buried at Sandy Hook, Maryland. Married twice: January 9, 1818 in Montgomery County, Maryland Mary Wilson and second to Sallie Sigler.

f. John Adams Watkins, born July 6, 1802; died October 27, 1886. Buried in Fultonham, Ohio. Married twice: Sarah Smith, and Sarah Jane Southard.

g.   Jetson Watkins. Perhaps the same individual reported married on November 24, 1841 in Montgomery County, Maryland, to Mary L. Grimes.
3.   Mary Ann Watkins, born May 6, 1756; married to Belt.
4.   Stephen Watkins, born February 28, 1758
5.   Elizabeth Watkins, born June 4, 1760
6.   Benjamin Watkins, born c.1762
7.   Margaret Watkins, born June 5, 1767. Apparently married to Ezekiel Phelps in 1794.

CHILD 2

Nicholas Watkins, Sr.
1691-1757/1770

This son of John Watkins, 3rd (died 1696) and Ann Gassaway was born in Anne Arundel County, Maryland, March 3, 1691 and died 1757 or 1770. Married Margaret Lamb, born December 1, 1703 and died about November 7, 1774, daughter of John Lamb and Elizabeth Belt Tydings. Their descendants will be discussed in more detail in Chapter 3, which see.

CHILD 3

Elizabeth Watkins
1693-

This daughter of John Watkins, 3rd (died 1696) and Ann Gassaway was born in Anne Arundel County, Maryland, April 11, 1693 and married January 27, 1714 to Samuel Smith. Nothing more is known of her descendants.

CHILD 4

Gassaway Watkins
1695-1746

This son of John Watkins, 3rd (died 1696) and Ann Gassaway was born in Anne Arundel County, Maryland, March 31, 1695, and died July, 1746. In 1739, under the will of his grandfather, Colonel Thomas Gassaway, this individual received "the farm on which he now lives." Married Elizabeth Ijams (or Elizabeth Rawlings), and had children:

1. John Watkins, baptized August 6, 1718. Perhaps married to Ann Hall Rutland under license dated October 27, 1791 in Anne Arundel County, as her second husband (see above). Three children:
    a. Rachel Watkins, born August 5, 1792
    b. Julia Anna Watkins, born October 22, 1794
    c. Elizabeth Watkins, baptized August 24, 1801
2. Anne Watkins, born January 4, 1719, married John Hammond Lore.
3. Elizabeth Watkins, born September 16, 1720
4. Margaret Watkins, born February 11, 1722
5. Gassaway Watkins, born July 3, 1723. Married Elizabeth Rawlings, daughter of Aaron Rawlings and Susannah Beard.
6. Mary Watkins, born c.1727
7. Thomas Gassaway Watkins, born c.1729; died May 30, 1800
8. Jane D. Watkins, baptized May 9, 1731.
9. Nicholas Watkins, baptized May 9, 1731

CHILD 5

Ann M. Watkins

This daughter of John Watkins, 3rd (died 1696) and Ann Gassaway was born in Anne Arundel County, Maryland. Nothing is now known of her life or descendants.

CHAPTER 3

Nicholas Watkins, Sr.
1691-1757/1770

This son of John Watkins, 3rd (died 1696) and Ann Gassaway was born in Anne Arundel County, Maryland, March 3, 1691 and died 1757 or 1770. Married Margaret Lamb, born December 1, 1703 and died about November 7, 1774, daughter of John Lamb and Elizabeth Belt Tydings. They had children:

1. Nicholas Watkins, Jr., born August 20, 1722, of whom more.
2. John Watkins, born November 27, 1724.
3. Elizabeth Watkins, born November 19, 1727. Married at All Hallows Parish, Anne Arundel County, Maryland, to Henry Hall on December 27, 1748; son of Major Henry Hall (1702) and Martha Bateman (1709). Henry was born c.1727 and died January 11, 1770. He was elected to the Lower House in 1762, serving through 1767. He was a merchant, and a money lender. He owned extensive lands in Queen Anne's Town and tracts called *Elizabeth's Fancy, Hall's Delight,* and *Chaney's Adventure,* as well as *Burrage's End* and *Middle Plantation.* His will, dated December 22, 1769, was probated March 9, 1770. The will mentions that he also owned land on Bennett's Creek in Frederick County, Maryland. His will indicates that he was a slave holder, and had nine children, born in Anne Arundel County, Maryland:
   a. Henry Hall, titled Captain, married December 27, 1774 Margaret Howard, born March 17, 1752, daughter of Joseph Howard and Margaret Williams. Five children were born to the marriage. After the death of his first wife, Henry married second Rachel Harwood by license dated June 23, 1787. She was born February 19, 1764, a daughter of Captain Thomas Harwood of St. James Parish, and Rachel Sprigg. Four children were born to the second marriage. The will of Henry Hall, dated June 5, 1797, was probated January 7, 1799, and is on file in the

Hall of Records at Annapolis. It describes extensive land along the Patuxent River, a number of slaves, and personal property. His children were:

(1) Joseph Hall, married Harriett Ann Sellman, by license issued February 2, 1802 in Anne Arundel County. They had children:
   (a) Sophia Ann Hall, born March 8, 1803.
   (b) Effy Hall, married to Crawford.
   (c) Ephraim Worthington Hall.
   (d) John Henry Hall.

(2) Margaret Hall, married Richard Galen Stockett, born February 7, 1776, son of Dr. Thomas Noble Stockett (1747) and Mary Harwood; license March 28, 1799.

(3) Elizabeth Hall, married c.1805 to Basil Warren.

(4) Henry Hall.

(5) John Washington Hall.

(6) Thomas Harwood Hall.

(7) Richard Henry Hall.

(8) Osborn Sprigg Hall, born c.1797, died November 10, 1845.

(9) Mary Ann Hall, married her cousin, Thomas W. Hall, son of Edward and Martha Hall, by license in Anne Arundel County dated October 24, 1816. Thomas died after 1826, leaving one son:
   (a) Julius Hall, a doctor, practicing in both Anne Arundel and Calvert Counties. He was married December 2, 1843 to Jane Kent, and died September 4, 1899 at the age of 80.

b. Nicholas Hall, born c.1757 in All Hallows Parish, Anne Arundel County, Maryland. In 1770, he inherited from his father 300 acres of *Chaney's Adventure*. Some time prior to 1778, he settled in Frederick County, Maryland, near New Market, and on June 10, 1778, was appointed captain of the county militia. Married June 1, 1779 to Ann Griffith, who died April 13, 1815, daughter of Henry Griffith and Ruth Hammond. Henry Griffith later settled in Montgomery County, Maryland, and at his death, left lands there to some of his grandchildren. On June 8, 1781, Nicholas and his brother John Hall, conveyed *Chaney's Adventure.* The will of Nicholas, dated May 9, 1820, was probated in Frederick County, January 9, 1821. He freed many of his slaves, and named a number of his grandchildren, and his children, who were:

(1) John Henry Hall.
(2) Nicholas Hall, born 1783 and married to Anne McElfresh. Children:
    (a) John Henry Hall.
    (b) Nicholas Hall, married Elizabeth P. Hammond under license dated October 29, 1838 in Frederick County, Maryland.
    (c) Elizabeth Jane Hall.
    (d) Martha Jane Hall.
(3) Elizabeth Jane Hall, married the Reverend John Pitts, son of Thomas Pitts and Sussanah Lusby. His will, dated June 26, 1820, was probated February 26, 1821 in Frederick County, Maryland, naming the children:
    (a) Nicholas Hall Pitts.
    (b) John Lusby Pitts.
    (c) Anna Maria Pitts.
    (d) Thomas Griffith Pitts.
    (e) Charles Hall Pitts.
    (f) William Pitts.
(4) Martha Ann Hall, married Thomas C. Shipley. They had children, including:
    (a) Rachel O. Shipley, married January 9, 1823 to Rezin Hammond Worthington.
    (b) Anne G. Shipley, married Alfred L. Moore.
    (c) Minerva O. Shipley, married to Milton M. Welsh.
    (d) Elizabeth Hall Shipley, married John Edward Bromwell.
    (e) Nicholas Shipley, married Margaret Contee.
    (f) Nimrod O. Shipley, married November 3, 1867 to Elizabeth Wright.

(g) Mary Shipley, married May 6, 1833 to her brother-in-law, Rezin Hammond Worthington

c. William Hall, born c.1755 in Anne Arundel County, Maryland. Married to Martha Duckett, under an Anne Arundel County license dated April 6, 1782. He lived in Frederick County, Maryland, at least for a time, and died in 1822. The widow of Martha was probatedMarch 9, 1829 in Anne Arundel. They had ten children:

(1) Richard Henry Hall, moved to Ohio.

(2) Elizabeth Hall.

(3) Margaret Hall.

(4) Mary Hall.

(5) Nancy Hall, married Samuel G. Hopkins by a license dated October 18, 1814, Anne Arundel

(6) Sophia Hall, married Benjamin M. Duckett. License July 13, 1835, Anne Arundel County

(7) Lucy Hall, married Thomas Hodges; license dated September 28, 1829, Anne Arundel.

(8) Basil Duckett Hall.

(9) Caroline Hall, married Richard Higgins by a license dated January 1, 1824, Anne Arundel.

(10) Harriett Hall, died young.

d. John Stephen Hall, married Elizabeth D. Boyd by license granted November 5, 1789, Anne Arundel County.

e. Martha Hall, born March 27, 1755, died June 11, 1815. Married July 4, 1771 to Joseph Howard, born March 13, 1749, died 1791, son of Joseph Howard and Margaret Williams. The will of Joseph Howard, there styled Jr., was dated December 17, 1790 and probated April 20, 1791 in Anne Arundel County. His personal estate, including two negroes, was valued at one thousand, two hundred and forty-three pounds. According to the 1783 tax list, he owned substantial lands, including 119 acres of *Snowden's Search*, 215 acres of *Plumpton*, 100 acres of *Foreland*, and 21 acres of *Snowden*. The following year he inherited 64 acres of *Howard's Angle* on South River. His will also mentions land in Frederick County. Upon the death of Joseph, his widow, Martha, married

Benjamin Howard, his brother, who died prior to April 21, 1791, when his will was probated in Anne Arundel. Joseph and Martha had children:

(1)   Henry Hall Howard, born July 12, 1772
(2)   Joseph Howard, born July 1, 1786. Married twice.
(3)   Eleanor Howard, died 1849, single.
(4)   Martha Howard, single.
(5)   Margaret Howard, who was married twice: to Allen Bowie Duckett and to Daniel Clarke.
(6)   Kitty Howard, single.
(7)   Marjorie Howard, died 1857, single.
(8)   Elizabeth Howard, who married Dr. Richard Duckett by license date December 20, 1804 in Anne Arundel County, Maryland.

f.   Margaret Hall, single.
g.   Elizabeth Hall; married John Watkins by license dated January 7, 1783 in Anne Arundel County.
h.   Mary Hall, married David Stewart.
i.   Anne Hall, married Thomas Rutland, by license issued July 26, 1784 in Anne Arundel County and had three children. Thomas Rutland was born July 27, 1765, the son of Thomas Rutland, Jr. and Margaret Howard, probably at *Middle Plantation*. She was married second to John Watkins, under a license dated October 27, 1791, in Anne Arundel. He was probably the John Watkins who was baptized August 6, 1718, eldest son of Gassaway Watkins (1695), based on the fact that Thomas Gassaway Watkins, brother of John, approved the inventory of the estate of John Watkins February 27, 1805. Three children were born to the union:

(1)   Rachel Watkins, born August 5, 1792
(2)   Julia Anna Watkins, born October 22, 1794
(3)   Elizabeth Watkins, baptized August 24, 1801

4.   Ann Watkins, born June 17, 1730; married Phillip Pindell.
5.   Gassaway Watkins, born November 13, 1731, died October, 1732.

6. John Gassaway Watkins, born April 25, 1733, died September 24, 1803, a second use of the name. Married November, 1758 to Dinah Smith. He had children, including:
   a. Margaret Gassaway Watkins, born 1765 and died September 7, 1829. Married January 27, 1788 to William Henry Hall of Anne Arundel County, born November 19, 1762, son of John Hall (1716) and Ann Wells.
   b. Gassaway Watkins, born 1771, died May 2, 1816. Married May 19, 1793 to Rebecca.
7. Joseph Watkins, born February 23, 1734, of whom more.
8. Thomas Watkins, born February 14, 1736.
9. Jeremiah Watkins, born March 8, 1743 (or February 12, 1739), of whom more in Chapter 4, which see.

Nicholas Watkins, Jr.
1722-

This son of Nicholas Watkins, Sr. (1691) and Margaret Lamb (1703), was born August 20, 1722, and married c.1743 to Ariana Worthington, born 1729, the daughter of Thomas Worthington and Elizabeth Ridgely, and removed to his wife's estate near Clarksville. Ariana and her brothers and sisters had each inherited parts of *Worthington's Range* near Clarksville, and *Partnership*, between Highland and Fulton. In *The Founders of Anne Arundel and Howard Counties, Maryland*, by J. D. Warfield, A.M., originally published in 1905 and reprinted in 1967 and 1973 by Regional Publishing Company, Baltimore, Nicholas is said to be of Clarksville, Maryland, and the progenitor of many of the Watkins families now found in that area and elsewhere in Maryland. After the death of Nicholas Watkins, Jr., his widow married secondly to John Ijams. In 1761, she deeded her estates of *Worthington's Range* and *Altogether* to her sons. Nicholas had children, of whom at least three sons served in the Revolution:
1. Margaret Watkins, born c.1744 and died 1814 in Rowan County, North Carolina. Married first April 20, 1789 Benedict Dorsey, who died c.1812, son of Thomas Dorsey and Mary Warfield, and had three children. Married second to Basil Gaither, by whom she had a son:

a. Thomas Dorsey.

b. Washington Dorsey, moved to Wilmington, Delaware, and married Hannah Chapman, having children:

    (1) George Washington Dorsey, married Mary Ann McKee, and had children:

        (a) Emily Dorsey, married to W. J. Ellison of Wilmington.

        (b) Anna Dorsey.

        (c) Bessie Dorsey.

        (d) George Washington Dorsey, Jr., married to Lizzie Spence of New York.

    (2) Thomas Dorsey.

    (3) Robert Dorsey.

    (4) William Dorsey.

    (5) Lizzie Dorsey.

    (6) Tamer Dorsey.

c. Elizabeth Ann Dorsey, born October 20, 1795. Married George Wilmer, the son of John Wilmer and Milicent Hyland, by license dated November 22, 1814, Baltimore County, Maryland. Lived in Cecil County, Maryland.

d. Nathan Gaither, who was a member of the Constitutional Convention of Kentucky.

2. Thomas Watkins, born c.1746 and died c.1786. Captain in the Revolution. Married January 24, 1767 to Elizabeth Jones, and second January 17, 1778 to Elizabeth Sprigg (or Lucy Belt). He was High Sheriff of Anne Arundel County, Maryland, and lost his estates. He had children, including at least:

a. Margaret Gassaway Watkins, born October 24, 1767.

b. Nicholas Watkins, born c.1771

c. Thomas Jones Watkins, born May 5, 1773; died c.1857

3. Elizabeth Watkins, born c.1748, married to a Gaither.

4. John Watkins, born c.1749, died 1822 in Jefferson County, Tennessee. Married c.1769 Mary Beall, daughter of Ninian Beall, and had five children. Married second November 28, 1787 to Mary Jones in Rowan County, North Carolina, and had ten children, all listed in order following:

a. Nicholas Beall Watkins.

b. John B. Watkins, who had children, including:

(1) Margaret W. Watkins, married November 25, 1817 to Ninian Chamberlain.

c. Thomas G. Watkins, a doctor; died January 1, 1830; married October 19, 1802 to Susan W. Jackson, daughter of Samuel Jackson.

d. Gassaway Watkins.

e. Andrew Watkins.

f. Isaac Jones Watkins, born August 19, 1788, died March 15, 1840. Married February 16, 1817 to Peggy Reese in Jefferson County, Tennessee, and second August 14, 1821 to Margaret Chamberlain. Father of:

(1) John Milton Watkins, born July 15, 1822 and died January 7, 1916. Married 1850 Belvadra Combs.

(2) Margaret Watkins, born March 13, 1824 and died August 12, 1892. Married to J. Albert Cardwell.

(3) William Wirt Watkins, born April 1, 1826, died January 15, 1898. Married to Mary Crump.

(4) Albert G. Watkins, father of:

(a) Isaac George Watkins, born September 24, 1842. Married twice: Nancy E. Milner and Nannie Carter

(b) William Brazelton Watkins, born July, 1850 and married Elizabeth James.

(c) Sarah Louise Watkins, born May, 1856, and died September, 1932. Married November 13, 1878 to John Alexander Galbraith.

(d) Reese Lee Watkins, born 1860 and died 1938. Married July 22, 1885 to Lula A. Sanders.

(e) Nancy Elizabeth Watkins, born March 1, 1848, died July 4, 1875

(f) Drucilla Lyttle Watkins, born January 18, 1854, and died December 25, 1942

(5) Thomsy Watkins, born November 10, 1829 and died May 31, 1904. Married Robert W. Cardwell.

(6) Lawson or Lawrence Clark Watkins, married Eliza Cocke.

g. Margaret Jones Watkins, married November 25, 1817 to Ninian Chamberlain.

h. Mary B. Watkins.

i. Abraham Watkins, born c.1793, and died February 14, 1868; married Mary E. Staples. Went to Carroll County, Arkansas in 1849 (now Boone County). Buried in the Gaither Cemetery at Gaither, Arkansas near Harrison. His wife's mother was a Gaither.

j. Nancy J. Watkins, born c.1794

k. Ariana Watkins, born May 13, 1799. Married to John Cardwell.

l. Richard Watkins, died c.1837; married March 4, 1823 to Martha Caldwell.

m. Thompsy Watkins.

n. Elizabeth Gaither Watkins, born June 7, 1802, and died September 29, 1885. Married April 30, 1827 to John G. Crump.

o. Osborne Ridgely Watkins, born March 6, 1804; died September 26, 1898. He is said to have been originally named Basil Gaither Watkins, but his name was changed by his half-brother, Dr. Thomas G. Watkins, who raised him from the age of thirteen. Married September 11, 1830 to Adaline McFarland.

5. Nicholas Watkins, 3rd, a Sergeant, born c.1751 and died 1822. Married Ann Jones; other sources report his wife as Sarah Disney, although that does not seem to be the case, based on reports found at pages 240 and 241, *Mareen Duvall of Middle Plantation*, by Harry Wright Newman. Children:

a. Fayette Watkins.

b. Isaac Watkins.

c. Sarah Watkins.

d. William Pitt Watkins, married Harriet Burgess, daughter of Captain Vachel Burgess (1756) and Rebecca Dorsey of Triadelphia. After the death of William Pitt, his widow married second Jeremiah Howard. William Pitt Watkins had at least one son:

(1) Oliver Watkins.

6. Gassaway Watkins, a Colonel, born in 1752 near Annapolis, Maryland, and died July 14, 1840. He enlisted at the beginning of the Revolution as corporal in Colonel William Smallwood's

regiment. He was said to be six feet, two inches tall, with a very strong, well developed build, and towered over his men in battle, causing many who knew him to fear for his safety. He took part in many battles; including Long Island, White Plains, Germantown, Monmouth, Cowpens, Camden and campaigns around West Point and Staten Island. Commissioned ensign of the 3rd Maryland Regiment in December, 1776; as Lieutenant May 1, 1777; and captain in 1782. Commanded a company at the battle of Cowpens under Colonel John Eager Howard. For his service, he received a warrant for 300 acres of land in Knox County, Kentucky, issued May 11, 1790, although he never perfected his title. Under the Acts of 1788, the State of Maryland granted him four lots of 50 acres each, in what is now Garrett County, Maryland, which were held as late as 1900 by his grandsons, Edwin Warfield and John Warfield. He was married three times: first to Sarah Jones, daughter of Colonel Isaac Jones of South River, and settled on the tract called *Richlands*. She died one year later, and he married second February 28, 1788 to Ruth Dorsey; by whom he had four sons and three daughters; daughter of Colonel John Dorsey (1734) and Anne Dorsey, of *Brown's Chance*; which he later acquired, and upon which he is said to have built the stone mansion house called *Walnut Grove* in 1803. Married third April 26, 1803 Eleanor Bowie Clagett, born c.1782 and died 1871, the daughter of Wiseman Clagett and Priscilla Bowie Lyles of Prince George's County, Maryland. By his third marriage, he had eight daughters and two sons, for a total of seventeen reported. They included:

a. Gassaway Watkins, a Lieutenant in the War of 1812, who died on duty in North Carolina. Married to Rebecca Richardson, the daughter of Richard Richardson and Elizabeth Thomas. Children, including:
    (1) Richard Gassaway Watkins, born March 3, 1794
b. Bonaparte Watkins, who died early
c. Charlotte Watkins, married Alfred Coale.
d. Harriet Watkins, married Basil Crapster of Glenwood and had a number of children and grandchildren. One of her children was:

(1)   Thaddeus Crapster, who married his first cousin, Eleanor Grieves.

e.   Thomas Watkins, who moved to Kentucky, and had at least one son:

(1)   Thomas Watkins, Jr., who became a prominent merchant in Louisville.

f.   Turenne Watkins, married Eleanor Stockett, daughter of Doctor Thomas Noble Stockett, and moved to Kentucky.

g.   Ann Elizabeth Watkins, married Lot Linthicum, a widower who was first married to Catherine Warfield, by whom he had four children. Lot was born March 3, 1784, son of the Reverend Slingsby Linthicum and Mary Griffith. Ann Elizabeth was the mother of:

(1)   Eliza Linthicum, deceased before 1905, single

(2)   Ruth Ann Linthicum, born September 13, 1822. Married Dr. Roberts and moved to Missouri.

(3)   Gassaway Watkins Linthicum.

(4)   Charles Linthicum.

(5)   Harriet Linthicum, married William Nichols, who was a druggist in Baltimore.

h.   Caroline Watkins, born in 1804, lived to be ninety-two years of age. She was the first of the second family of ten children, and was married to Julius Watkins, probably the same Julius who was a twin, born May 20, 1802, son of Richard Watkins (died 1842).

i.   Camsadel Watkins, married to Dr. Horatio Grieves of Hagerstown, formerly of Wales, and had two daughters:

(1)   Eleanor Grieves, married her first cousin Thaddeus Crapster of *Ellerslie,* the youngest son of Basil Crapster and Harriet Watkins. No children.

(2)   Daughter, married Dr. Moorland.

j.   Eleanor Watkins, married William Ridgely Warfield of *Springdale,* a son of Beale Warfield and Emily Ridgely, and had children, not necessarily listed in birth order:

(1)   Eleanor Amelia Warfield, married the Reverend William Crapster, a minister and teacher, and had children, married second Captain Richard Watkins. Her children were:

(a) William Channing Crapster.
(b) Emma Crapster, married Taylor.
(c) Florence Crapster, married Shields.
(2) Rosalba Warfield, married Reverend Mosely Beale of Mississippi, and had a daughter:
(a) Bertha Mosely.
(3) Beale A. Warfield, a surveyor, married Cordelia England, daughter of Abram England. No children.
(4) Bowie Clagett Warfield, married to Julia Gregory and lived at Sandoval, Illinois. Children:
(a) Alverta Warfield, who married Rhodolphus Crapster.
(b) Alice Warfield.
(5) Gassaway Watkins Warfield, died single.
(6) Emma Warfield, married John R. Kenley, manager of the Atlantic Coast Line Railway. Children:
(a) Edna Kenley.
(b) Nelly Kenley.
(7) Camsadel Warfield, married George England, son of Abram England. Children:
(a) Elizabeth England, married Sollers of Calvert County
(b) Cordelia England.
(8) Alberta Clay Warfield, married Samuel Sharretts, and died as a bride.
(9) William Ridgely Warfield, Jr., a hydraulic engineer and was in charge of the Harlem River Tunnel.
(10) Georgietta Warfield, married Mortimer Dorsey Crapster, the only son of Rhodolphus Crapster and Elizabeth Dorsey. Children:
(a) Rhodolphus Crapster.
(b) Ernest Crapster.
(c) Eleanor Crapster.
(d) Mary Blanche Crapster.
(e) Thaddeus Crapster.
(f) Mortimer Dorsey Crapster, Jr.
(g) Alice Crapster.
(h) Emma Crapster.

        (i)   Bowie Crapster.

        (j)   Robert Gordon Crapster.

k.   Amanda Watkins, married Thomas Watkins and had at least one son:

        (1)   Harry W. Watkins.

l.   William Washington Watkins, born 1810, and died 1880. A doctor, and the eldest son of his father's third marriage, he was married 1837 to Laura Louise Watkins, born May 5, 1812, died November 11, 1850, daughter of Thomas Watkins, and lived at *Richland*. He married second to Eleanor Harwood, of West River. He was a delegate to the Legislature in 1838, urging the creation of the new county of Howard, and when it was created in 1851, he was chosen its first state Senator. For twenty-five years served as Clerk of the Court for Howard County. He had children:

        (1)   Thomas Gassaway Watkins, who married Catharine Welling, only daughter of William Welling of *White Wine and Claret*, and had children:

                (a)   Henry Watkins.

                (b)   Kate Watkins.

                (c)   Laura Watkins.

                (d)   Maude Watkins.

        (2)   William Washington Watkins, Jr., also a doctor, and married a Watkins cousin.

        (3)   Lewis Jones Watkins, who succeeded his father as Clerk of the Court of Howard County in 1873, 1879 and 1885. Married Mary Tinges Brocchus. Children, including:

                (a)   Mary Louise Brocchus Watkins, married to William Bell Wood.

        (4)   Harwood Watkins, the youngest son, was a lawyer and editor of *The Times*. He died young.

        (5)   Ellen Elizabeth Watkins, married Joshua Warfield Dorsey, and had children:

                (a)   James Malcolm Dorsey, an attorney.

                (b)   J. Worthington Dorsey, a Baltimore merchant

                (c)   Benjamin Dorsey, an attorney.

(d) William R. Dorsey of Ellicott City, Maryland
(6) Amanda Watkins, youngest daughter, married to Thaddeus M. Sharretts, of Baltimore. She was the only living child in this family as of c.1905.

m. John S. Watkins, who married Amanda Linthicum, daughter of Wesley Linthicum (1792) and his first wife, Mary Meriweather. He inherited the home place of *Walnut Grove*, and was state Senator of Howard County at the outbreak of the Civil War. After his death, the property was sold to Edwin Warfield, governor of Maryland at the beginning of the twentieth century. He later purchased the adjoining property known as *Hayland* from William Clark. Two daughters:
(1) Caroline Watkins, married Richard Owings, son of Major Henry Owings of Howard County, and his second wife, Elizabeth Dorsey.
(2) Daughter, married John Bracco.

n. Elizabeth Watkins, married William Watkins, son of Thomas Watkins.

o. Priscilla Watkins, married George T. Kenley.

p. Margaret Gassaway Watkins, died August, 1897, and married August 25, 1842 to Albert Gallatin Warfield, born February 26, 1817, died November 6, 1891, son of Joshua Warfield. In 1838, he built his home called *Oakdale* in Howard County, Maryland, and served as School Commissioner of the county for several years. He owned a number of slaves, but freed each of them when they reached the age of forty. Reportedly, there were ten children, but we can here report only eight:
(1) Albert Gallatin Warfield, Jr., born 1843, died 1883, who also served in the Confederate Army as a Major, and after the war, became a well-known civil engineer; went to Japan in 1873 as a member of the American Scientific Commission, and died in 1883, as a result of exposure in the mountains of West Virginia while taking part in construction of the West Virginia Central Railroad. Children:
(a) Albert Gallatin Warfield, III.

       (b)   Catherine Warfield.

       (c)   Frances Warfield.

(2)   Joshua Nicholas Warfield of Howard County, born September 3, 1845. Married to Lucy Hutton, the daughter of Enoch Hutton. Children:

       (a)   Margaret Warfield.

       (b)   Joshua Nicholas Warfield, Jr.

       (c)   Norman Warfield.

(3)   Gassaway Watkins Warfield, born 1846, who served in the Confederate Army; died in prison in 1864 at Camp Chase.

(4)   Marshall T. Warfield of Howard County.

(5)   Edwin Warfield, president of the Maryland Senate in 1886 and Surveyor of the Port of Baltimore. Governor of Maryland early 1900s, and president of the Fidelity and Deposit Company.

(6)   John Warfield, an attorney, and editor of the *Daily Law Record* of Baltimore.

(7)   Alice Warfield, who married M. Gillet Gill of the firm of Martin, Gillett & Co., tea importers. On their wedding trip, she visited Japan, being the first American lady on the island. Children:

       (a)   M. Gillett Gill, Jr.

       (b)   Howard Gill.

       (c)   Royal Gill.

       (d)   Mildred Gill.

(8)   Margaret G. Warfield, married Herman Hoopes of West Chester, Pennsylvania. Children:

       (a)   Marian Hoopes.

       (b)   Edward Hoopes.

       (c)   Albert W. Hoopes.

q.   Albina Watkins, married William Clark, son of David Clark and Rachel Warfield of Anne Arundel County. At least these six children:

(1)   William Clark.

(2)   Thaddeus Watkins Clark, a doctor in Baltimore. He served as a captain in the Fifth Maryland Regiment during the Spanish War. Married Florence C.

Mathews, daughter of Judge William Mathews and Harriet Howard of *Glenwood*, in Howard County, Maryland.

(3)   Thomas Clark, formerly editor of the *Ellicott City Times*. Married the only daughter of John Hardy and had several children.

(4)   Daughter, married William Gorman.

(5)   Daughter, married Whitney.

(6)   Nora Clark, who died as a young woman.

Joseph Watkins
1734-1788

This son of Nicholas Watkins, Sr. (1691) and Margaret Lamb (1703), was born February 23, 1734, and died 1788. Married November 21, 1762 to Ann Brown, and had children:

1.   Nicholas Watkins, born October 8, 1763

2.   Archibald Washington Watkins, who had children:
  a.   Thomas Coke Watkins, born March 25, 1800 and died December 18, 1875. Married three times: Elizabeth Ann Warfield, Sarah Margaretta Patterson, and Elizabeth Ann Hersche. He had fourteen children, including:

   (1)   William Francis Asbury Watkins, born June 22, 1816

   (2)   Thomas Bascom Watkins, born September 18, 1824

   (3)   William McKendree Watkins, born June 27, 1828, died November 28, 1890. Married Ann Rebecca Greentree, born March 5, 1830 in Frederick, and died April 26, 1904 in Baltimore. At least a son:
     (a)   Millard Fillmore Watkins, born in Baltimore, Maryland, August 19, 1856, of whom more.

   (4)   George Washington Watkins, born January 21, 1835.

   (5)   Wilbur Fiske Watkins, born July 7, 1836

   (6)   George Rust Watkins, born February 1, 1840.

   (7)   Robert Emory Watkins, born June 13, 1842

   (8)   Helen Maria Watkins, born December 16, 1844.

        (9)   Francis Dungar Watkins, born March 25, 1847.

        (10)   Mary Louise Watkins, born January 5, 1850.

        (11)   Kate Cochran Watkins, born September 9, 1853.

    b.   Rebekah Watkins, born September 5, 1802

    c.   Margaret Watkins, born March 5, 1805

    d.   Sarah Watkins, born February 2, 1815

    e.   Mary Ann Watkins, born June, 1820

    f.   John Quincy Adams Watkins, born April 9, 1825.

    g.   Joseph Pendell Watkins, born in the 1820s

3.   Gassaway Watkins, born August 12, 1781, who had at least:

    a.   Gassaway Watkins.

    b.   John Wesley Watkins.

4.   Thomas Spencer Watkins, born May 2, 1769 and died 1858. Married April 24, 1798 to Catherine Magruder, and had four children. Married second January 30, 1812 Mary Magruder, cousin of his first wife, and had a fifth child. About 1829, Thomas Spencer took work on the C. and O. Canal project as a contractor, with three of his sons as his assistants, including the youngest, Samuel Brewer. When Thomas Spencer retired, his sons retained the business. His will, dated June 30, 1855 is filed in Liber WTR 2 at folio 381, will records of Montgomery County, Maryland. He leaves his home farm to the children of his son, Greenbury M. Watkins, naming five of them, and "any other children my son and his wife Helen may have." He provides further that his negro women Linny and Lucy and their children are not to be sold or hired out outside the state, and that the males are to be set free at age thirty-five, and the women at age thirty. He leaves his negro man William to his grandson Spencer Watkins. Next, he leaves to his three grandsons who are sons of his sons; Wilson, Joseph and Samuel; and named after him, each the sum of one hundred dollars. Finally, he leaves bequests to his sons, Joseph and Wilson, and to his grandson, Edgar G. Watkins. Children:

    a.   Greenbury M. Watkins, born c.1808, died March 26, 1876. He served two terms in the state legislature, and as chairman of the committee on ways and means. He was a delegate to the constitutional convention of 1867. Married four times: first October 6, 1831, Kitty Ann Gatton, who died 1839; second June 13, 1842 to Helen Gatton, died 1855, daughter of Zachariah Gatton; third to Susan Venable, born c.1824, died July 3, 1862 at *Boscage*; the daughter of William H. Venable of *Hickory Grove*, Prince Edward County, Virginia; and fourth to Margaret Jackson Duvall, born 1828, died June 2, 1890 in the District of Columbia. He appeared as head of household in the 1850 census for the Clarksburg District of Montgomery County, with his second wife, Helen, and five children. He appears again in the 1860 census for Darnestown District, apparently as a widower, with four of his children. There is also present in the household, one Emma Martin, born c.1827, born in England, and listed as governess. There is also Patrick Flinn, born c.1833, the farm manager. His will was dated February 3, 1876 and probated April 4, 1876 in Liber RWC 6 at folio 114, will records of Montgomery County, Maryland. He leaves to his wife, Margaret J. some Richmond City bonds valued at six thousand, five hundred dollars, and her selection of three thousand, five hundred dollars in mortgages he holds at the time. She is also granted the home place of *Boscage* for her lifetime. He mentions five children, apparently four of them having been born to his first marriage to Helen Gatton, and the youngest, Maggie, to his wife Margaret Jackson Duvall. He leaves to his two sons, the farms known as *Boscage* and the *Sufborough* place, totalling about 535 acres, which he values at seventy dollars per acre. The farm was located near Chevy Chase, in Montgomery County. He also mentions that any advancements he may have already made were received by him through their mother Helen. There is also a special bequest of cash to his sons Edgar and Spencer out of any money coming to the firm of Watkins and Sons. There is also a codicil to the will, dated February 12, 1876, changing slightly some of the dollar amounts of bequests, but also providing that his lands in Missouri are to go to his daughter Kate, and the lands in Kansas to his daughter, Alice. The codicil also mentions "my other lands in Montgomery County" not included in the specific bequests; it is to be sold and the proceeds go to his two sons. There is also two hundred dollars per year to "my uncle, Robert W. Magruder." Children, including:

(1)   William Mansfield Watkins, born c.1835 (1850 census), and apparently died before his father made his will, although he is specifically named in his grandfather's will.

(2)   Robert W. Watkins, born c.1837 (1850 census)

(3)   Spencer Watkins, born c.1844 (1850 census) on the family farm, upon part of which was later built the well-known Chevy Chase Lake, and died November 5, 1904 in Washington. In 1867, he went to Mississippi, but returned to Maryland after three years. With his father, he built three miles of the Metropolitan branch of the B. and O. Railroad, and later, with his brother, built the railroad from Hagerstown to Williamsport. He sold a part of his property to the Chevy Chase Land Company, who developed the communities along Connecticut Avener. He appears in the 1900 census for Bethesda, Montgomery County, Maryland, with his wife and two daughters. His will, dated February 10, 1897, was filed in Liber HCA 4 at folio 167 in Montgomery County will records. He names his wife, two of his sisters, a brother, two daughters, and a sister in law; Annie E. Vedder. Spencer was married June 14, 1870 to Maria W. Brooke, eldest daughter of General E. H. Brooke. They had children:

(a)   Helen Watkins, born 1873

(b)   Ann Watkins, born 1878; married A. D. V. Burr.

(4)   Catherine E. Watkins, born c.1847 (1850 census). Married November 15, 1869 to Thomas D. Skiles and lived in Minneapolis, Minnesota.

(5) Alice Johnston Watkins, born 1849 (1850 census). Married July 22, 1872 to Judge McDowell R. Venable and lived in Los Angeles, California.

(6) Edgar P. Watkins, born c.1853 in the Bethesda District of Montgomery County, and died July 1, 1907 in Washington. Married April 22, 1878 to Lucretia Batchelor. The *Sentinel* abstracts report his name as Edward. She died March 31, 1894 in Washington, D. C., at the home of her brother-in-law, W. H. Rapley.

(7) Maggie Watkins. Not named in her grandfather's will, and apparently born after that date. Married to Frank Fields, and lived in Washington, D. C.

b. Joseph Magruder Watkins, born 1806 and died 1884. Married twice, first January 22, 1833 in Tennessee, Lavenia Penn, and second to Margaret Linster. Children:

(1) Thomas W. Watkins, born c.1834. Children:
    (a) Thomas Watkins.
(2) John Watkins, born c.1836
(3) Martha Watkins, born c.1838
(4) Mary Watkins, born c.1840
(4) Joseph Watkins, born c.1842
(6) Harry Watkins, born c.1858
(7) Wilson Lee Watkins, born c.1865

c. White Watkins, died before 1858

d. Wilson Lee Watkins, married December 24, 1833 in Tennessee to Caroline Wade. Apparently at least one son:

(1) Thomas Spencer Watkins.

e. Samuel Brewer Watkins, born on Easter Sunday, April 18, 1813, near Rockville, Montgomery County, the only child of his father's second marriage; died February 2, 1908. As mentioned above, he worked on the Chesapeake and Ohio Canal with his father and two of his half-brothers, until 1840, when he boarded a sailing vessel for the west to engage in prospecting, landing in Galveston, Texas, after seventeen days voyage. He traveled in Texas for several months, and then began to head for home, overland, stopping in Tennessee to visit with his half-brothers, Wilson and Joseph. There he met Mary Ann Wade, daughter of Walter Wade and Susan Tinnon, and they were married December 22, 1842, and returned to Maryland on horseback. She died about 1877, being a cripple during the last seven or eight years, resulting from a fall. On his return, he found that his investment in Canal stock had been totally wiped out, and in 1844, he and his wife purchased a farm near Murfreesboro. He was a Confederate sympathizer, and during the war, his home was burned to the ground during the night, with the family escaping with little other than their lives. They were the parents of three sons and a daughter, including:

- (1) James Elwood Watkins, killed while serving the Confederacy, near his home
- (2) Robert Watkins, died at age fourteen
- (3) Thomas Spencer Watkins, married Maggie Turner and died in 1897.
- (4) Mary Watkins, married William Roberts, a cotton buyer of Nashville, Tennessee, and died in 1906, having had four children, the only descendants of her father. They included:
  - (a) Anne Roberts, who lived with her grandfather until his death in 1908.
  - (b) Margaret Roberts, married McFerrin.

5. Margaret Watkins, born March 6, 1765; married March 9, 1787 to Joshua Dorsey.
6. John Watkins, born March 2, 1767
7. Martha Watkins, born January 21, 1771
8. Joseph Watkins, born February, 1776. A colonel, he married Ann Gray and had children:
   - a. John Nelson Watkins, born September 24, 1790, an 1811 graduate of St. John's College in Annapolis, and later the Adjutant-General of Maryland.
   - b. Sophia Watkins, born March 2, 1792, died young
   - c. Mary Watkins, born August 12, 1793
   - d. Richard Watkins, born August 11, 1797 and died about August 17, 1799.

e. Sophia Watkins, born November 8, 1799, second use of the name, died April 11, 1839. Married November 17, 1825 to Joseph Noble Stockett, his third wife. He was one of the ten children of Dr. Thomas Noble Stockett and Mary Harwood. Children:

   (1) John Shaaff Stockett, born September 17, 1826, married Georgette Stockett.
   (2) Charles James Stockett, born 1828, died 1830
   (3) Thomas Richard Stockett, born March 20, 1830. Married April 28, 1859 to Jemima O. Edmond of England.
   (4) Mary Sophia Stockett, born November 16, 1831. Married first to Dr. Richard Harwood Cowman, Navy Surgeon; and second John Thomas Stockett, only son of George Lee Stockett (1800).
   (5) Charles William Stockett, born March 19, 1833, a doctor, married Maria L. Duvall, only child of Dr. Howard Mareen Duvall.
   (6) Lewis Stockett, born 1834, died 1836
   (7) Ann Stockett, born April 27, 1836. Married July 16, 1861 Francis S. Kent Penn, and reportedly married also to Roderick Warfield, of *Warfield's Range*, in Howard County. Removed to Kentucky.
   (8) Eleanor Stockett (or Ellen), born February 6, 1838 married Turenne Watkins, the son of Colonel Gassaway Watkins (1752) and Ruth Dorsey, and moved to Kentucky. Also reported to have married Marshall Chapman of Charles County, Maryland, on October 18, 1859, perhaps a first marriage.
   (9) Sophia Stockett, born April 10, 1839, and died September 11, 1888. Married June 25, 1863 at St. Anne's Church to John H. Sellman, USN.

9. Richard Watkins, born June 15, 1784

Millard Fillmore Watkins
1856-1934

This son of William McKendree Watkins (1828) and Ann Rebecca Greentree (1830), was born in Baltimore, Maryland, August 19, 1856, and died July 27, 1934. A copy of his family Bible was found in family folder files of the Montgomery County Historical Society library in Rockville, Maryland. From entries there, we assume that he was the son of William McKendree Watkins, (born June 27, 1828, died November 28, 1890) and Ann Rebecca Greentree (born March 5, 1830 in Frederick, died April 26, 1904 in Baltimore). Millard Fillmore was apparently married twice: first July 16, 1882, Mary Catherine Fowner, born February 1, 1867 in Clifton, Maryland, and died March 16, 1893 in Baltimore. Married second June 12, 1894 to Anna May W. Zile, born May 30, 1871, all of Baltimore. He had children, born in Baltimore:

1. Ann Rebecca Watkins, born November 2, 1884, died April 5, 1963. Married December 30, 1908 to Lloyd Horatio High, born November 5, 1887, died September 13, 1943. Children:
   a. Millard Lloyd High, born January 6, 1911, died March 7, 1914
   b. Lloyd Robert High, born March 26, 1915; married September 21, 1935 to Rita Ann Elizabeth Pagano, and had children:
      (1) Ann Elizabeth High, born July 28, 1930
      (2) Margaret Mary High, born August 21, 1938
      (3) Catherine High.
   b. Paul Arthur High, born December 19, 1926 and married November 12, 1946 Sarah Ann Albrecht. Children:
      (1) Dorothy Ann High, born May 18, 1948
      (2) Deborah Alice High, born May 5, 1954
      (3) Diana Andrea High, born September 25, 1957
      (4) Dana Alison High, born July 31, 1965
2. William McKendree Watkins, born August 21, 1886, and died June 26, 1906 in Baltimore, after being crushed between two cars.
3. Willie Oswil Myers Watkins, born February 21, 1889
4. Albert James Watkins, born July 12, 1892 in Baltimore

CHAPTER 4

Jeremiah Watkins
1743-1833

This son of Nicholas Watkins, Sr. (1691) and Margaret Lamb (1703), was born March 8, 1743 in Anne Arundel County, Maryland, and died May 3, 1833 in Montgomery County, at the age of 90 years, 1 month and 25 days. Buried in the Maurice Watkins graveyard at Browningsville in Montgomery County. Married May 30, 1762 in Frederick County, Maryland, Elizabeth Waugh, born c.1745 in Anne Arundel County, and died October 18, 1823 in Montgomery County, daughter of James Waugh and Alice Green. He held land in Frederick County called *Solomon's Contrivance*, and was a tobacco farmer with large holdings in Frederick County, and in Montgomery County near Browningsville. Jeremiah appears to be the progenitor of the Watkins families later found in Montgomery and nearby counties of Maryland, and was the father of eleven children. Prints from pages of the family Bible were found in the family folder file of the Montgomery County Historical Society library in Rockville, providing much information relative to the family. There were eleven children, the first, sixth, seventh, and last of whom will be treated in more detail following the listing:

1. Nicholas Watkins, born November 1, 1763; see Child 1.
2. Jeremiah Watkins, Jr., born August 20, 1765; married Deborah Purdy.
3. Richard Watkins, born November 23, 1766, died 1814
4. Joseph Watkins, born October 25, 1768
5. Margaret Watkins, born April 4, 1770; died young
6. Gassaway Watkins, born November 2, 1772; see Child 6.
7. Thomas Watkins, born March 9, 1774; see Child 7.
8. Margaret Watkins, born May 7, 1776, second use of the name. Married D. Lewis.
9. Ann Watkins, born March 6, 1778
10. Elizabeth Watkins, born March 9, 1780
11. John W. Watkins, born August 24, 1782; see Child 11.

CHILD 1

Nicholas Watkins
1763-1848

This son of Jeremiah Watkins (1743) and Elizabeth Waugh (1745), was born November 1, 1763, died c.1848. Married March 13, 1787 to Rachel Lewis, daughter of Jeremiah Lewis (born March 30, 1745; died November 22, 1822) and his wife Jane Lewis (died March 9, 1814). The will of Nicholas, there styled Nicholas Watkins, Sr., was dated October 25, 1845, and filed originally in Liber HH 1 at folio 485, and rerecorded in Liber VMB 4 at folio 463, in will records of Montgomery County, Maryland. He leaves his entire estate to his wife, Rachel, for life, and then makes several other legacies. To his son, Jeremiah, he leaves his silver watch, with the request that it be passed on to the man in his family who should seem to him to merit it. He mentions his other four sons, commenting that each of them owes him a sum of money, and that for purposes settling the debt with his estate, he establishes a value less than that actually owed. He then provides that upon the death of his wife, the personal estate is to be divided between his ten children. The number ten is mentioned more than once, and the children are all named more than once, but there are only nine of them named. The fact seems to be that he had a total of thirteen children, at least three of whom are known to have predeceased their father. At the death of his wife, he directs that his land, consisting of about 360 acres is also to be sold and the ten children are to share and share alike. His children included:

1. Jeremiah Watkins, born November 26, 1787, of whom more.
2. Gassaway Watkins, born May 1, 1789. This is probably the same individual found as head of household in the 1850 census of Clarksburg District, Montgomery County with a wife, Ara A. Watkins, born c.1790, and two others who may be children, or family members. They include Ruth Watkins, born c.1836; and Stephen Watkins, born c.1824.
3. Daniel Lewis Watkins, born March 1, 1791. The 1850 census for Clarksburg District, Montgomery County, has a household headed by John W. Lewis, born c.1823, with a wife, Lucretia

Watkins, born c.1829, and two small children. There was a Lucretia A. Watkins, born June 10, 1829 and died July 6, 1885; buried at Montgomery Chapel cemetery, Claggettsville, Maryland. Records also state that her husband was J. W. Watkins. Also in the household is Daniel L. Watkins, of the proper age to be this individual. Following his name are two older children, suggesting that Daniel is widowed, with his two youngest children still living; the three of them in the household of his oldest married son. We then construct the children of Daniel Lewis Watkins as being, at least:

a. John W. Watkins, born about 1823, married to Lucretia A., born c.1829. They appear again in the 1860 census for Damascus District, with more of their family; in the 1870 census of Damascus with a number of children; and in the 1880 census for Clarksburg District with three of the children. In the 1860 census, there is one John Sheckles, born c.1822, living with them. At least these children:

   (1) Martha E. Watkins, born c.1847. She was perhaps married December 10, 1868 to Richard H. Becraft at the home of Owen Watkins. She was found in the home of her father in the 1880 census, with at least one daughter:

   (a) Susie Becraft, born c.1871

   (2) George E. Watkins, born c.1848.

   (3) Juliann Watkins, or Julia Ann, born c.1850

   (4) Ellen L. Watkins, born c.1852

   (5) Mary M. Watkins, born c.1854. The 1880 census for Damascus, then in the Clarksburg District of Montgomery County, lists the household of Julius A. Crockett, born c.1834, who was a worker in the custom house. He has a wife, Mary M., aged 24; two children; and a sister in law, Julia A. Watkins, age 29, listed as a laundress. We believe these to be Mary M., listed here, and her older sister, found elsewhere as Juliann. Note, however, that the first child listed was either a son of a first marriage of Julius Crockett, or was born when Mary Watkins

was barely thirteen years of age, which is rather unlikely, even for the times. It appears then that Mary was married to Julius A. Crockett, and had at least one child:

    (a) Henry W. Crockett, born c.1869

    (b) Ida H. Crockett, born c.1877

(6)   Georgianna Watkins, born c.1856. In the 1900 census, she was found in the home of John H. Bellison, listed as a sister-in-law.

(7)   John W. C. Watkins, born c.1859. He was listed in the 1900 census for Damascus, with a wife, Sarah C., born c.1862, and one son:

    (a) Elbert L. Watkins, born c.1888

(8)   Alfred W. Watkins, born c.1864

(9)   Reuben E. Watkins, born c.1865, died February 4, 1905 at the age of 40 years, 4 months and 4 days. He is buried at Montgomery Chapel cemetery at Claggettsville, with his name appearing on the same stone as that of Rodolphus Grafton Watkins (1846). It appears that Reuben was married February 12, 1889 to Eudolphia Claggett Watkins (1840), widow of Rodolphus, and the family has perhaps put both her husband's names on a single tombstone. No reported children.

(10) Alice M. Watkins, born c.1866

(11) Enoch S. Watkins, born January 3, 1870 and died February 16, 1894, buried at Montgomery Chapel, Claggettsville, Maryland. Married February 14, 1893 Mary Edna Moxley in Montgomery County, born February 2, 1861, died December 22, 1945, and buried with her husband. Children, including at least:

    (1) Blanche Sheridan Watkins, born October 25, 1893, from Church records; December 19, 1893 from family Bible. Married to Albert Thompson, and had one child:

        (a) Leona Thompson, married to George Walter Buckingham.

b.   Christy O. Watkins, born c.1834

c.   Ruth A. Watkins, born c.1841

4.   Stephen Watkins, born March 11, 1793, died July 14, 1819.

5.   Richard Watkins, born January 25, 1795, died May 4, 1814.

6.   Delilah Eliza Watkins, born November 23, 1796. Married to Thomas Sedgwick, born October 16, 1774. Children:

a.   Jerusa Ann Sedgwick, born December 27, 1825

b.   Elizabeth Emley Sedgwick, born July 25, 1826

c.   Emmanuel Thomas Sedgwick, born March 21, 1835

7.   Margaret Watkins, born October 8, 1798, died November 23, 1811.

8.   Aleatha Watkins, born October 14, 1800, and married January 18, 1821 William Moxley, born c.1794. They appear in the 1850 census of Montgomery County, with two of their children. In the 1860 census, Aleatha appears alone, suggesting the death of her husband between 1850 and 1860. In the 1870 census of Damascus, she appears in a household headed by William A. Moxley, who is apparently her son, with her known son, Mahlon, also there. In addition, there is one George W. Beall, aged 5 (born c.1865), who is not otherwise identified. Her children included:

a.   Mahlon Moxley, born c.1820

b.   William A. Moxley, born c.1823

c.   Asbury Moxley, born May 26, 1828

d.   Rachel Moxley, born c.1838

e.   Lucinda Moxley, born c.1845

9.   Nicholas Watkins, born December 24, 1802

10. Rachel Watkins, born November 2, 1804, married January 5, 1826 to Lloyd Hilton, born c.1798, son of Thomas I. Hilton, Sr. (1773) and Lely Griffin. Lloyd had a log cabin on Scott Branch at *Wolf Den*, property he was renting. They had their children at the cabin. The family appears in the 1850 and 1860 census of the Laytonsville District, Montgomery County. Children:

a.   Richard Washington Hilton, born January 5, 1827 and married January 27, 1864 to Louisa Jane Shipley.

b.   Willie Elizabeth Hilton, born September 24, 1829. This daughter was married to a Hilton, and had at least one son:

(1)   Filmore Hilton, born c.1853

c.   Thomas Samuel Hilton, born April 16, 1831

d.   Henry Clay Hilton, born November 3, 1833

e.   William Harrison Hilton, born March 13, 1836, died July 1, 1919. Served as a private in Co. B, 5th Maryland Regt, and in Co. C, 13th Maryland. Married to Elizabeth A. Warfield, born August 14, 1841, died December 22, 1919. Buried Damascus Methodist Church.

f.   Sarah E. Hilton, born c.1839, married William Young.

g.   Susannah Ruth Hilton, born c.1842, married Edward Dyer.

h.   Eldridge Jesse Hilton, a daughter, born c.1847

11.   Levin Belt Watkins, born November 5, 1806. He is shown as head of household in the 1850 census for the Clarksburg District of Montgomery County, at that time with a wife, and four children. His wife was Mary E. Wharton, born c.1806. In the 1860 census, it appears that only Levin and his wife are in the household, with their son, Julius and his wife, Amanda, and their first born child, Tobias. In the 1870 census, just the elderly couple appear alone. Levin Belt Watkins had children, including:

a.   Julius Watkins, born c.1833, of whom more.

b.   William Watkins, born c.1841

c.   James Watkins, died June 6, 1842, and not shown in the census.

d.   Edmund Watkins, born c.1845

e.   Nicholas Watkins, born c.1848

12.   Deborah Watkins, born February 25, 1809, married March 10, 1827 Montgomery County, Maryland, Walter Applebee. They had children:

a.   Levi Thomas Applebee, born December 28, 1828

b.   Sarah Moriah Applebee, born September 2, 1830

c.   Rufus Henry Applebee, born August 23, 1832

d.   Nicholas Watkins Applebee, born March 9, 1834

e.   Harriet Ann Applebee, born March 27, 1836

f.   Mary Ann Applebee, born April 24, 1838

g.   Summerset Waters Applebee, born August 13, 1847

13.   Elizabeth Hall Watkins, born January 29, 1811. Married to Owen Brown, according to her father's will, of whom more.

Julius Watkins
1833-1896

This son of Levin Belt Watkins (1806) was born c.1833, and died 1896. Married to Amanda, born 1841, died 1920. Both are buried at Bethesda United Methodist Church cemetery, Brownings-ville, Maryland. He appears as head of household in the 1870 and the 1880 census for the Clarksburg District of Montgomery County. In the 1900 census for Damascus, Amanda appears as a widow, with five of their children. Tobias C. Watkins and Joseph G. Watkins were Administrators of the estate of Amanda, with final accounts filed August 9, 1921 in liber HCA 23 at folio 397 in the wills office of the county. The heirs are named there. They had a number of children, according to church records filed at the library of the Montgomery County Historical Society, including:

1.   Tobias C. Watkins, born c.1859, died c.1949. Tobias lived near Lewisdale, Maryland, and married October 11, 1883 to Catherine C. Swartz. In the 1900 census for Clarksburg, To-bias is listed with his wife, and four of their children. Also listed is Basil D. Swartz, born c.1878, a stepson, indicating that the wife of Tobias was married earlier to Swartz. The will of Tobias was dated December 22, 1948, and probated June 15, 1949 and filed in Liber WCC 13 at folio 251 in the will records of Montgomery County. He does not mention a wife, nor does he specify children, leaving his estate by specific be-quests. To Leanna Day, he leaves his antique chandelier lamp; to Merhl Lawson, his antique guns. The rest of the estate is to be sold and the proceeds divided between Mamie Boyer; Rus-sell Watkins; the heirs of Jemima C. Lewis; Vivian M. Law-son; and Basil Dorsey Schwartz. The first four of these are his children; Basil Dorsey Schwartz was his stepson. Children:

a.   Mamie Cleveland Watkins, born July 6, 1884, married December 25, 1906 to Norman D. Boyer.

b.   Russell C. Watkins, born September 18, 1886, died September 14, 1971; buried at Bethesda United Methodist Church cemetery, Browningsville, Maryland. His wife was Louise L., born February 26, 1879, died May 29, 1956; buried with her husband. They had children:
   (1)   Dorothy Watkins, married Ball; daughter of the first marriage of Louise L.
   (2)   Josephine Watkins, married Schlesinger; also a daughter of the first marriage of Louise L.
   (3)   Mildred M. Watkins, married Pauley.
c.   Catherine Jemima Watkins, born April 15, 1891
d.   Vivian Myrtle Watkins, born November 28, 1894 and married to Lawson, and probably parents of:
   (1)   Merhl Lawson.
2.   Hezekiah Watkins, perhaps, baptized December, 1862 at the home of Julius Watkins, his father. He is not named in the administration of estate of his mother, and was perhaps an infant death, if he belongs in this family at all.
3.   Edward E. Watkins, born February 21, 1861 and died January 29, 1900. Married December 7, 1888 in Montgomery County, Maryland, to Cordelia B. Mullinix, born January 23, 1870 and died May 30, 1937. Buried at Bethesda United Methodist Church at Browningsville. The family appears in the 1900 census for Browningsville, with the three youngest children; they had four children. After his death, she was married second to Oscar Thomas Mullican, born 1886, and had four children. Children of Edward E. Watkins included:
a.   P. Madge Watkins, born February 26, 1890, died January 24, 1895.
b.   Maynard Wilson Watkins, born September 6, 1894, and died November 3, 1973. Married Elsie Beall, born January 21, 1900, died February 16, 1982. Both buried in cemetery of the Bethesda United Methodist Church, Browningsville. At least two sons:
   (1)   Royce Maynard Watkins, born June 27, 1923, and died October 30, 1975 at Washington County Hospital, in Hagerstown, Maryland, buried in cemetery of Bethesda United Methodist Church at

Browningsville. His wife was Mary Virginia, born August 9, 1927. Children:

    (a) Royce Maynard Watkins, Jr.; Browningsville.

    (b) Daughter, married John Hardy, of Damascus.

  (2) Ernest E. Watkins, of Frederick.

c. Pearl L. Watkins, born c.1897; married Beall.

d. Rosie M. Watkins, born c.1898

4. Annie D. Watkins, born c.1864; died before 1921. Married Mullinix and had children:

a. Urna R. Mullinix.

b. Robert E. Mullinix.

5. Joseph G. Watkins, born 1866, according to the census. He probably is Joseph Grant Watkins, born February 23, 1866 and died February 22, 1928, Joseph Grant was married February 17, 1893 to Nettie F. Beall. She was born December 3, 1872 and died August 12, 1937. They are buried at Bethesda United Methodist Church cemetery, Browningsville, Maryland. There is an unnamed infant buried with them, with no dates. They appear in the 1900 census for Clarksburg, with their son, Lester. He is the only known surviving child:

a. Lester Steele Watkins, born June 23, 1895, died March 19, 1966. Married June 1, 1921 Mazie Nadine Brandenburg, born November 18, 1897, the daughter of Bradley Jefferson Brandenburg (1865) and Valerie Eveline Hyatt (1867). Buried in cemetery of Bethesda United Methodist Church, Browningsville. They had children:

  (1) Eloise Nadine Watkins, born September 11, 1925 and died September 29, 1925.

  (2) Lester Edsel Watkins, born October 21, 1927, and married October 15, 1949 Peggy Woodfield, born April 3, 1928, daughter of William Robert Woodfield and Grace Rogers. They had children:

    (a) Steven Edsel Watkins, born July 16, 1952 and married June 28, 1974 to Shirley Tucker, born January 16, 1952, of Annapolis, the daughter of Joseph Lester Tucker and Josephine Benning. One child.

　　　　(b)　Dennis Wayne Watkins, born June 2, 1955
　　　　　　and married October 2, 1982 Tania Moxley,
　　　　　　born January 22, 1962. Two children.
6.　Samuel C. Watkins, born 1868, according to the census. He is
　　probably the same individual who is buried with his wife in the
　　cemetery of Bethesda United Methodist Church at Brown-
　　ingsville, as are numerous other members of the Watkins fam-
　　ily. She was Josephine Lee, born 1877 and died April 21,
　　1947, and they were married September 24, 1898 in Mont-
　　gomery County, Maryland. Josephine was received into mem-
　　bership at Mountain View Methodist Church July 1, 1906;
　　Samuel on February 9, 1908. They appear in the 1900 census
　　for Clarksburg, with their first child. They had children:
a.　Roby Selman Watkins, born March 6, 1899 at Lewisdale,
　　died April 19, 1975 at Montgomery General Hospital in
　　Olney, Maryland. Buried at Mountain View cemetery,
　　Purdum. He was survived by his wife, Margaret C.
　　Runkles, born February 6, 1914, died December 18,
　　1985; four grandchildren, and two children:
　　　　(1)　Nancy Lee Watkins, married MacKenzie of Mt.
　　　　　　Airy.
　　　　(2)　Wayne Sellman Watkins, born May 15, 1938 near
　　　　　　Lewisdale. Married May 9, 1962 to Evelyn Louise
　　　　　　Day, born April 7, 1943, daughter of Hanford
　　　　　　Perry Day (1916) and Marie Allen Chick (1921).
　　　　　　They had children:
　　　　　　(a)　Catherine Marie Watkins, born June 15,
　　　　　　　　1963; christened at the Mountain View
　　　　　　　　Church, Purdum, Maryland.
　　　　　　(b)　Patricia Lynn Watkins, born August 12, 1967
b.　Nellie Irene Watkins, born May 10, 1901; married Octo-
　　ber 24, 1918 to Elias Dorsey Lawson.
c.　Samuel Calvin Watkins, born October 12, 1905. Also
　　found as Calvin S. Watkins, he died October 13, 1973.
　　His wife was Nettie Emily Burdette, born March 12,
　　1911, daughter of George H. Burdette (1870) and Sarah
　　Elizabeth Watkins (1871). Buried Montgomery Chapel,
　　Claggettsville. They had at least one daughter:

(1)   Rosie Elaine Watkins, born August 9, 1939. Married July 6, 1957 to Bernard Oscar Cordell, born March 22, 1937 at Clarksburg, son of Welty Cordell.

7.   Caroline Clark Watkins, born February 16, 1870 and died April 22, 1953. Married to Samuel V. Broadhurst, born September 10, 1866 and died May 21, 1956.

8.   Morgan H. Watkins, born November 8, 1874, died December 24, 1930. Bethesda United Methodist Church cemetery at Browningsville.

9.   Mary Francis Watkins, born November 8, 1873, and married to Beall.

10.   Julius M. Watkins, born 1876. This is probably Julius Monroe Watkins, who lived in Browningsville, and was married there April 4, 1900 at the home of J. L. Watkins, to Martha Ann Burdette. Mention of the home of J. L. Watkins suggests that his father, Julius, had a middle name beginning with the letter L., although we have not found that in the records. He was listed as a farmer, and she as a servant. He was born 1876 and died 1962; she was born 1877 and died 1967. Both are buried in the Bethesda United Methodist Church cemetery at Browningsville, Maryland. Her will, dated January 30, 1962 at Monrovia, was probated February 29, 1968 and filed in will book WES 104 at folio 178 in Montgomery County. She names two daughters, and at least one child was buried with his parents:

a.   Infant son, died November 5, 1901

b.   Ada Frances Watkins, born September 27, 1911 at Lewisdale, Maryland.

c.   Vertie Watkins, married to Moxley.

11.   Martha A. Watkins, born c.1878, appearing in the 1900 census with her widowed mother.

12.   Rosetta May Watkins, born January 11, 1879 and died 1940. Married to George Cutsail. At least one daughter:

a.   Fannie Cochel Cutsail, born there July 13, 1900, and died April 26, 1977 at the Frederick Nursing Center; buried with her husband. In Church records at the Historical Society, her middle name is spelled Coachell. Married December 7, 1917 to Ira Lansdale Burdette, born January

5, 1900, died April 11, 1970; buried at Bethesda United Methodist Church near Browningsville, where he had been a Trustee since the age of eighteen, and a former superintendent of the Sunday School. He was a son of Abraham Lincoln Burdette (1864) and Georgia Ellen Waters King (1867). A daughter:

(1) Olive Virginia Burdette, born January 23, 1919, died April 16, 1995 at home in Damascus. Married September 2, 1939 to Glenwood Dawson King, born c.1918, died May 6, 1996 in Damascus, and was son of R. Delaney King (1874) and Mary Sybil Ward (1880). Glenwood was, for many years, chief of employee services for the Montgomery County government, prior to his retirement. He was also a Nationwide Insurance agent for 44 years, and chairman of the board of the Bethesda United Methodist Church, where he and his wife are buried. Children:

(a) Bonnie Elaine King, born June 16, 1940 at Browningsville, and married Delmas Foster of Damascus. Two daughters:
1. Penny Sue Foster, born 1961
2. Tammy Lynn Foster; May 21, 1964
(b) Judy N. King, and married to Thomas Knoll and had a child:
1. Troy Knoll.

13. Richard Watkins, a Captain, of California
14. Hattie G. Watkins, born August 29, 1882. Married December 9, 1908 at Clarksburg, Maryland to Ernest H. King. Both said to be from Lewisdale.
15. Cora J. Watkins, married to Burns. Named in administration of the estate of her mother.

Jeremiah Watkins
1787-1856

This son of Nicholas Watkins (1763) and Rachel Lewis was born November 26, 1787. In the 1850 census for Clarksburg District of Montgomery County, there is a household headed by Jeremiah Watkins, born c.1787. There is also one Susan Watkins, born c.1800, who is perhaps his wife, as well as Christopher Johnson, born c.1836, and black. His will, dated February 16, 1855, was probated September 15, 1857 and recorded in Liber WTR 2 at folio 349, will records of Montgomery County. He there styles himself as Jeremiah Watkins of N. He leaves to his two eldest sons, Richard and Caleb Watkins, the lands on which they then reside, known as part of *Mt. Radnor*, containing two hundred and fifty acres. To his youngest son, Grafton Watkins, he leaves another part of *Mt. Radnor*, whereon he resides, containing 100 acres, and a twenty acre tract on which his negro man Harry then lives, providing that Harry is permitted to remain there for life, rent free. Grafton also receives a negro boy, also named Grafton. He leaves to his daughter, Ara Ann Watkins, wife of Lorenzo D. (Dow) Watkins, his negro girl, Margaret. To his daughter Margaret Becraft, he leaves a negro girl, Sarah. He directs that two other negroes, Nelson Hammond and Lydia Elizabeth, be sold to the highest bidder of the five children. Finally, he leaves to his son, Richard, the silver watch "left to me by my father, Nicholas Watkins." From the will, we see that his family consisted of:

1. Richard Watkins.
2. Caleb H. Watkins, born about 1816. The 1850 census of Clarksburg District has a household headed by Caleb Watkins, born c.1818, probably this individual. He has a wife, Sally, born c.1809, and four children. Also in the household is one George W. Lovejoy, born c.1829, a farmer. The wife of Caleb was Sarah J. Lovejoy, by whom he had one son. Apparently her brother was living with the family in 1850. The 1860 census for Damascus District also lists the family, with his wife now called Sarah, and three of their children, including Joanna as the then youngest. The 1870 census of Damascus lists Caleb at the age of 52, with Louisa J. Watkins, age 26, and four very young children. This is Caleb's second wife, Louisa J. Brown, by whom he had seven children. The 1880 census for Cracklin District includes the household of Luther E. Clagett, born c.1851. His wife, Joanna, and several children appear there, and there is also one Caleb H. Watkins, age 64

(born c.1816), listed as father-in-law. Additionally, there is Elmore E. Watkins, age 16, brother-in-law; and Amanda C. Watkins, sister-in-law. The children of Caleb were:

a. Jeremiah Columbus Watkins, born December 25, 1841, and of whom more following.

b. Rebecca Watkins, born c.1843

c. Sarah C. Watkins, born c.1845

d. Joanna Watkins, born c.1848, married December 23, 1869 in Montgomery County, to Luther Edward Claggett, born c.1851. As mentioned above, they appear in the 1880 census of Cracklin District, with several of their children, and members of Joanna's family. Children:
  (1) Robert E. Claggett, born c.1871
  (2) Alfred S. Claggett, born c.1872
  (3) Rosie B. Claggett, born c.1874
  (4) Alvertis Claggett, born c.1876
  (5) George Claggett, born c.1878
  (6) Joseph E. Claggett, born c.1880

e. Elmore Everett Watkins, born 1863, died 1950. Married to Margaret E. Becraft, born 1865 and died 1941. Both buried at Montgomery Chapel, Claggettsville, Maryland. In the 1900 census for Damascus, he is listed as Elmon E. Watkins, with his wife, and one child:
  (1) Cora E. Watkins, born c.1891

f. Tobias Calvin, found simply as Calvin in several records, was born about 1865 and died in 1954 at Kemptown, in Montgomery County, Maryland. He and his wife are buried at Providence Cemetery at Kemptown. He is listed as Calvin in the 1900 census for Howard County, with his wife and three children. Married to Mary Roberta Brandenburg, born c.1866, daughter of Jesse B. Brandenburg (1824) and Sarah Rebecca Purdum (1829). Children:
  (1) Grover Sim Watkins, born May 14, 1892
  (2) Oakley Massarene Watkins, born February 3, 1895. The name is spelled Oaksly on church record cards of the library of Montgomery County

Historical Society in Rockville, but Oakley in the 1900 census.

    (3)   Infant Watkins, born May 10, 1897; died June 1, 1897.

    (4)   Virgie I. Watkins, born c.1899

    (5)   Infant Watkins, born August 24, 1900; died October 4, 1900.

g.   William Eldridge Watkins, born c.1867 and died April 1, 1943. Married November 7, 1894 to Emma Rose Buxton, born August 21, 1874 and died June, 1957; daughter of Basil F. Buxton (1843) and Charlotte Lavinia Brandenburg (1851). William and his wife are buried at Montgomery Chapel, Claggettsville, Maryland. His will, dated May 23, 1924, was probated May 12, 1950 and filed in will book WCC 49 at folio 166, Montgomery County. They had children:

    (1)   Myra Lavinia Watkins, born February 16, 1896, died 1987. Married December 28, 1915 at the parsonage in Kemptown Emory Cross Woodfield, born June 17, 1889, died December 9, 1934, son of Thomas Griffith Woodfield (1856) and Emma Cassandra Boyer (1868), and had children:

        (a)   Eldridge Woodfield.

        (b)   Rose Woodfield.

        (c)   George Woodfield.

    (2)   Nellie Mae Watkins, born July 4, 1897; married to Mullinix.

    (3)   Albert Dewey Watkins, born January 28, 1899, and died December 12, 1968; buried Forest Oak Cemetery, Gaithersburg, Maryland. Married Helen Mobley, who predeceased him.

    (4)   Cora Elaine Watkins, born March 1, 1901; and married Solomon.

    (5)   Anna Louise Watkins, born February 16, 1903 and married Shoemaker.

h.   James Henning Watkins, born December 15, 1868 and died August 20, 1952. Married November 22, 1892 to Mary E. Burdette, born June 30, 1873 and died March

20, 1942. Both are buried at Montgomery Chapel, Claggettsville. The couple appear in the 1900 census for Damascus, where he is listed simply as Henning. They have two young children at the time. He was perhaps married twice, according to marriage and newspaper records of Montgomery County, Maryland. There is a second marriage reported under this name: in July, 1908 to Annie E. Woodfield of King's Valley. The latter report stated that James H. was of Cedar Grove, and the marriage took place at Laytonsville Methodist Church. This last marriage is not believed by the author to be the individual under study, but a coincidence in names that has not been resolved. Our James Henning had children:

(1)   Alonzo Watkins, born c.1896
(2)   Gladys Watkins, born c.1899
(3)   Bertha Catherine Watkins, born April 23, 1900
(4)   Daphnia Marie Watkins, born August 23, 1904
(5)   Winfred Watkins, born November 28, 1905, died September 4, 1991 at his home in Mount Airy, Maryland. Buried at Pine Grove Cemetery, Mount Airy. His obituary lists his name as we have it here; church records list Winfield. His wife was Daisy Leatherwood. One daughter survived him:
   (a)   June Marie Watkins, married Doyle and had children:
      1.   Deidre Doyle.
      2.   Tina Doyle, married Faecke, of Mount Airy. One daughter.
(6)   James Russell Watkins, born January 3, 1908
(7)   Irving Bromwell Watkins; September 13, 1913
i.   Amanda C. Watkins, born c.1871
j.   Annie E. Watkins, born 1872, died 1923. Married Oliver M. Hood, born 1864, died 1907. Both buried at Prospect cemetery, Mt. Airy, Maryland.
k.   Jessie Watkins, born 1874.
3.   Grafton Watkins, born c.1823, of whom more.
4.   Ara Ann Watkins, born 1814, married July 8, 1837 in Frederick, Maryland, to Lorenzo Dow Watkins, born 1807 (who was

perhaps her cousin), son of Thomas Watkins (1774) and Charity King (1769). In the 1880 census for Cracklin District, Lorenzo appears alone, said to be 70 years of age and widowed. He is listed as a doctor, and under health, is said to be bilious. They had children:

a.   Charity A. Watkins, born c.1838
b.   Martha T. Watkins, born c.1839; married October 8, 1857 to Luther M. Watkins, a cousin, born March 2, 1831, died April 15, 1900, the son of Alpha Watkins (1803) and Harriet Ann Lewis (1805). The family appears in the 1870 census for Damascus, in Clarksburg District, with five children. In the *Sentinel* death notice, Luther M. Watkins was said to have been a school teacher for forty-two years, a minister for thirty years, a gauger at King's distillery, a census taker for three times, and at the time of his death, a justice of the peace. The family appears in the 1870 census for Damascus, in Clarksburg District, with five children. Martha was the mother of at least:
    (1)   Laura V. Watkins, born 1859, perhaps died young
    (2)   Agnes E. Watkins, born c.1862
    (3)   Spencer J. Watkins, born c.1864
    (4)   Willie M. Watkins, born c.1866
    (5)   Elsie M. Watkins, born c.1869
c.   Eveline K. Watkins, born c.1846
d.   Mary C. Watkins, born c.1848
e.   May B. Watkins, married William J. Lewis; a child:
    (1)   Russell Lewis.
5. Margaret Watkins, married to James Becraft.

Jeremiah Columbus Watkins
1841-

This son of Caleb Watkins (1818), was born December 25, 1841. In the 1870 census, he appears in his father's household, with his wife, Annie W., born c.1848, and their first child. This is apparently the same Jeremiah who appears as head of household in the 1880 census of Cracklin District, Montgomery County, said to be 38 years old (born c.1842). His wife was Ann Wilson Moxley, born about September 28, 1847, died September 10, 1887, daughter of Risdon Moxley (1812) and Eleanor Mullinix (1821).

1. Edward Watkins, born c.1867
2. Sylvester Watkins, born December 7, 1869, of whom more.
3. Sarah Elizabeth Watkins, born c.1871, of whom more
4. Milton Watkins, born c.1873, of whom more
5. Louisa Agnes Watkins, born August 13, 1874, died September 10, 1954, single. Buried Prospect United Methodist Church cemetery at Mt. Airy, Maryland.
6. Lucinda Walker Watkins, born c.1877, died 1978. Married to William Hardy, born 1876, died 1957. Both buried at Howard Chapel United Methodist Church cemetery. Four children:
   a. Arthur R. Hardy, died June 5, 1899, infant death
   b. William A. Hardy, died September 6, 1901, infant death
   c. Norman Henry Hardy, married to Helen Smith and divorced. Married second Helena Lenora DeGrange Hull, born July 24, 1906, died May 12, 1989, the daughter of Thomas F. DeGrange and Erma V. Heffner. One child:
      (1) Joan Lucy Hardy, married Henry Degano; a child:
          (a) Henry Degano, born January 19, 1973
   d. Annie Hardy, married first Elmer Smith, and after his death, married second Charles Brown. No children.
7. Josephine Watkins, born October 30, 1879, died 1965, Married Noah W. Phillips, born 1874, died 1942. Buried at the Montgomery United Methodist Church cemetery Claggetsville, Maryland. They had children:
   a. Edwin Worthington Phillips, born June 1, 1903, died June 12, 1938
   b. Ruth Naomi Phillips, born 1907, died 1932
   c. Annie Harriett Phillips, born 1911, married Thomas Stinson Hilton, born March 31, 1914, son of Thomas Garfield Hilton (1880), and had children:
      (1) Stanley Hilton.
      (2) Jeanette Hilton.
      (3) Brice Hilton.
      (4) George Hilton.

d. Irvin Woodrow Phillips, born April 9, 1914, and died March 2, 1934. Married Annie Pearl Luhn, daughter of Wilbur Luhn, and twin sister of Myrtle Luhn. After the death of Irvin, Annie married second Carl Warren Miller. Irvin and Annie had one child:

    (1) Naomi May Phillips, born April 29, 1933. Married Allen Clark Edge, born March 29, 1932, and had two children:

        (a) Allen Clark Edge, Jr., born February 25, 1953. Married July 1, 1978 to Barbara Ann Mawdsley.

        (b) Nancy Ann Edge, born August 31, 1955. She married July 18, 1977 Alexandro Dillanueva Hipano, Jr., and had one child.

e. Nowlin S. Phillips, born December 18, 1915. Married December 24, 1939 to Hattie Bell Lugenbeel, born May 10, 1923. Four children:

    (1) Ruth Naomi Phillips, born May 21, 1941. Married September 17, 1960 to Wells Clinton Hay and had two children. She married second September 15, 1978 to Melvin T. Waskey, no children. Her two children from the first marriage were:

        (a) Roxanne Carol Hay, born May 30, 1961, and married May 10, 1985 to Perry Jerdin. They had one child:

            1. Leah Nicole Jerdin, born July 31, 1983

        (b) Diane Lynn Hay, born December 24, 1962. Married May 15, 1985 to Steve James Sears and had two children:

            1. Jessica Leigh Sears; January 1, 1986

            2. Shana Leanne Sears: November 1, 1988

    (2) R. Wayne Phillips, born July 11, 1943. A doctor, he married June 30, 1965 to Alice Ruth Adams, and had one child. He married second November 25, 1978 to Miriam Ruth Anderson, and had two children, twins. His three children were:

        (a) Rebecca Lynne Phillips, born October 13, 1968.

          (b)   Linsey Christine Phillips: February 16, 1983

          (c)   Ashley Violet Phillips: February 16, 1983

    (3)   Richard Nowlin Phillips, born July 7, 1946 and married January 23, 1971 to Mary Carol Thomas. Two children:

          (a)   Shannon Dana Phillips: May 29, 1976

          (b)   Nathan Jonathan Phillips: May 10, 1983

    (4)   Paul Wesley Phillips, born December 19, 1952 and married May 14, 1974 to Georgene Barbara Frisoli. Two children:

          (a)   Geoffrey Paul Phillips; March 9, 1976

          (b)   Kristen Thersa Phillips; August 1, 1978

8.   Jeremiah M. Watkins, born 1881, died 1941. Married Bessie American Lowman, born January 29, 1886 in Carroll County and died October 11, 1957. They first lived in Unionville and then moved to Mt. Airy, where they are buried in Pine Grove cemetery. One child:

    a.   Etta Viola Watkins, born April 17, 1910. Married first to Paul Snyder, born February 2, 1907, died December 9, 1963 and had one child. On April 8, 1972, Etta Viola married second John Walter Hart, born April 6, 1916 and died April 26, 1983. He had two daughters from a prior marriage. Etta's one child was:

          (1)   Paul Edward Snyder, born October 26, 1942 and married June 27, 1964 to Doris Ann Franklin, born February 24, 1946, of Winfield, Maryland.

9.   Nicie Watkins, also known as Unice Watkins, born 1884 and married to Harry Gue. Nicie died giving birth to their child:

    a.   Harry Willard Gue, infant stillbirth 1884.

10.   Marcellous, or Morris, Watkins, born May 9, 1886, died August 10, 1971. Married December 24, 1910 to Anetta Gue, born August 19, 1883, died October 23, 1970, daughter of Hamilton Gue. Two children:

    a.   Nevlon Marcellous Watkins, born December 11, 1917. Married August 24, 1940 to Georgetta Rippeon, born August 2, 1922, the daughter of Charles A. Rippeon and Beulah Molesworth. Three children:

(1) George Nevlon Watkins, born September 8, 1946, married April 24, 1976 to Cynthia Glenn, born December 5, 1954. Three children:
    (a) Kathryn Marie Watkins; June 6, 1978
    (b) Emily Dawn Watkins; April 12, 1981
    (c) Lisa Diane Watkins; June 16, 1983

(2) Brenda Lee Watkins, born December 19, 1952 and married December 19, 1980 to Ernest Eugene Kisner. He was born September 15, 1951 and they had one child:
    (a) Joseph Brandon Kisner; November 22, 1981

(3) Deborah Kay Watkins, born February 28, 1955. Married May 10, 1973 Mark Preston Bowman and had two children:
    (a) Leah April Bowman; April 16, 1976
    (b) Terri Marcella Bowman; March 9, 1981

b. Albert Lewellys Watkins, born February 9, 1922, and married February 8, 1947 to Loretta Estelle Molesworth, born August 31, 1926, daughter of Eli Thomas Molesworth (1898). Two children:

(1) Ronald Eugene Watkins, born August 23, 1947 and married October 30, 1969 to Marie Ridgely, born February 19, 1949, of Woodbine. They had two children:
    (a) Thomas Andrew Watkins, born November 20, 1970 in Indiana.
    (b) Shannon Marie Watkins, born July 15, 1974

(2) Linda Diane Watkins, born July 15, 1950. Married May 21, 1977 to Donald C. Brightwell, born July 16, 1942. No children.

Sylvester Watkins
1869-1950

This son of Jeremiah Columbus Watkins (1841) and Ann Wilson Moxley (1847), was born December 7, 1869, died November 2, 1950. Married December 28, 1897 to Helen E. Buxton, born March 2, 1880 and died January 16, 1961, at the bride's home near

Kemptown. Both buried in the cemetery of Montgomery Chapel, Claggettsville. She was the daughter of Basil Francis Buxton and Charlotte L. Brandenburg. Children, including:

1. Rudy Edward Watkins, born August 13, 1898, died October 7, 1982. Married Delma Viola Mullineaux, born 1893, died 1966, the daughter of Eldridge Mullineaux and Rosene E. Merson. Another report (cemetery record) states that the wife of Rudy was Delma Viola Buxton, born 1893, died 1966, the daughter of Upton Buxton and Jane Wolf. After the death of Delma, Rudy Edward married second Hazel Viola Hall, who had been previously married and was from Kansas. Two children born to his first marriage:

   a. Betty Lee Watkins, born September 22, 1924. Married Clayton Otis Smith of New Market, born June 10, 1913, had two children, and was divorced. Married second Eric Leopold Van Glabeke, born September 28, 1924. Clayton married second Joyce Anne Norwood, born September 9, 1938. The two children of Betty Lee Watkins from her first marriage were:

      (1) Gerald Edward Smith, born September 10, 1947.
      (2) Sharon Lee Smith, born May 8, 1951. Married to Merhle Wayne Warfield, born December 15, 1950, and had children:
         (a) Jason Edward Warfield, born April 8, 1979
         (b) Kristin Leeann Warfield, born July 26, 1984

   b. Rudell Edward Watkins, born April 29, 1932. Married June 14, 1952 to Norma Lee Lewis, born November 7, 1932, daughter of Eugene Francis Lewis (1910) and Linda Amelia Bennett (1913). Two children:

      (1) Bruce Edward Watkins, born March 5, 1957.
      (2) Debra Lee Watkins, born February 27, 1958. Married February 11, 1978 to Gary Ray Estapinal, born January 15, 1955; divorced. One son:
         (a) Justin Ray Estapinal, born November 11, 1983

2. Norman Sylvester Watkins, born December 17, 1900 and died February 9, 1986. Buried at Laytonsville Methodist Church cemetery. Married July 27, 1929 to Ethel Hilda Mount, born

July 17, 1911, daughter of Wilfred Edgar Mount and Nona Augusta Burns. Three children:

a. Mary Jean Watkins, born January 17, 1931. Married March 30, 1967 Homer W. Akridge, born March 10, 1929. No children reported.

b. Shirley Lee Watkins, born August 26, 1933, died August 2, 1984. Married March 8, 1952 to Donald Eugene Butt, and had children:

   (1) Donald Eugene Butt, Jr., born June 30, 1955. Married July 18, 1979 to Ann Kelly Willard.

   (2) Mark Timothy Butt, born December 8, 1958. Married August 21, 1982 to Susan Marie Holz, born June 12, 1959, daughter of Dr. Richard G. Holz of Frederick, and had children:

      (a) Kathleen Lee Butt, born February 21, 1984

      (b) Jacob Watkins Butt, born March 14, 1987

c. Barbara Ann Watkins, born September 5, 1938. Married August 27, 1954 to Bedford Ashley Dodson, born March 29, 1936, and had a son. Barbara Ann married second on June 8, 1968 to Charles Junior Reed, born September 28, 1940. Her one child was:

   (1) Norman Bedford Dodson, born December 31, 1954. Married Shirley October 24, 1981; a son:

      (a) Adam Charles Dodson, born May 3, 1983

3. Addie Watkins, born December 5, 1902. Married to Gary U. Stull, born September 27, 1899, died April, 1954. They had nine children:

a. Eloise Stull, born February 5, 1923. Married Sterling McQuay and had children:

   (1) Jane McQuay.

   (2) Jean McQuay, married Warnick and had children:

      (a) Susan Warnick.

      (b) Gail Warnick.

   (3) Sterling McQuay, Jr.

   (4) Terri Lynn McQuay, married Pickett. Children:

      (1) Bruce Pickett.

      (2) Bridgett Lynn Pickett, born c.1988

   (5) Kelly McQuay.

b. Gary U. Stull, Jr., born March 15, 1927. Married Marion and no children reported.
c. Miriam Stull, born April 26, 1928. Married to Norman Shipley and had children:
   (1) Robin Shipley, married Graham.
d. Charles Stull, born March 30, 1929, married and had four children:
   (1) Deborah Stull, married Myers, and had children:
       (a) Ericka Myers.
       (b) Nicole Myers.
       (c) Tiffany Myers.
   (2) Charles Stull, Jr.
   (3) Pamela Stull, married Graham.
   (4) Brian Keith Stull, died 1988
e. Mary Stull, born June 22, 1930. Married Kenneth Haines and had children:
   (1) Sharon Haines, who marrried Robinson and had children:
       (a) Jessica Robinson.
       (b) Brian Robinson.
   (2) Michael Haines, married and had children:
       (a) Nathaniel Haines.
       (b) Camrell Haines.
   (3) Bonnie Haines, married McEvoy.
f. Dorothy Stull, born October 13, 1931. Married George Long.
g. Stanley Stull, born July 4, 1934; married Shirley, and had a daughter:
   (1) Bonnie Stull.
h. Lois Stull, born July 17, 1938. Married Richard Ford.
i. George Stull, born June 30, 1940. Married Jo Ann and had a son:
   (1) Michael Stull.
4. Anna Reba Watkins, born January 2, 1908. Married January 28, 1942 in Frederick, to John Wesley Thompson, born October 26, 1900, died August 29, 1965. No children.
5. Lester Basil Watkins, born April 3, 1910, died November 14, 1968. Married Ruth Evelyn Swartzbaugh, born July 21, 1914,

died November 20, 1984. Buried at Montgomery Chapel. Children:

a. Lois Evelyn Watkins, born August 24, 1931, married January 27, 1951 to Walter Lee Cline, born August 18, 1926, son of Carl Albert Cline (1898) and Esther Leith Moxley (1898). They had children:
    (1) Michael Lee Cline, born June 30, 1951
    (2) Robin Lynne Cline, born November 9, 1954

b. Mildred Colleen Watkins, born January 12, 1933. Married first to Ronald Max McPherson and second on December 22, 1979 to Charles Peter Schuettler, born February 20, 1919. Children from her first marriage:
    (1) Stephen Duane McPherson, born July 29, 1956
    (2) Ronald Max McPherson, Jr., born April 7, 1959. Married December 7, 1984 to Cynthia Thompson, who was previously married to Granahan. She was born February 28, 1958. One child:
        (a) Matthew Ronald McPherson, born September 16, 1985.

6. Lucy Marian Watkins, born June 16, 1914. Married to John Roland Swartzbaugh, born July 9, 1908, and had children:

a. Doris Elaine Swartzbaugh, born April 11, 1931. Married George Raymond Sauble, Jr., and had children:
    (1) George Roland Sauble, born January 26, 1950. Married Kathy Sue Adamson, born August 16, 1950, and had children:
        (a) Kristin Anne Sauble, born June 26, 1976
        (b) Janis Elaine Sauble, born April 14, 1979
    (2) Scott Randal Sauble, born December 17, 1954. Married to Sharon Kosenski, and had children:
        (a) Scott Randal Sauble, II: November 8, 1983
        (b) Justin Raymond Sauble: October 17, 1985

b. Betty Swartzbaugh, born April 23, 1938, died April 14, 1990. Married Fred Dioquino and had children:
    (1) Timothy Dean Dioquino, born May 20, 1958. An officer in the Coast Guard, he married Judith Lynn Ott, born March 23, 1958.

        (2)   Teresa Rene' Dioquino, born November 29, 1960. She was a deputy sheriff in Pinellas Park, Florida.

7.   Robert Watkins, an infant death at five months.

8.   Helen Elizabeth Watkins, born June 26, 1917. Married November 28, 1936 to Herbert Gervis Miller, born December 21, 1914, and had seven children:

    a.   Joyce Ann Miller, born August 18, 1937. Married November 10, 1956 to Allen Bliss, born March 18, 1932, and had a daughter:

        (1)   Dawn Bliss, born February 25, 1958. Married to Michael Montlenone and had one child. Married second September 5, 1985 to Glenn Michael Miller, born December 19, 1958. Her child was:

            (a)   Dawn Bliss (Montlenone) Miller, who was born January 25, 1979.

    b.   Elsie Miller, born October 2, 1938. Married first Dale Thomas Clickner, born November 25, 1930; and second on June 13, 1983 to George Hogan. Children from first marriage only:

        (1)   Dale Thomas Clickner, Jr. born February 10, 1960 and married August 9, 1986 to Christina Polansky, born November 23, 1962.

        (2)   James Andrew Clickner, born September 7, 1961

    c.   Helen G. Miller, born October 5, 1941. Married April 22, 1958 to Robert Jessie Rawles, born March 28, 1935, and had children:

        (1)   William Douglas Rawles, born June 14, 1960 and married January 29, 1980 to La Brenda Ashley, born August 12, 1961, and had children:

            (a)   Jennifer Hope Rawles: November 23, 1981

            (b)   Marci Ann Rawles: May 23, 1984

        (2)   Robert Cleon Rawles, born February 19, 1964. Married December 9, 1985 to Tiffany Swartout, born May 28, 1966, and had children:

            (a)   Jessica Rawles, born February 2, 1989

        (3)   Carl Rawles, born May 6, 1966. Married June 28, 1968 to Carla Ingram, and had children:

            (a)   Cody Allen Rawles, born January 28, 1986

d. Mary Miller, born August 28, 1943. Married first Zollars who died, and second June 24, 1986 to Larry Simmons, born July 12, 1946. They lived in Louisiana; no children.

e. Herbert Allen Miller, born December 30, 1945. Married May 16, 1968 to Melva Gerhart, born August 28, 1948 and had two children:
   (1) Patricia Ann Miller, born January 2, 1971 and died January 8, 1971.
   (2) David Allen Miller, born October 17, 1982

f. Beverly Jo Miller, born March 14, 1947. Married to Frederick Miller, born November 16, 1933; divorced after two children:
   (1) Michael Allen Miller, born January 25, 1967.
   (2) Glenn Scott Miller, born October 6, 1974

g. William David Miller, born January 25, 1950. Married August 3, 1974 to Beverly Lowe, born October 14, 1947. She had two children by a prior marriage.

9. Alvin Rudell Watkins, born January 17, 1921 and married August 30, 1945 to Maizie H. Haines, born April 12, 1925, the daughter of Walter Edward Haines (1890), and Rosie Smith (1895). Children:

a. Alvin Rudell Watkins, Jr., born November 20, 1946. Married July 24, 1971 to Ruby L. Wisner, born May 1, 1953, the daughter of Paul and Mildred Wisner of Frederick. Three children.

b. Glenda Eileen Watkins, born July 5, 1950. Married February 14, 1978 David Devilbiss. No children.

c. Bernard Lee Watkins; March 3, 1960.

Sarah Elizabeth Watkins
1871-1913

This daughter of Jeremiah Columbus Watkins (1841) and Ann Wilson Moxley (1847), was born c.1871 and died 1913. Married to George H. Burdette, born 1870 and died 1942. They lived on Penn Shop Road, near Mt. Airy, Maryland. Both are buried at the Montgomery cemetery, Claggettsville, where her stone gives the date of birth as 1875, which may be correct. Six children:

1. Raymond W. Burdette, born August 17, 1892, died December 10, 1934. Married to Fannie M., born March 18, 1895, died November 17, 1974. They are both buried at Montgomery Cemetery at Claggettsville, and had several children.

2. Lillian Mae Burdette, born April 16, 1894, died March 28, 1987. Married Roby Byrd Miles, born May 23, 1888, died August 11, 1975. Buried at Damascus Methodist Church. Roby was the only child of James F. Miles (1853) and Emily Catherine Rabbit (1856). Children:

   a. Dorcas Miles, born June 14, 1915, died August 30, 1969. Married April 16, 1941 to Druid Andrew Clodfelter, born August 29, 1912. They had four children:

      (1) Druid Miles Clodfelter, born February 9, 1942. Married January, 1962 Dawn Lopp of Thomasville, North Carolina. They had three children. He was married second in 1973 at Durham, to Julie Johnson, and had one child. He married third on December 13, 1986 to Linda McCormack. His children were:

         (a) Sheryl Kimberly Clodfelter, born December 26, 1962, in Durham, North Carolina.
         (b) Lori Dawn Clodfelter, born June 18, 1964 in Olney, Maryland. Married August 13, 1988 Robert James Larrabee.
         (c) Druid Douglas Clodfelter, born May 29, 1970 in Durham, North Carolina.
         (d) Kellie Miles Clodfelter, born February 17, 1975 in Durham, North Carolina.

      (2) James Robert Clodfelter, born April 23, 1943 in Frederick, Maryland. Married 1967 in Mississippi to Elizabeth Joyce Wright, and had a son:

         (a) Christopher Andrew Clodfelter, born October 16, 1986.

      (3) Dorcas Eugenia Clodfelter, born March 22, 1951. Married March 6, 1976 to Aris Mardirossian, born January 3, 1951 in Iran of Armenian parents. He is a well-known businessman in Montgomery County and present owner of the *Flaming Pit Restaurant*

and other ventures. They have three children, born in Olney, Maryland:

- (a) Emily Dorcas Mardirossian, born January 30, 1978.
- (b) Toni Mardirossian, born February 22, 1980
- (c) Tracy Mardirossian, born August 6, 1984

    (4) Emily Virginia Clodfelter, born January 9, 1953. Married August 13, 1977 to Raymond C. Sherman

  b. Emily Eugenia Miles, born August 30, 1920. Married March 13, 1971 to Druid Andrew Clodfelter (1912) the widower of her sister, Dorcas Miles (1915).

3. John William Burdette, born July 4, 1895, died April 7, 1969
4. Nicie Burdette, married Sokol. Lived in Baltimore, and had no children.
5. Carrie Louise Burdette, born September 13, 1908, died April 20, 1978. Married February 19, 1925 to Joseph Stanislaus Knott, born June 13, 1904, died August 10, 1987, son of Francis Alexander Knott (1848) and Louise Albine Merz (1869). He first opened a blacksmith shop in Urbana, and later expanded the business to become Knott's Garage, finally as Knott and Geisbert, Inc., Machine Shop. Children:

  a. Catherine Louise Knott, born July 18, 1926. Married first Walter Z. Gibbs and second to Leonard Martin Kemper, born January 12, 1929, having children by both:

    (1) Frances Ann Gibbs, born November 26, 1945, and married July 11, 1965 to Steven Eugene Wert, born August 4, 1943. One son:

      (a) Robert Allen Wert, born June 5, 1972

    (2) Milton Paul Gibbs, born March 25, 1950. Married February 14, 1970 to Patricia Ann Rossbach, born March 16, 1952 and divorced after two children. He married second August 22, 1986 ro Kristis Jane Wetzel, born July 18, 1956. His two children:

      (a) Milton Paul Gibbs, Jr.: September 21, 1970.

      (b) Kathryn Anne Gibbs: January 4, 1975

    (3) Leonard Martin Kemper, II, born December 9, 1957. Married to Roxanne Marie Warhime, born May 2, 1962, and had children:

        (a)   Sondra Marie Kemper: October 29, 1979

        (b)   Crystal Lynn Kemper: February 28, 1984

    (4)   John Albert Kemper, born September 2, 1961. Married September 5, 1987 to Tammy Lynn Bridges, and had a child:

        (a)   Samantha Lynn Kemper: May 16, 1988

    (5)   Wanda Sue Kemper, born December 2, 1962

b.   Evelyn Frances Knott, born February 2, 1930. Married February 14, 1953 to Theodore Edward Reynolds of Brunswick, Maryland, born February 17, 1919, and died January 21, 1984 and had a child:

    (1)   Patricia Ann Reynolds, born May 23, 1956.

c.   Joseph Stanislaus Knott, II, born May 4, 1945. Married first to Connie L. Warrenfeltz of Frederick and divorced after one child. Married second Donna Jean Taylor, born February 15, 1949, and had two children. His children were:

    (1)   Lea Deanne Knott, born June 24, 1972

    (2)   Joseph Stanislaus Knott, III, born April 14, 1979

    (3)   Edward Nathan Knott, born July 16, 1984

6.   Nettie Emily Burdette, born March 12, 1911. Married July 27, 1929 to Calvin Samuel Watkins, born October 12, 1905, died October 13, 1973, son of Samuel C. Watkins (1868) and Josephine Lee (1877). One child:

a.   Rosie Elaine Watkins, born August 9, 1939. Married July 6, 1957 to Bernard Oscar Cordell, born March 22, 1937 at Clarksburg, son of Welty Cordell.

Milton Watkins
1873-1965

This son of Jeremiah Columbus Watkins (1841) and Ann Wilson Moxley (1847), was born February 13, 1873, and died April 13, 1965. Buried at Pine Grove cemetery, Mt. Airy, Maryland. Married Dora E. Phebus, born March 14, 1877, and died October 22, 1946, and had two children:

1.   Emily Catherine Watkins, born October 19, 1903, and died November 27, 1967. She was a school teacher, serving in sev-

eral smaller schools in Montgomery County. Married July 13, 1925 to Clifton Webster Burns, born February 23, 1925, died June 2, 1979. She is buried in Pine Grove cemetery at Mt. Airy; he is buried at Mt. Olivet cemetery, Frederick. They had four children, and were divorced. The children were:

a. Charles Meredith Burns, born January 30, 1929. Married November 11, 1951 to Joan Marie Hoade, born September 6, 1931 at Mt. Airy. They had children:

    (1) Karen Kristine Burns, born April 18, 1953. Married first November 7, 1976 to John Shaffer, born May 1, 1941, and divorced after one child. She was married second June 2, 1984 to Thomas Joel Stansfield, born December 4, 1953, and had two children. Her three children were:

        (a) Liana Marie Shaffer: September 22, 1977

        (b) Timothy Joel Stansfield: May 8, 1986

        (c) Samuel Andrew Stansfield: July 11, 1988

    (2) Marcie Lee Burns, born April 18, 1955. Married April 26, 1975 to Raymond Franklin Harne, born March 12, 1954 at Mt. Airy, and had children:

        (a) Alyssa Renee' Harne: July 16, 1981

        (b) Nicholas Ryan Harne: November 5, 1983

        (c) Jacob Daniel Harne: July 3, 1986

    (3) Wendy Sue Burns, born December 30, 1957. Married October 4, 1980 to Thomas Cross, born October 4, 1947 at Mt. Airy, and had children:

        (a) Jason Thomas Charles Cross: April 20, 1982

        (b) Adam Christian Cross: December 26, 1985

    (4) Lori Gail Burns, born May 17, 1960

    (5) Beverly Jill Burns, born May 16, 1966

b. Richard Courtney Burns, born January 13, 1932. Married March 8, 1952 to Dolores Pauline Stup, born June 3, 1932, of Frederick, and had children:

    (1) Vicki Lynn Burns, born December 9, 1952. Married March 22, 1980 to Jonathan F. Bland, born November 19, 1952, and had children:

        (a) Lauren Rebecca Bland: July 7, 1980

        (b) Courtney Alcutt Bland: June 18, 1985

       (2)   Ann Renee' Burns, born August 20, 1958. Married September 10, 1983 to Samuel Connor Bland, born July 11, 1955, and had children:

           (a)   Alexandra Connor Bland: January 2, 1986

           (b)   Connor Richard Bland: August 31, 1988

c.   Ann Yvonne Burns, born July 22, 1933. Married August 17, 1951 to Robert Lincoln Gosnell, born September 17, 1930, died April, 1984, and had children:

       (1)   Joyce Ann Gosnell, born May 17, 1953. Married to Charles Keller Watkins. No children.

       (2)   Robin Michelle Gosnell, born April 7, 1958. Married September 17, 1977 to Kevin Richard Hubble, born September 15, 1957, son of Marvin W. Hubble, and had two children:

           (a)   Robert Andrew Hubble: March 5, 1980

           (b)   Kevin Daniel Hubble: November 19, 1986

d.   Catherine Jane Burns, born August 26, 1935. Married October 2, 1953 to Robert Eugene Lowman, born November 19, 1933, and had children:

       (1)   Robert Dale Lowman, born January 20, 1954. Married October 27, 1979 Deborah Mae Mullinix, born June 29, 1954, and a son:

           (a)   Jeffrey Dale Lowman: March 15, 1981

       (2)   Lisa Ann Lowman, born March 8, 1958. Married April 7, 1979 to Robert Michael Smith, born January 27, 1956, and had children:

           (a)   Ryan Michael Smith, born May 12, 1985

           (b)   Chad Robert Smith, born December 25, 1987

       (3)   Cheri Jean Lowman, born August 10, 1959. Married May 2, 1980 Russell Dods and had children:

           (a)   Meghan Renee' Dods, born May 27, 1984

           (b)   Derek Russell Dods, born April 24, 1987

       (4)   Gina Yvonne Lowman, born April 20, 1962

2.   Velma Winifred Watkins, born October 22, 1906, and died May 6, 1986. Married twice, first December 22, 1925 to Raymond J. Spurrier, born August 6, 1897, died August 15, 1939. She married second to Claude Fillmore Brandenburg, born January 19, 1904, died August 13, 1979. He had been

previously married to Mary Angeline Spurrier (1902), by whom he had four children. Three children were born to the first marriage of Velma:

a. Mary Elizabeth Spurrier, born August 12, 1927. Married William F. Shock, born April 29, 1923, and had children:

    (1) Leslie Winifred Schock, born August 25, 1949. Married twice, first to Peter Bortz, and second to John Christopher.

    (2) Stephen Kelly Shock, born March 12, 1952. Married Mary D. Fulton, born October 8, 1953, and had a son:

        (a) William Jackson Shock: July 17, 1986

    (3) Joseph Francis Shock, born November 18, 1955. Married to Jo Ann Baker, born August 31, 1957.

b. Milton Eugene Spurrier, born July 1, 1928, and blind from birth, and was the first blind student to graduate from Towson State College. Married December 26, 1953 to Carole Dentz, born July 14, 1935. Five children:

    (1) Ellen Ann Spurrier, born April 9, 1955

    (2) Lisabeth Ann Spurrier, born July 29, 1957. Married Lawrence Richardson, born June 27, 1956, and had children:

        (a) Joshua Richardson, born August, 1982

        (b) Zachary Richardson, born March 15, 1984

    (3) Michael Eugene Spurrier, born September 17, 1961. Married Linda Lee Landgraf, born April 8, 1953.

    (4) Barbara Ann Spurrier, born June 22, 1963

    (5) Laura Ann Spurrier, born May 21, 1965. Married Kirk Damon, born June 22, 1964

c. Catherine Winifred Spurrier, born December 5, 1929. Married March 29, 1953 to Rodney Thomas Gist, born January 23, 1930 of Baltimore, and had children:

    (1) David Thomas Gist, born May 19, 1954

    (2) Kathryn Denise Gist, born April 9, 1957. Married to James Farinholt, born May 27, 1954.

(3)   Kimberly Ann Gist, born August 10, 1959. Married May 20, 1978 to Aldon Lednum, and had children:

       (a)   Patricia Ann Lednum: October 8, 1979
       (b)   Christopher Aldon Lednum: August 9, 1982

Grafton Watkins
1823-1881

This son of Jeremiah Watkins (1787), was born c.1823. The 1850 census of Clarksburg District, Montgomery County, and the 1860 census of Damascus District, includes a household headed by Grafton Watkins, born c.1824, which could be this person. In the 1870 census of Damascus, he appears with his wife, and ten children. He appears also in the 1880 census for Clarksburg District, with his wife and nine children, and two other individuals. They are Martha Becraft, born c.1857, listed as a daughter, and Lucie Becraft, born c.1871, listed as a granddaughter. He is listed as constable, and has a wife, Rhoda A. Watkins, born c.1830. She was Rhoda Ann Mullinix. The couple are buried at the Montgomery Chapel cemetery, near Claggettsville. He died December 31, 1881 at the age of 58 years, 8 months and 16 days (born April 15, 1823). His wife died January 19, 1890 at 60 years, 9 months and 8 days (born April 11, 1829). From the census reports, Grafton could have been born between 1824 and 1828.

Various records relative to the estate of Grafton exist in the office of the Register of Wills for Montgomery County, Maryland. There is an inventory of the personal estate, submitted January 24, 1882 by Cornelius Watkins, Administrator, and recorded in liber RWC 13 at folio 90. It is rather lengthy, but provides an excellent view of what was required to operate a farm in that period of our history. For that reason, it is included here, just as it was submitted:

Dining table	$ 3.00	Safe	2.50
Oil cloth cover	.25	1 clock, brass	1.50
Waiters, small	.05	Lamps	.50
Knives and forks	.75	Table	.75
1/2 dozen slip chairs	.75	Desk	.75

Spinning wheel & reel	1.25		Lot crocks	.50
Trundle bed	5.00		Cook stove complete	6.50
Lot tin ware	.25		Kitchen safe	1.50
2 benches	.25		Bedstead	2.50
Shot gun	3.00		2 baskets	.25
Bedstead	1.50		1 bread tray	.50
5 barrels	.50		1 trunk	.30
1 chest	.25		Lot old books	.50
Saddle pockets	.25		Saw and hatchet	.25
Parlor stove	6.00		Clock, wooden	2.00
Lounge, frame	.25		Book stand	.50
Looking glass	.50		1 bureau	4.00
Table oil cloth	.25		Lot old carpet	.50
2 strand sleigh bells	1.50		Bedstead	2.50
Bedstead	1.50		Corner cupboard	4.00
1 Saber and pistol	.25		2 rocking cradles	1.00
Lot old china and table	.50		Lot boxes and barrels	1.50
Lot boards	4.00		Wagon and bed	15.00
Jersey wagon	25.00		Wheelbarrow	2.50
Lot sacks	1.50		2 log chains	2.00
Maul, wedges & 2 rings	.75		1/2 bushel	.25
Set single harness & whip	2.00		Digging iron	.75
Grindstone	.75		1 sled	.75
Scythe & cradle	1.50		Hoes, shovels	1.75
Rakes and mattock	.75		Single & double trees	1.00
Lot old iron	.50		Tar bucket	.10
Wagon sheet	.75		About 6 barrels of corn	16.50
Pair hames and axe	1.00		Lot chesnut shingles	6.00
Hay carriage	2.00		Two bar plows	2.00
Single & double shovel			Harrow & cultivator	4.00
plow and corn cover	3.00		Lot tobacco	125.00
Lot tobacco sticks	4.50		Lot rye straw	25.00
Lot growing wheat	115.00		2 stacks hay	25.00
Lot fodder	5.00		1 sleigh	4.00
1 wheat fan	8.00		Cutting box	1.50
Lot rye	28.00		Lot forks	.40
Lot fertilizer	5.50		Lot shucks	1.00
Lot chaff	.50		Two cows	27.00
Bay mare	20.00		1 black colt	45.00
1 brown horse	60.00		1 wagon saddle	2.50
Breeches, 2 sets	18.00		Lead gear, 2 sets	4.00
Lot bridles	3.00		Lot collars	1.50

| Plow gears, line & halter 3.00 | Sheep | 16.00 |
| Sow and shoats 26.00 | Lot growing rye | 40.00 |

On May 2, 1882, an estimate of the value of the real estate of Grafton Watkins, deceased, was filed with the Register of Wills, in liber RWC 13 at folio 188. Assessment was made by Jackson Day and John Warfield, who reported that the deceased was owner of a farm of 175 acres, of which 35 acres was wooded. It was improved by 2 dwelling houses, barn, 4 tobacco houses, corn crib, wagon house, garden and orchard; "all in fair condition." The appraisers set an annual value of one hundred and twenty dollars, which we assume represented the estimated rental yield per year. Cornelius Watkins filed a final accounting on February 13, 1883, listing the net value of the estate, and the list of heirs for distribution, being ten children, all named, who each received one dollar, fifty-four and one fifths cents from the personal estate. On September 9, 1890, first and final accounts of the estate of Rhoda A. Watkins were filed by Darius F. Watkins, and recorded in liber RWC 19 at folio 240 in the wills office of Montgomery County. That report includes the names of ten children, all of whom were then living, with the exception of Cornelius. The known children were:

1. Martha Watkins, born c.1847, not included in the distribution of her father's estate. Married Becraft and had at least one daughter:
   a. Lucie Becraft, born c.1871
2. Augustus Watkins, born c.1850; also shown in the census abstracts as Augustine. A newspaper abstract from the Montgomery County Sentinel, dated August 5, 1921, states that Augustus was then visiting relatives in Montgomery County, and that he was from Winnebago, Minnesota, but a native of Damascus, having moved to Minnesota c.1881. He is listed in the accounts of his mother's estate.
3. Darius Franklin Watkins, born May 9, 1851, and died May 25, 1923; buried in the Montgomery Chapel cemetery, at Claggettsville, Maryland. Married July 10, 1886 in Montgomery County, to Fidelia E. Reed, born August 1, 1862, died April 15, 1944 and buried with her husband. In the 1900 census for Damascus, Fidelia's mother, Rachel A. Reed, born

c.1840, is living in the household. Fidelia filed final accounts December 5, 1923, recorded in liber HCA 28, at folio 423 in the wills office of Montgomery County. Six children are listed as heirs; we have identified seven, one of whom must have been an early death:

a. Cornelius Herbert Watkins, born c.1888. This individual's wife was I. E. Watkins, and they had children, born near Kemptown, Maryland, including:
    (1) Edna Vernonice Watkins; March 8, 1916.
    (2) Earl Cornelius Watkins; December 8, 1918

b. Amos F. Watkins, born c.1890. Married December 30, 1914 to Marcie F. Snyder.

c. Della A. Watkins, born c.1892; married Burdette.

d. Amanda Zerah Watkins, born February 19, 1893. Married to Long.

e. Bates Ewing Watkins, born March 4, 1894 and died May 19, 1970; lived on Ridge Road in Damascus, Maryland. Married June 9, 1917 to Rebecca Waters Allnutt, born April 23, 1894 and died July 14, 1969. Their tombstone carries the same birth dates given here, but report his death as May 19, 1976, and hers as July 19, 1965. Buried at Montgomery Chapel cemetery at Claggettsville. They had two children, born near Kemptown:
    (1) Eleanor Rebecca Watkins, born October 23, 1919. Married April 6, 1940 John Raymond Molesworth, born March 26, 1918. Two children:
        (a) John Raymond Molesworth, Jr.
        (b) Jennifer Molesworth.
    (2) Audrey Jean Watkins, born September 3, 1927. Married March 18, 1950 Charles Carroll Parker, born May 10, 1925. Four children:
        (a) Randall Charles Parker.
        (b) Barry Ewing Parker.
        (c) Timothy Lee Parker.
        (d) Peter Alan Parker.

f. Darian Fidelia Watkins, a twin, born December 10, 1898. Not listed in the final accounts, nor in the 1900 census for the family. This is perhaps an inaccurate report. Note that the birth date is the same as for the child following, and that the middle initial of the following child is F., which could be Lottie Fidelia Watkins. Or, of course, the two could have been twins, and this child died.

g. Lottie F. Watkins born December 10, 1898 at Damascus, Maryland, and died June 5, 1979. Married December 3, 1919 at the Kemptown parsonage to James Herbert Mullinix, born November 13, 1894 and died December 7, 1980, son of James Asbury Mullinix (1861) and Fannie Ernestine Mullinix (1868). Buried at Howard Chapel. Lottie was the mother of six children:

   (1) James Albert Mullinix, born January 20, 1921 and died November 22, 1994 at Sun City Center, Florida. Married to Vina Patton.
   (2) H. Winford B. Mullinix, born June 5, 1928
   (3) Margaret E. Mullinix, born December 16, 1929
   (4) Edward L. Mullinix.
   (5) David R. Mullinix.
   (6) Robert B. Mullinix.

4. Cornelius Watkins, born c.1853, of whom more.
5. Susan E. Watkins, born c.1855
6. Lavinia Watkins, born c.1857
7. Ellen M. Watkins, born c.1858, or Ella M. Watkins. She is not included in the distribution of her father's estate; but is listed in her mother's accounts, there listed as M. E. Watkins.
8. Alice B. Watkins, born c.1860; married Gardner.
9. Hepsie P. Watkins, born c.1863; married Harrison.
10. David W. Watkins, born c.1868, died September 29, 1900. Montgomery Chapel, Claggettsville.
11. Fannie G. Watkins, born c.1868 (or Fannie E.). Married to Mullinix.
12. Marsh Watkins, born c.1869. A son, the name was hard to read on the census microfilm, and could be an error. Final accounts of the estate of Grafton Watkins include a daughter named Missouri E. Watkins, who may well be this child. No other child listed in those accounts could have been.

Cornelius Watkins
1853-1883

This son of Grafton Watkins (1823) was born c.1853. Probably the same who was married May 18, 1875 to Ida M. Merson, and died April 8, 1883 at the age of 29 years, 5 months and 11 days. They appear in the 1880 census of Clarksburg District, Montgomery County, with three children. Buried in the Montgomery Chapel cemetery, at Claggettsville.

Inventory of his estate was filed by William C. Merson, Administrator, on April 24, 1883, indicating a fairly prosperous young man, who died so early. William C. Merson was perhaps either the father or a brother of the wife of Cornelius. It is of interest, for comparison to that of his father, above, and to our own personal holdings in todays society.

Bread tray	$ .50	Preserving kettle	$ .25
Single straw tick	.20	Trundle stead	.75
Stabler lantern	.20	Bedstead	1.50
Bedstead, straw tick		Writing desk	1.00
and pillows	2.50	Pair quilting frames	.25
Shot gun, single	1.00	Turn back kitchen table	2.00
Half dozen wooden		Kitchen table	.25
bottom chairs	1.50	Safe	2.00
Set knives and forks	.50	Lot dishes	1.00
Coffee mill	.25	Rocking chair	.10
Cooking stove complete	15.00	Lounge complete	7.50
Lot tin ware	1.00	Butter print	.10
Ice cream freezer	.50	Dining table and cover	2.00
Sideboard	1.50	Rag carpet, 18 yds	1.50
30 hour clock	1.50	Dining room stove	3.00
3 cromos framed	.25	Coat rack	.05
8 cane seat chairs	2.50	Set goblets & butter dish	.25
Lounge	.25	Dozen glass jars	.50
Chest	.50	Grindstone & hangings	.50
Lot tubs	.10	Churn	.25
15 bushel potatoes,		Earthen crocks	.25
early and late	5.25	2 rakes and shovel	.10
Hoes, mattocks	.25	2 axes	.50
Plow	5.00	Double & single tree	.25

Double shovel plow	.50	Tar bucket	.05
Corn coverer	.75	Single shovel plow	.50
Two horse harrow	2.00	Slide	1.00
Bed for hauling tobacco	.25	Road wagon	25.00
Lot boxes and barrels	1.00	Grain cradle	1.50
15 barrels of corn	37.50	Lot buckwheat	.50
Lot guano sacks	.25	Corn basket	.10
2/3 of lot clover hay	12.00	Half bushel measure	.25
Riding saddle & bridle	4.00	2 blind bridles	2.00
2 sets backbands & traces	1.50	2 horse collars	1.00
2 sets breeching	12.00	2 horse halters	.25
Rope plow line and		Wagon saddle	3.00
curry combs	.10	Sorrel mare, Doll	125.00
Bay mare and colt	75.00	7 shoats	49.00
1 buffalo cow	25.00	2/3 crop of tobacco	60.00
2/3 crop rye growing,		2/3 crop 15 acres of	
2 and 1/6 acres	8.65	wheat growing	80.00
Hay carriage	2.00	Wash board & jugs	.37
Coal oil can	.10		

The personal estate of Cornelius was appraised by John Warfield and Nathan J. Burdette. In the settlement of his mother's estate, dated September 9, 1890, liber RWC 19, folio 240, Cornelius is said to be deceased, leaving a widow and four children to divide his share of the estate. The known children of Cornelius Watkins, and Ida M. Merson, were:

1. Annie E. Watkins, born c.1876
2. William C. Watkins, born c.1878
3. Ada E. Watkins, born c.1880

Elizabeth Hall Watkins
1811-

This daughter of Nicholas Watkins (1763) and Rachel Lewis was born January 29, 1811, and married to Owen Brown, born c.1816. They had one daughter, according to information received in 1997 from Rodney H. Darby of Rockville, Maryland. However, the 1850 census of Montgomery County included the family, with numerous children. The 1860 and 1870 census for Damascus, then in the Clarksburg District, includes the family also. Children:

1. Rhoda Brown, born c.1827
2. Ephraim Brown, born c.1828
3. Thomas G. Brown, born c.1831
4. Rachel A. Brown, born c.1837
5. William G. Brown, born c.1839
6. Richard G. Brown, born c.1841
7. Sarah E. Brown, born c.1843
8. Mary Elizabeth Brown, born c.1844, married to George M. Moxley, born 1836, of whom more.
9. Louisa J. Brown, born c.1844
10. Anna Brown, born c.1846
11. Owen Cornelius Brown, born c.1848
12. Christina Brown, born c.1849
13. Lucretia V. Brown, born c.1850
14. Catherine Brown, born c.1854
15. Elizabeth Brown, born c.1855
16. Margaret E. Brown, born c.1856
17. James T. Brown, born c.1856

Mary Elizabeth Brown
1844-

This daughter of Elizabeth Hall Watkins (1811) and Owen Brown, was married to George M. Moxley, born 1836 and died 1896. They had eight children:
1. Cornelius Edward Moxley, born 1861. Married Florence Poole, born 1863, and had children:
   a. Elsie Leonie Moxley, born 1884, died 1978. Married to Mullinix.
   b. Emory Dorsey Moxley, born 1888, died 1968
   c. James Golden Moxley, born 1890, died 1963. Children:
      (1) Golden Jane Moxley, born 1925. Married Brown.
      (2) Ruby Lee Moxley, born 1928. Married Phillips.
   d. Floyd Simms Moxley, born 1895, died 1974. Children:
      (1) Floyd Keen Moxley, born 1928. Children:
         (a) Glenn Floyd Moxley, born 1953
         (b) Nancy Lee Moxley, born 1957; married Hood

e. Nellie Estelle Moxley, born 1897, died 1963. Married to Mullinix.
f. Vernie Lansdale Moxley, born 1900. Married Madeline Buxton.
g. William Cornelius Moxley, born 1903. Married Hilda Moxley.
h. Edgar Maynard Moxley, born 1907.
2. Anna Belle Moxley, born 1863. Married Flemming.
3. Asbury Moxley, born 1865.
4. William Seymour Moxley, born 1866
5. James Oscar Moxley, born 1868, and had at least one son:
a. George Clyde Moxley.
6. Orville Moxley, born 1871
7. George Crawford Moxley, born 1875, died 1972. Children:
a. Virgie B. Moxley, born 1903
b. May Moxley, married Tittsworth.
c. Thomas Moxley.
d. Gertrude Moxley.
e. Bernice A. Moxley, born 1928. Married Morris.
8. Ira Dorsey Moxley, born 1876, died 1940. Children:
a. Della Moxley, born 1902
b. Edna Moxley, born 1904
c. Pearl Elizabeth Moxley, born 1912

CHILD 6

Gassaway Watkins
1772-

This son of Jeremiah Watkins (1743) was born November 2, 1772, married Arianna Norwood, and had children:
1. Silas B. Watkins, born c.1814, of whom more. This son of Gassaway Watkins was born c.1814 in Montgomery County, Maryland. Appearing as the head of household in the 1850 census of Clarksburg District, Montgomery County, Maryland, Silas was born c.1814, and had a wife, Sarah E. Watkins, born c.1814, and seven children. He appears again in the

1870 census, with his wife, and just two of the children, all of whom were:

a.   Mary E. Watkins, born c.1837
b.   Oliver Watkins, born c.1839.
c.   Emily J. Watkins, born c.1841
d.   Lucinda Watkins, born c.1844
e.   Susan R. Watkins, born c.1845
f.   William Edward Watkins (or William A., born c.1847, according to some records). However, the 1870 census of his father's household; and the 1880 census for the Clarksburg District carries William E. Watkins, born c.1855, with a wife, Fannie L. Watkins, born c.1861. In their home there is one Sarah E. Watkins, age 65, listed as mother. That could be the household of this individual. If so, William Edward was born March 22, 1855 and died June 10, 1930, as reported in the *Sentinel* newspaper of June 20, 1931. He appears in the 1900 census for Damascus with his wife, and four children. Married to Fannie Leannah Hyatt, born January 29, 1861, and died October 29, 1927. Both are buried at the Montgomery Chapel, Kemptown, Maryland. She was a daughter of Thomas A. Hyatt (1831) and Alcinda Moxley (1839). Her will, dated March 18, 1927, was probated November 29, 1927 and filed in Liber PEW 9 at folio 402 in the will records of Montgomery County. She names her husband, and one son. They also had at least four daughters, as stated in Fannie's death notice in the Sentinel, but we now know only three of them. The children were:

(1)   Morgan Herbert Watkins, born January 13, 1882, died February 21, 1952, of whom more.

(2)   Bessie May Watkins, born April 29, 1884 and died August 30, 1975. Married November 15, 1900 to Jesse Becraft, born March 26, 1879 and died July 24, 1962, the son of Grafton Becraft and Senora Clagett. One child:

    (a)   Mable Watkins Becraft, born April 12, 1901 and died March 21, 1987. Married December 25, 1917 Robert Lee Etchison, born August

21, 1898, died May 14, 1976, son of John Osborne Etchison, and Mary Virginia Penn. One child:

1. Ramona Etchison, born February 13, 1929. Married April 12, 1975 to Jack Driskill, born April 24, 1924, a barber and real estate agent, now deceased. As a personal aside, Jack was the barber who gave the author's youngest son his first haircut about 1959. Ramona had been previously married, with two children.

(3) Mamie Alice Watkins, born December 25, 1886, died January 24, 1969. Married to Ernest Davis Duvall, born March 3, 1883, died May 26, 1960, son of Joseph Duvall. Children:

(a) Idell Genevieve Duvall, born August 4, 1915. Married June 8, 1936 Carl Emile Dornheim, Jr., born October 15, 1912, died October 14, 1973, son of Dr. Carl Emile Dornheim (a veteranarian) and Mary Catherine Weidman. Idell had one son:

1. Carl Emile Dornheim, III, born February 25, 1945, died September 20, 1970. He was married to Carol Ann Boone, and had one son.

(4) Lola Leanna Watkins, born September 17, 1897, died March 17, 1980. Married December 25, 1915 to Harry Clifton Stanley, born January 19, 1895, died November 28, 1949, son of Harry and Fannie Stanley. Lola married second July 30, 1952 to Sterling Elwood Day, born April 1, 1891, and died November 17, 1984, son of Columbus Washington Day (1859) and Leanna Adelaide Hobbs (1862). Lola and Harry Clifton Stanley adopted two sisters without legal process or name change.

g. Rhinaldo Watkins, born March 13, 1850, died August 2, 1926 and buried in the Damascus Methodist Church cemetery. His wife is buried with him, Airy C., born

March 4, 1853, died February 10, 1915. He appears in the 1880 census of Frederick County, and the 1900 census of Damascus, Montgomery County. They had at least two children:

(1) William S. Watkins, born c.1878, died 1947. probably the same who was married November 27, 1902 to Blanche S. Pearce, born 1882, died 1960, daughter of Levi Pearce. Damascus Methodist Church cemetery. At least one child, an infant death, buried with them:

(a) William L. Watkins, infant death March 24, 1918

(2) Bertha Watkins, born 1889, married Lewis Duvall.

2. William Watkins, head of household in the 1850 census for Clarksburg District, Montgomery County, Maryland, William was born c.1817, and has a wife, Ann Watkins, born c.1822 to 1826, and four children. Also in the household is Perry G. Watkins, born c.1826, his brother. In the 1870 census, Ann appears alone, with three of her children. They appear again in the 1860 census of Damascus District, with more of their family. Children:

a. Sarah A. Watkins, born c.1842

b. William H. Watkins, born c.1845

c. Mary E. Watkins, born c.1847. This is perhaps the same Mary E. Watkins who was born August 13, 1846, and died June 8, 1911. Married December 18, 1865 in Montgomery County, Maryland, to Charles C. King, born September 18, 1846, and died February 12, 1920, son of John A. King (1808). Both are buried at Clarksburg United Methodist Church. At least one record reports their marriage as October 15, 1866. They appear in the 1870 census of Damascus, Montgomery County, with two children. Also in the household is George G. King, born c.1854, not otherwise identified. The 1880 census includes the family, with five of their children. The children were:

(1) Bradley T. King, born c.1867 and died 1959; married June 14, 1892 to Sarah Wilson Dowden,

85

born May 31, 1867 and died 1948, daughter of Zachariah Dowden, III (1829) and Rebecca Miller (1831). Bradley and Sarah are buried at Salem United Methodist Church at Cedar Grove. They had children:

- (a) Wallace C. King, born 1903 at Cedar Grove, and died March 13, 1977. Buried with his parents.
- (b) Bertie Madeline King, born 1897; died 1983. Married May 26, 1937 William E. Crutchley, born 1868 and died 1942; no children were reported. He was apparently first married to Lydia M., born 1870 and died 1933, the mother of his children. The family is buried at the Clarksburg Methodist Church cemetery.

- (2) Hannah M. King, or Annie M. King, born c.1869, and married December 12, 1894 John E. Harding.
- (3) Norris M. King, born c.1871. Married March 13, 1907 to Elizabeth Penner, both of them being of Montgomery County.
- (4) Florence G. King, born c.1875
- (5) Maggie M. King, born c.1877
- (6) George King.
- (7) Bud King.

d. Lyde A. Watkins, a son, born c.1849. The 1880 census for Clarksburg District contains a family headed by Lyde Watkins, born c.1851 according to the census, listed as a laborer, who is probably this individual. His wife, Amanda E., was born c.1836, appreciably older than he was. They also appear in the 1900 census for Barnesville, with their youngest son. Five children:

- (1) Cora L. Watkins, born 1873
- (2) Richard Watkins, born 1875
- (3) Mary Watkins, born 1877
- (4) Theopholis, a son, born May, 1880.
- (5) Robert Watkins, born c.1882

e. Mordecai Watkins, born c.1851 to 1858. He is listed in the 1880 census of Damascus District, with his wife, Lavana W., born c.1855, and two children:
   (1) Lillie W. Watkins, born c.1874
   (2) Florida B. Watkins, born c.1877. Married on February 27, 1895 Vachel H. Davis.
   (6) Greenbury Watkins, born c.1853
f. Margaret S. Watkins, born c.1857
g. Philemon G. Watkins, born c.1859, according to census records. However, he is probably the same Philemon G. Watkins who was born March 4, 1862, died November 15, 1919. Married May 7, 1886 Amelia A. Kinder, born June 8, 1865, died February 28, 1936. In 1900 census of Laytonsville; no children listed. She married second Charles T. McClure. Montgomery Chapel, Claggettsville.
3. Perry G. Watkins, born c.1826. He was first married in Montgomery County, Maryland, April 24, 1851 to Dorothy A. Hilton, born February 8, 1828 and died January 11, 1892; buried in the Damascus Methodist Church cemetery. He married second December 5, 1899 Mrs. Emily Lewis; he was then seventy, she was sixty years of age. They appear in the 1900 census for Clarksburg, with no others in the household. There is a Perry G. Watkins listed as head of the household in the 1860 census for Damascus District, born c.1828, which could be this individual. However, his wife is listed there as Ruth A. Watkins, born c.1834. There are four small children, and two other individuals listed: Lloyd Ridgely, born c.1845; and E. A. Watkins, a female, born c.1804, who is perhaps the mother of Perry. But, in the 1870 and 1880 census, he is listed with his wife, Dorothy, which is clearly his first wife, with several children. There is yet another report we have found that lists his wife as Teresa, which we can not now explain. From all available records, it appears that his children were:
a. Oliver Watkins, born August 19, 1838 and died April 2, 1923. Buried at Montgomery Chapel cemetery in Claggettsville, Maryland, with his wife, and four sons, who died young. His wife, Susanna Ruth Etchison, was born November 15, 1844, died July 19, 1926, daughter of

Greenbury S. Etchison and Rachel Wood (the name Susanna appearing in census records). The 1870 census of Damascus includes the couple, with one infant. Also in the household is Hezekiah Burdette, aged 70 (born c.1800), listed as a farm laborer. The 1880 census for Clarksburg District, Montgomery County, includes the family, with three children. In the 1900 census for Damascus, Oliver and his wife appear with their youngest child. There were at least five:

(1)   Caroline E. Watkins, born c.1869, died 1933. Married to Jesse Darby Boyer, born October 7, 1866, died 1949. At least one daughter:
    (a)   Ruth L. E. Boyer, born July 18, 1896, died June 13, 1918.

(2)   Harry G. Watkins, born c.1874, died September 11, 1882 at age 8 years, and 7 days.

(3)   Ira H. Watkins, born c.1878, died September 20, 1882 at age 4 years, 7 months and 11 days.

(4)   Wilbur E. Watkins, born January 29, 1885, and died September 7, 1891.

(5)   Bernard Lee Watkins, born May 27, 1887, died February 15, 1904 at age 16 years, 8 months and 18 days.

b.   Cordelia A. Watkins, born c.1853; married Francis C. Beall, born c.1852, and had at least one son. The three of them are living in her father's household during the 1880 census. The one known son was:

(1)   Ernest W. Beall, born c.1878

c.   Thomas F. Watkins, born c.1854, as it appears in the 1880 census. However, in the 1870 census the name appears as Francis T., with the correct attained age. His proper name was perhaps Francis Thomas Watkins.

d.   Vernon U. S. Watkins, born c.1856

e.   Robert Bart Watkins, born c.1859, died 1906; buried at Damascus United Methodist Church. Married Sallie Merson, born March 25, 1868, died July 11, 1954. They lived in Bartholows, Maryland where he was a saloon keeper, and where their children were born. In the 1900 census for Damascus, the wife of Robert is listed as Lillie L., which is probably correct, considering that the first child bore that name. After the death of Robert Bart, Sallie (or Lillie) married second Clay F. Jones, born c.1879, and died October 27, 1910. After the death of Clay, Sallie married third to William Edward Watkins. Robert Bart's children were:

(1)   Lillie May Watkins, born c.1886. Married Ernest M. Moxley.

(2)   Harvey Lansdale Watkins, born 1888, died November 23, 1916. Married Bertie Olivia Bellison, born July 24, 1888, died August 8, 1948, daughter of Edward Leander Bellison and Hattie Virginia Moxley (1872). Harvey and Bertie had three children. After the death of her husband, Bertie married second Claud C. Hurley, born April 8, 1888, died October 26, 1969, son of Harry Mankin Hurley (1853) and Rosa Brown (1860). No children. He had been previously married also, to Ethel Mae Bellison. The three children of Harvey Lansdale Watkins were:

(a)   Lelia Edward Watkins, born October 14, 1907 and died November 23, 1916.

(b)   Robert Lee Watkins, born March 8, 1910 and died March 15, 1910.

(c)   Lorraine Virginia Watkins, born January 9, 1912. Married February 22, 1941 to Howard Greenwood Taylor, Jr., a dentist, born January 9, 1913, died April 29, 1977, son of Howard Greenwood Taylor (1875), and Flora A. Rippeon (1874). He was a Lieutenant Commander in the Navy, and later played trumpet in the bands of Joe Stephens, Dave Hagan and Clark Sheetenhelm. One child:

1.   Tamara Olivia Taylor, born November 25, 1944. Married on May 23, 1964 to Richard Thomas Newman, born May 21, 1943 in Virginia, son of Everett Emory

Newman (1919) and Billie Corby Dillon
(1919). One child.
(3)   Emma Lee Watkins, born c.1890; married Spencer
       G. Jones, born 1889, died 1954.
(4)   Raymond F. Watkins, born August 14, 1893, died
       May 9, 1953. Married to Ethel, and had one son:
       (a)   Thomas Watkins.
(5)   Herman Watkins, born December 10, 1895, and
       died February 8, 1958. Married to Beatrice Bell
       Chaney, born July 11, 1893, died March 11, 1978.
       Both are buried at the Marvin Chapel Methodist
       Church, Mt. Airy.

Morgan Herbert Watkins
1882-1952

This son of William Edward Watkins (1855) was born January 13, 1882, died February 21, 1952. Morgan was buried in the
Damascus Methodist Church cemetery. Married December 22,
1904 Mary Catherine Pearce, born June 15, 1883, died June 18,
1963, daughter of Levi W. Pearce. Children, including at least:
1. Edward Levi Watkins, born February 14, 1911, died July 15,
    1969. Buried at Montgomery Chapel, Claggettsville. Married
    Gladys Irene Watkins, born November 25, 1916, widow of
    Charles Wilson Covington. After the death of Edward Levi,
    she was married third to Hilton B. Nehouse. Gladys was the
    daughter of Ira Dorsey Watkins and Florence Elizabeth
    Molesworth. No children.
2. Wilfred Morgan Watkins, born October 12, 1914, died Octo-
    ber 10, 1978. He was married June 26, 1937 to Edith Pauline
    King, born December 18, 1915, daughter of James Rufus
    King (1871) and Della Waters Woodfield (1879). Children:
    a.   John Edward Watkins, born October, 1940, and married
          June 30, 1962 Sandra Mae Keilholtz, born July 9, 1941.
          Children:
          (1)   Stephen Edward Watkins, born December 8, 1964,
                 and married to Jeanne Weller, daughter of Alvie L.
                 Weller of Union Bridge, Maryland.

  (2) Douglas Allen Watkins, born September 11, 1966

  (3) Wayne Stuart Watkins, born July 4, 1968

  (4) Crystal Elaine Watkins, born January 12, 1970

 b. Richard Morgan Watkins, born 1944; died June 15, 1948 of leukemia. Buried in Damascus Methodist Church cemetery.

 c. Rachel Paulette Watkins, born November 26, 1949. Married February 3, 1968 William Donald Wivell, born July 26, 1946, and had children:

  (1) Todd Anthony Wivell, born October 5, 1970

  (2) Timothy Albert Wivell, born April 17, 1973

 d. Deborah Susan Watkins, born November 10, 1954. Married December 23, 1976 to William Charles Clarke, born January 8, 1954, and had children:

  (1) Amanda Marie Clarke, born November 9, 1979

  (2) Michael Richard Clarke, born October 9, 1986

CHILD 7

Thomas Watkins
1774-

This son of Jeremiah Watkins (1743) and Elizabeth Waugh was born March 9, 1774, and married April 30, 1803 to Charity King, born c.1769 in Frederick County, Maryland, in an area which became Montgomery in 1776, daughter of Edward King (1740) and Rebecca Duckett (1742). They apparently lived in the Purdum area of Montgomery County, and were ancestors of large numbers of the Watkins family still living in the county. His will, dated February 28, 1855, was probated September 16, 1856 and recorded in Liber WTR 2 at folio 293 in the will records of Montgomery County. He signed the will as Thomas Watkins of Jeremiah, firmly establishing his lineage, and names his three children, leaving a small bequest to his son, Alpha, and the lands and houses equally to his other two children. Their children included:

1. Alpha Watkins, born c.1803, of whom more in Chapter 5

2. Elizabeth A. Watkins, born c.1805. She was single, and her will, dated April 29, 1867 and probated September 27, 1870

was recorded in liber JWS 1 at folio 334 in the will records of Montgomery County. It was witnessed by Middleton King and James W. Burdette, and states that she has lived most of her life with her brother, Lorenzo D. (Dow) Watkins, and that she leaves her one half interest in the land and house to him, and at his death to two of his daughters, both named. She also leaves a small personal legacy to her sister-in-law, Ara Ann Watkins, spelled Ary in the will.

3. Lorenzo Dow Watkins, born c.1807; married in Frederick County, Maryland, July 8, 1837, to Ara Ann Watkins, born 1814. He was no doubt named for the famous Methodist minister, as were many other young men of this period. His family appears in the 1850 and the 1860 census of the Clarksburg District of Montgomery County, listing him as the head of household, with his wife, and four children (following). Also in the household are his father, Thomas Watkins (1774) at the age of 75; his sister Elizabeth A. Watkins (1805); and a cousin, John Thomas Watkins (1834), then fifteen years old and listed as a laborer. In the 1870 census for Damascus, Lorenzo and his wife appear, with their daughter, Mary C. Watkins and Lorenzo's sister, Elizabeth. However, there is a child, Ulysses G. Watkins, born c.1868, who is not otherwise identified, but appears to be a child of Mary C. Watkins. In the 1880 census for Cracklin District, Lorenzo appears alone, said to be 70 years of age and widowed. Listed as a doctor, and under health, said to be bilious. Lorenzo Dow had children:

a. Charity A. Watkins, born c.1838; married October 19, 1858 at the home of her father, to Benjamin F. Burdette, born December 16, 1832, died August 17, 1895. Buried at Damascus Methodist Church. They had children:

(1) Annie M. Burdette, born April 16, 1861, and died January 7, 1887.

(2) Benjamin F. Burdette, born c.1876, died February 17, 1953. Married to Amanda M., and had at least one son:

(a) George I. Burdette, died February 29, 1908 at the age of fourteen days.

      (3)   Anita E. Burdette, born July 29, 1879, died August 17, 1879.

  b.   Martha T. Watkins, born c.1839; married October 8, 1857 to Luther M. Watkins, a cousin, born March 2, 1831, died April 15, 1900, the son of Alpha Watkins (1803) and Harriet Ann Lewis (1805). The family appears in the 1870 census for Damascus, in Clarksburg District, with five children. In the *Sentinel* death notice, Luther M. Watkins was said to have been a school teacher for forty-two years, a minister for thirty years, a gauger at King's distillery, a census taker for three times, and at the time of his death, a justice of the peace. They had children:

      (1)   Laura V. Watkins, born 1859, perhaps died young
      (2)   Agnes E. Watkins, born c.1862
      (3)   Spencer J. Watkins, born c.1864
      (4)   Willie M. Watkins, born c.1866
      (5)   Elsie M. Watkins, born c.1869

  c.   Eveline K. Watkins, born c.1846
  d.   Mary C. Watkins, born c.1848; perhaps the mother of:
      (1)   Ulysses G. Watkins, born c.1868.

CHILD 11

John W. Watkins
1782-1866

This son of Jeremiah Watkins (1743) and Elizabeth Waugh (1745), was born August 24, 1782 in Frederick County, Maryland, died September 19, 1866. Buried at Browningsville Methodist Church, Montgomery County, Maryland. Enlisted April 3, 1814 as a private in Lieutenant Thomas' detachment, 2nd regiment, infantry, commanded by Major Daniel Hughes. Discharged at New Orleans April 9, 1815. Received a bounty land warrant of 160 acres. Married Frederick County, December 8, 1829, Eleanor C. Hitchcock, born February 15, 1797 in Baltimore County, Maryland, and died Frederick County, November 7, 1860, daughter of Asael Hitchcock, Jr. (1746). The 1850 census of Clarksburg District,

Montgomery County, Maryland includes the household, with John then being 68 years of age, his wife, Eleanor is 54 years old, and only their daughter is still with them. Three children:

1. Josiah W. Watkins. This is perhaps the same individual who is buried at Bethesda United Methodist Church near Browningsville. He was born May 22, 1832, and died October 7, 1897. Married to Mary Ann, born October 7, 1830, died August 17, 1911, and buried with him. They appear in the 1860 census of Damascus District, with two children; and again in the 1870 census with eight children; and in the 1880 census for Clarksburg, with nine children. In the 1900 census for Damascus, Mary Ann is head of household, with four of her children still at home. The children were:

    a. Frances V. Watkins, born 1858. Her middle name is perhaps Virginia, and she may be the sister married to Beall as mentioned in the obituary of her brother, Album.

    b. Sarah E. Watkins, born 1859

    c. Album H. Watkins, born 1861. This child has been reported in some records as Allen H. Watkins, but this spelling of Album appears to be correct. He was born September 6, 1861 and died February 2, 1961. Buried in the cemetery of Bethesda United Methodist Church at Browningsville, as are his wife and children. According to his obituary, he was the brother of Martha P. Watkins, born 1858, died April 19, 1931; Mrs. Virginia Beall; and Catherine Watkins. He married Nettie B., born February 26, 1869, died October 10, 1956. However, in the 1900 census for Damascus, Album appears with four of the known children, but his wife is listed as Sarah J., born c.1869. Children were:

        (1) Flossie I. Watkins, born c.1892

        (2) Ann D. Watkins, born c.1895

        (3) Winfred C. Watkins, a daughter, born c.1896

        (4) Marshall J. Watkins, born July 8, 1900, lived ten months.

        (5) Clarence Gordon Watkins, born February 25, 1910, died February 10, 1915.

d. James W. Watkins, born May 25, 1864 and died April 17, 1924. Married to Addie E. Shipley, born July 18, 1887 and died December 26, 1966. Buried in the cemetery of Bethesda United Methodist Church, Browningsville. Children:

   (1) Ruth Estelle Watkins, born July 28, 1919.
   (2) James Oliver Watkins, born July 19, 1921 at Browningsville and died February 9, 1949. Buried at the Bethesda United Methodist Church

e. Joshua W. Watkins, born May 29, 1865, died February 18, 1939. Married Martha P., born August 19, 1867, died April 19, 1931. Both buried in cemetery of Bethesda United Methodist Church, Browningsville.

f. Mary R. Watkins, born 1868

g. Martha P. Watkins, born 1868

h. Catharine M. Watkins, born 1870

i. Ida P. Watkins, born 1873

2. Margaret A. Watkins, born c.1841

3. John Thomas Watkins, born September 5, 1834, and of whom more

John Thomas Watkins
1834-1908

This son of John W. Watkins (1782) and Eleanor C. Hitchcock (1797), was born September 5, 1834 in Frederick County, Maryland, and died there November 6, 1908. Buried at Providence Methodist Church. He was a miller, and was married in the county August 27, 1857, to Mary Burton Baker, born March 30, 1838 and died February 21, 1915 in Frederick County, a sister of Susan S. Baker (1848), and daughter of Thomas Baker (1800) and Anne Burton (1812). The family appears in the 1860 and 1880 census for Clarksburg District of Montgomery County, and in the 1900 census for Damascus. Five children:

1. Francis Washington Watkins, born May 13, 1858, and died November 17, 1934. Married on August 31, 1897 at Layhill, Montgomery County, to Florence P. Davis, born 1859 and died November 18, 1923, the daughter of Mrs. Mary J. Davis

(1825). Both are buried at the Rockville cemetery. The couple appear in the 1900 census of Wheaton, with the mother of Florence living in the household. The will of Florence, dated April 28, 1914, was probated May 9, 1924 and filed in Liber PEW 2 at folio 69 in the will records of the county, naming only her husband, Francis Watkins. There is, however, a report in the *Sentinel* newspaper, issue of November 1, 1929 reporting the marriage of Francis Watkins on October 26, 1929 to Mary E. Green of Clarksburg at the home of her brother, Robert Green, which is apparently a second marriage for Francis. The death notice appearing in the Sentinel of November 22, 1934, mentions the widow, Mary E. Watkins, and three known brothers of Francis Washington Watkins.

2. Martha Virginia Watkins, born c.1859. She married John H. Burdette.

3. Thomas Ellsworth Watkins, born March 11, 1862, and of whom more.

4. Vernon Dorsey Watkins, a land surveyor, born November 5, 1865, died April 9, 1956. As a young man, he lived in the Etchison area of Montgomery County; educated in the public schools and attended National Normal University in Lebanon, Ohio. Taught ten years in the county schools, after which he retired to his farm and to surveying. Ran for office of the County Surveyor, but failed to unseat the Maddox family. The author of these papers is also a surveyor, and on several occasions saw Mr. Watkins practicing his craft, well into his later years, even using crutches! Some of the men I knew called him "screwdriver" Watkins, since he had developed a means of measuring distances without an assistant, simply by fastening the measuring tape to a screwdriver and sticking it in the ground; then walking away for the desired distance. When he had completed his measurement, he just pulled harder on the tape, and dragged the screwdriver up to the new location. He was married to Blanche Etchison, according to his will, dated May 4, 1948, and filed in Liber EA 70 at folio 512 in the will records of Montgomery County, Maryland. She is the only person named in the will.

5. Arthur Reese Watkins, died June 2, 1951, married September 12, 1902 in Gaithersburg, to Ettie Elizabeth Bell, died September 21, 1955, daughter of William Louis Bell and Wilma G. Bell. His estate was filed in Case Number 9982 and that of Ettie Elizabeth in Case 9983. In both cases, their son is the Administrator, and two daughters are named. The children were:

    a. Russell C. Watkins, born c.1912 in Washington Grove, Montgomery County, Maryland, Russell died January 13, 1987 at Shady Grove Hospital near his home. Buried in Kemptown cemetery, Frederick County. His wife was Ruby G., and they had two children:

        (1) Patricia A. Watkins, married Mundy; and lived in Germantown.

        (2) Ronald L. Watkins, living in Hamilton, Virginia.

    b. Wilma Louise Watkins, married Louis S. Ulmer.

    c. Mary Elizabeth Watkins, married Bogar.

Thomas Ellsworth Watkins
1862-1949

This son of John Thomas Watkins (1834) and Mary Burton Baker (1838) was born March 11, 1862 in Frederick County, Maryland, and died February 20, 1949 in Carroll County. Married 1882 in Frederick County to Rosa Medora Moxley, born June 30, 1865 in Frederick County and died January 19, 1934 in Carroll. She was a daughter of Robert Bromwell Moxley (1840) and Susan S. Baker (1848). Thomas Ellsworth and his wife appear in the 1900 census of Damascus, with four of their children. They were parents of six children:

1. Ira Dorsey Watkins, born September 10, 1883 near Kemptown, in Montgomery County, Maryland; died February 1, 1982. His wife was Amy Bell Dietrich, born December 26, 1886, died April 8, 1980. In 1982, a new town park in Mt. Airy was named *Watkins Park* in his honor. He was president of the Peoples Lumber Supply Company of Mt. Airy, a member of the Maryland Historical Society, and several other civic and fraternal organizations. There were no children.

2. Raymond Watkins, born March 10, 1885, died September 12, 1962. He was associated for a number of years with Peoples Lumber Supply Company, a family owned business. Later, he purchased the family farm on Kemptown Road, where some of his descendants still live. Married September 18, 1913 in Rockville to Osca Pearl Brandenburg, born January 31, 1892, daughter of Ezra Brandenburg (1868), and Tillie Wren. His will, dated April 11, 1956, was probated November 13, 1962 and filed in will book VMB 155, at folio 598, in the county. They had children:

    a. Lois Virginia Watkins, born November 19, 1914; married June 17, 1934 to Francis Hahn and divorced without children. Married second in 1946 to James L. Bolger, born July 21, 1903, died November 27, 1989. No children; she lived in Miami, Florida.

    b. Janice Pearl Watkins, born March 21, 1917; married April 6, 1937 at Montgomery Methodist Church to Raymond Carl Lewis, of Kemptown, Maryland. He was born January 7, 1915, died March 24, 1972, without children.

    c. Margaret Rae Watkins, born December 13, 1919, and died March 20, 1982 in Miami, Florida. Buried at the Providence Cemetery in Kemptown, Maryland. Married December 12, 1942 to Seth Edward Bishop, and had at least one son, followed by divorce:

        (1) Ray Edward Bishop, born December 28, 1949

    d. Thomas Ellsworth Watkins, born May 9, 1922, and married December 31, 1946 Marjorie May Miles. Lived at Kemptown, divorced, no children.

3. Asa Hull Watkins, born February 12, 1887, died January 13, 1967. Married December 25, 1909 to Jessie Fay Brandenburg at her home near Kemptown, Montgomery County. She was born January 6, 1892, died September 27, 1963, daughter of Bradley Jefferson Brandenburg (1865) and Valerie Eveline Hyatt (1867). They had children:

    a. Rose Eveline Watkins, born October 18, 1915. Married December 30, 1939 to William James Kiefer, born September 16, 1914, died November 29, 1965 in a tractor accident. After his death, Rose married second Richard

Albert Mott, born February 8, 1917. Two children were born to her first marriage:

    (1)   Patricia Dale Kiefer, born September 3, 1943

    (2)   William James Kiefer, Jr., born July 2, 1947 and died April 7, 1973 in a highway accident. He left one child:

        (a)   Diana Kiefer, born c.1970

b.   Bradley Ellsworth Watkins, born June 24, 1918 and died July 6, 1981. Married Margaret Virginia Stauffer, born January 11, 1920, of Frederick, Maryland. They had two children:

    (1)   Sally Fay Watkins, born September 22, 1939 and married Ronald A. Lennox, born October 14, 1936 and were divorced in 1987, after three children:

        (a)   Valerie Ann Lennox, born March 19, 1963 and married September 28, 1986, to Douglas Alan Dailey.

        (b)   Laura Beth Lennox, born April 17, 1968

        (c)   Ronald Watkins Lennox, born August 27, 1972

    (2)   Bradley Ellsworth Watkins, born September 29, 1947. Married Marsha Lynn Cantrell, born November 28, 1946, the daughter of Verdin Smith Cantrell and Drucilla Iona Mitchell of Salisbury, Maryland. One child:

        (a)   Bradley Mitchell Watkins, born November 16, 1974.

c.   Jessie Nadine Watkins, born January 29, 1921. Married Donald Edward Grigsby, born June 16, 1918, and died August 27, 1977. They had two children:

    (1)   Don Ellsworth Grigsby, born December 28, 1942. Married Beverly Ann Nelson, daughter of William C. Nelson of Frederick. Don owned and operated Great Eastern Concrete, Inc. in Frederick. They have two children:

        (a)   Don Ellsworth Grigsby, Jr.; March 20, 1964

        (b)   Heather Lea Grigsby; July 10, 1973

 (2) Christopher Hull Grigsby, born April 23, 1949 and died September 12, 1980. Married Deborah Ann Magers, daughter of Howard Magers. They were divorced after one child. He married second Vickie and had a son. His two children were:
  (a) Heidi Grigsby, born May 28, 1972
  (b) Shane Gribsby, born November 6, 1973

4. Donald Elsworth Watkins, born October 21, 1899, died April 12, 1973. Married July 5, 1924 Elsa Corrine Bennett, born January 6, 1901 at Lonaconing, Maryland, the daughter of Burman Bennett (1869) and Margaet G. H. Linn (1869). Elsa and Donald were both teachers.

5. Robert Malcolm Watkins, born September 8, 1901, died July 3, 1954; buried at Pine Grove cemetery, Mt. Airy, Maryland. Married June 3, 1925 Hazel Owings Murray, born October 6, 1905, died October 8, 1987; buried at Howard Chapel. She was a daughter of Joseph Murray (1865) and Hannah M. Owings (1870). Robert Malcolm, known as Bunt, was an instructor of speech at the University of Maryland, and a land developer and builder. The *Watkins Memorial Park* in Largo, Maryland, was dedicated in his honor. One child:

a. Robert Malcolm Watkins, Jr., born February 21, 1932. Married first to Patricia and divorced after one child. Married second Jasmine DeBan, and had a second child:
 (1) Hannah Watkins, a musician.
 (2) Shannon Watkins, born May 1, 1966.

6. Maybelle Geraldine Watkins, born October 2, 1903 in Frederick County, and died there May 20, 1971. Married in 1920 in Virginia, to Omar John Dubel, born January 12, 1898 in Frederick County, Maryland; died September 20, 1947 in Baltimore City, son of Tyson David Dubel and Amanda Catherine DeLauter. Buried Thurmont, Maryland. They had one child, and were divorced:

a. Robert Ellsworth Dubel, born March 3, 1921 at Mt. Airy. Married in 1940 to Mary Amelia Hilton, born July 7, 1922, daughter of George Earl Hilton (1901) and Estelle W. Mullinix (1905). Robert and Mary were divorced after having one child, and she was married second to Francis Patrick Lyons of Baltimore, who adopted the son. Robert was married second April 9, 1949 to Sherley Louise Fleming, born July 5, 1930, and they had two daughters. The three children of Robert, from his two marriages, were:

(1)   Robert Ellsworth Dubel, Jr., changed to Lyons, born October 6, 1941 at Olney, Maryland. Married September 5, 1964 at Laurel, Maryland, Cynthia Anne Davies, born February 6, 1946 in Washington, D. C., daughter of Ronald E. Davies and Pauline Dion. They had two children:

    (a)   Lisa Ann Lyons, born April 13, 1965 at Baltimore; married May 9, 1987 C. Scott McDavid, born August 1, 1961 at Ashland, Kentucky, son of Charles Clayton McDavid and Betty Maggard.

    (b)   Erik Evan Lyons, born June 21, 1972.

(2)   Janet Fay Dubel, born February 19, 1956; married October 2, 1976 to Timothy Lee Duvall, born July 16, 1954, son of Sherwood Duvall and Hazel Butcher of Woodfield, Maryland.

(3)   Donna Jean Dubel, born October 19, 1963. She is an accomplished musician, performing at special church functions, and active in the Browningsville Band.

CHAPTER 5

Alpha Watkins
1803-1880

This son of Thomas Watkins and Charity King (1769) was born c.1803, probably on the family farm near Cedar Grove, in Montgomery County, Maryland, and died c.1880. He was married to Harriet Ann Lewis, born c.1805, and died c.1882. Inventory of her estate, dated December 5, 1882, was filed by Oliver T. Watkins, her son, and recorded in liber RWC 13 at folio 286 in the office of the Register of Wills for the county. The personal effects are rather meager, even by standards of that period, containing:

1 old wagon wheel	$ 2.50	1 cook stove	$ 1.00
1 dark cow	19.00	1 gun and tin engine	.25
1 log chain	.87	1 table	2.00
1 grindstone	.50	1 bedstead	1.25
1 safe	.25	1 cupboard	1.50
2 old steads	.25	1 note of B. F. Watkins	50.00
1 hand saw	.25		

On August 5, 1884, Oliver T. filed final accounts of the estate of his mother, recorded in liber RWC 14 at folio 206, and listed all the heirs, there being twelve living children, and the heirs of Mary S. Purdum, deceased. The family appears in the 1850, 1860 and 1870 census of Montgomery County, providing names of the children. In the 1880 census for Clarksburg District, three sons of this family were found living in adjoining households as the taker of the census listed them: Noah, James W. and Lorenzo D., each of whom are described following. The children will first be listed here, followed by detailed accounts of the families of each of those known to have had descendants:

1. Oliver T. Watkins, born c.1828, of whom more as Child 1.
2. Mary S. Watkins, born c.1829, and married December 17, 1850 to John Rufus Purdum, born c.1828. They appear in the

1860 census with seven children, in the household of his parents, John Purdum (1780) and Eleanor Purdum (1784). In 1870, they appear in their own household with nine children. Their children included, at least:

a.   Emily J. R. Purdum, born c.1852
b.   William R. K. Purdum, born c.1853
c.   Harriett Elizabeth Purdum, born c.1854
d.   Henrietta M. Purdum, born c.1856
e.   Charles W. (or L.) Purdum, born c.1857
f.   Margaret E. Purdum, born c.1858
g.   Henry Purdum, born c.1859
h.   Luther E. Purdum, born c.1865
i.   John Purdum, born c.1867
j.   James M. Purdum, born c.1870

3.   Luther M. Watkins, born March 2, 1831; died April 15, 1900. In the *Sentinel* death notice, Luther M. Watkins was said to have been a school teacher for forty-two years, a minister for thirty years, a gauger at King's distillery, a census taker for three times, and at the time of his death, a justice of the peace. He was married three times; first October 8, 1857 to his cousin, Martha T. Watkins (1839), daughter of Lorenzo Dow Watkins (1807) and Ara Ann Watkins (1814). They had a daughter, and he married second at the Methodist Church South in Gaithersburg on December 24, 1878 Mary Catherine Darby. He was married third on February 15, 1893 to Mary Rebecca Eller at the Upper Seneca Baptist Church in Cedar Grove. She died about June 27, 1931, and was buried at Upper Seneca Baptist Church at Cedar Grove. The 1880 census of Damascus District contains the family of Luther M. Watkins, born c.1831, which could be this individual. However, we read the microfilm as listing his wife's name as Margaret, born c.1841, reasonably close to the reported birth of Martha T. Watkins, above. There were three children listed in the household, all of whom would have been born to that first marriage, if we are here dealing with the same couple. For the record, we will include them here, with one other child so far identified:

a.   Laura V. Watkins, born 1859; perhaps died young.
b.   Spencer J. Watkins, born c.1864
c.   Willie M. Watkins, born c.1866
d.   Elsie N. Watkins, born c.1869

4.   William Watkins, born June 12, 1832, died April 7, 1927. Married December 9, 1852 in Montgomery County to Rachel A. Hobbs, born December 17, 1830, died December 22, 1909, but had no children. They are buried together at Upper Seneca Baptist Church in Cedar Grove, Maryland. They appear in the 1860 census for the county in Clarksburg District, at which time they have living with them one Rezin F. Minn, aged 14. William is listed as head of household in the 1870 census for the district, with his wife, and several other individuals, who are not listed as family members. The couple are listed alone in the 1900 census for Clarksburg.

5.   Rebecca Watkins, born c.1834; married in Montgomery County, Maryland, December 9, 1852, to William Miller, born c.1830, and by occupation a miller. Married second May 29, 1867 to William Waters. She appears in the 1860 census of Montgomery County with her first husband, and five children:
a.   Washington Miller, born c.1849
b.   Harriett A. Miller, born c.1855
c.   Jonathan Miller, born c.1857
d.   Jacob Miller, born c.1858
e.   William P. Miller, born c.1860

6.   Lorenzo Dallas Watkins, born August 28, 1835, of whom more as Child 6, following.

7.   Edward King Watkins, born May 31, 1837, of whom more as Child 7, following.

8.   Levi Lewis Watkins, born c.1839, and died 1906. Buried at Neelsville Methodist Church cemetery. Married December 20, 1864 in Montgomery County to Elizabeth Jane Buxton, born c.1843, and died November 28, 1928 at her home in Gaithersburg. In the 1860 census, he was living alone in the Clarksburg District of the county, listed as a miller. He appears again in the 1870 census with wife and three children, and in the 1880 census with his wife, and seven of his children. He also appears in the 1900 census for Gaithersburg, with his

wife, and four of their children. The accounting of his estate was filed by his daughter, Helen R. Watkins, and his son, Grover Cleveland Watkins, accepted by the court July 23, 1907, recorded in liber HCA 7, at folio 152. Nine of his children are listed there. Children, including:

a.   Bettie M. Watkins, born c.1866, married Chase.
b.   Maggie L. Watkins, born c.1867; married Hawkins.
c.   Edgar M. Watkins, born c.1869, died 1900.
d.   Mary E. Watkins, born c.1871; married Hawkins.
e.   May B. Watkins, born c.1873; married Duley.
f.   William H. Watkins, born c.1876
g.   Malissa J. Watkins, born c.1878; married Higgins.
h.   Helen R. Watkins, born c.1881.
i.   Esther Blanche Watkins, born c.1883, died October 10, 1961, single. Buried at Neelsville Presbyterian Church cemetery. In the 1900 census of her parents' family, she is listed as Hester B., born c.1883.
j.   Alverta Watkins; married a Watkins.
k.   Grover Cleveland Watkins, born c.1886, died February 10, 1941. Married Florence Foster, who died July 3, 1977; buried at Parklawn near Rockville. He does not appear in the 1880 census with the family, but does in 1900. He had children:
    (1)   Stanley Watkins.
    (2)   Philip Lewis Watkins.
    (3)   Foster Watkins.

9.   Elizabeth A. Watkins, born 1841, married October 29, 1868 to John S. Leamon.

10.   Harriet Watkins, born c.1843; married November 25, 1862 near Cedar Grove to John Boyer (also found as Henry Boyer). Buried in Baltimore, at Louden Park Cemetery. Children:
a.   John Spencer Boyer
b.   Mollie Boyer; died 1918, single.
c.   Harry Boyer.

11.   Benjamin Franklin Watkins, born December 20, 1844, of whom more as Child 11, following.

12.   Noah Watkins, born August 23, 1846, of whom more as Child 12, following.

13. James Willard Watkins, born September 26, 1848, and of whom more as Child 13, following.

CHILD 1

Oliver T. Watkins
1828-1894

This son of Alpha Watkins (1803) and Harriet Ann Lewis (1805) was born c.1828, and died August 26, 1894. The 1879 *Atlas of Montgomery County*, by C. M. Hopkins, CE, clearly shows Oliver T. Watkins at the village of Cedar Grove, with his residence and his store and post office. A small box of Business Notices proclaims that he is a *"Dealer in General Mdse. Country Produce taken in Exchange for Goods. Dry Goods, Boots, Shoes, Liquors, etc."* Married December 23, 1851 in Montgomery County to Eleanor Jane Brewer, born c.1835, and died February 5, 1913, the daughter of Vincent Brewer and Catherine Lewis. Oliver and his wife were first cousins, and are buried together at the Upper Seneca Baptist Church in Cedar Grove, Maryland. They appear in the 1860 census of Damascus District, with the first two of their children; and in the 1870 and 1880 census for Clarksburg District, with three of them. Eleanor Jane appears as a widow in the 1900 census for Clarksburg, with her daughter, Ida C. (1872) and four of Ida's children. First and final accounts of the estate of Oliver T. Watkins were filed by Eleanor J. Watkins, Administrator, and accepted March 30, 1897, recorded in liber GCD 6 at folio 443. Four of their children are named (Laura is not). They had children:

1. Christopher E. Watkins, born June 10, 1854; died April 7, 1915. Married to Emma Jane Lewis, born July 12, 1857; died June 3, 1900. Both are buried at Upper Seneca Baptist Church cemetery. They appear in the 1880 census for Clarksburg with their first child. In the 1900 census, they have six children in the household. There is a burial record of Ellen R. Watkins, born August 3, 1867 and died May 26, 1931; buried at Grace Episcopal Church cemetery in Silver Spring, and said to be a wife of Christopher E. Watkins. Abstracts of the Montgomery County *Sentinel*, dated May 6, 1910, report the marriage of

Christopher Watkins of Clarksburg, April 27, 1910, to Ella Jones, daughter of Samuel C. Jones of Wheaton. The announcement also includes the statement that Oscar Watkins was a brother in law of the bride, thus the brother of her husband, although we have not found him as a child of this family. The Sentinel also carried the report of her death on May 28, 1931, here calling her Ella R. Watkins. The will of Christopher, dated February 19, 1912, was probated April 20, 1915 and filed in Liber HCA 14 at folio 454 in the will records of Montgomery County. There, he leaves his estate, consisting of the home and 22 acres at Clarksburg, principally to his wife, Ellen R. Watkins, for her lifetime. Upon her death, the estate is to go to his children. The final report of his estate was filed by Melvin E. Watkins, Administrator, April 18, 1916 and recorded in liber HCA 17 at folio 154 in the wills office of Montgomery County. The widow is Ella R. Watkins, clearly indicating a second marriage for Christopher. Six children were there listed as well as heirs. All except Melvin E. Watkins were deceased prior to Ella, and her death notice states that she leaves only one adopted daughter, Dorothy Watkins, and members of her own family. Children of Christopher were:

a. Melvin E. Watkins, born May 24, 1879; died 1945. Married Myrtle M. Stull.

b. Willie Watkins, born December 30, 1881, lived 19 days. Salem United Methodist Church, Cedar Grove.

c. Etta May Watkins, born c.1883; married Wells.

d. Oliver A. Watkins, Sr., born August 24, 1886 and died January 15, 1962; buried Upper Seneca Baptist Church, Cedar Grove, Maryland. His wife is buried with him; she was Nannie G., born August 31, 1886 and died February 21, 1939. With them is an infant daughter:
    (1) Bessie Watkins, February 20, 1923.

e. Angie I. Watkins, born c.1890; married Lewis.

f. Jesse H. Watkins, born February 10, 1893; died November 1912. Buried Upper Seneca Baptist.

g. McKinley H. Watkins, born November 14, 1896 and died October 10, 1918. Buried Upper Seneca Baptist.

h.   Alpha Watkins, born March 21, 1900 and died June 10, 1919. Buried Upper Seneca Baptist.

i.   Dorothy Watkins, apparently, based on the *Sentinel* newspaper article mentioned above.

2.   Laura V. Watkins, born c.1857, apparently died young.

3.   John Oliver Thomas Watkins, born November 3, 1860, and of whom more following.

4.   Ellen V. Watkins, born c.1870; married March 27, 1893 in Cedar Grove, to Frederick L. Tschiffely. Both she and her husband were deaf mute.

5.   Ida C. Watkins, born June 10, 1872; died May 17, 1942, and married December 26, 1889 to Bradley J. Riggs, born September 30, 1869, died February 9, 1920, son of William E. Riggs (1839) and Mary Ellen King (1843). She was living in her mother's household in the 1900 census of Clarksburg and there were four children listed there as grandchildren. They are assumed to be children of Bradley J. Riggs and Ida:

a.   Bessie J. Riggs, born c.1889

b.   Bradley C. Riggs, born c.1893

c.   Ada W. Riggs, born c.1895

d.   Ella J. Riggs, born c.1900

John Oliver Thomas Watkins
1860-1928

This son of Oliver T. Watkins (1828) and Eleanor Jane Brewer, was born November 3, 1860, and died January 11, 1928. Married March 19, 1883 Eva Lee King, born August 31, 1864 and died January 11, 1928. She also appears in some records as Eveline Lee King, and was the daughter of Edward J. King (1821) and Mary Jane Burdette (1825). John O. T. appears in the 1900 census of Clarksburg, with his wife, and nine children. His will, dated March 9, 1926, was probated January 24, 1928 and filed in Liber PEW 9 at folio 448 in the will records of Montgomery County. There, he leaves his estate for her lifetime to his wife, spelled Evie L. Watkins; and, after her death, to the children, not named in the will. They had children:

1. Frederick B. Watkins, born March 13, 1884, died February 14, 1968. His wife was Anna May, born December 5, 1891 and died February 7, 1982. Both buried at the Upper Seneca Baptist Church, Cedar Grove, Maryland.
2. James Norman Watkins, or John Norman Watkins, born September 27, 1885 and died January 15, 1975. Married to Vivian R. Woodfield, born September 7, 1891, died August 1, 1931, daughter of James Woodfield. Both are buried at Upper Seneca United Methodist Church in Cedar Grove, Maryland. They had children, including:
   a. Norman D. Watkins, died October 20, 1920 at four months, buried with his parents.
   b. James Gilford Watkins.
3. Eleanor Jane Watkins; married Thomas H. C. Flynn. In the 1900 census, she is found in her parents' household, listed as Ellen J., born c.1887.
4. Maynard Watkins, born c.1890
5. Mazie Marie Watkins, born c.1891. Married December 20, 1910 to John Dorsey Woodfield, born November 3, 1887; died July 25, 1953. They had children:
   (1) John Woodfield.
   (2) Thomas Woodfield.
   (3) Paul Woodfield.
   (4) Jane Woodfield.
   (5) Elizabeth Woodfield.
   (6) Grace Woodfield.
6. Dorsey M. Watkins, born March 2, 1893, died March 26, 1893. Buried at Upper Seneca Baptist church cemetery.
7. Eva Louise Watkins, born c.1894; married Joseph Waters Woodfield.
8. Archibald Brett Watkins, born c.1895. Montgomery County marriage records report the marriage of Archie B. Watkins on March 18, 1921 at Monrovia, to Marie King, born c.1903, which is this individual. He is shown in other records as being just Archer Brett Watkins, born July 16, 1895 at Cedar Grove. He was married March 15, 1921 to Amanda Marie King, born July 1, 1902, daughter of Edward Walter King (1869) and Fannie Dutrow (1876). They had children:

a. George Lacy Watkins, born March 29, 1922 at Purdum, single. Injured at birth by forceps; worked for the U. S. Army in Washington, D. C.

b. James Edward Watkins, born September 24, 1925 in Washington, D. C.; married June 6, 1947 to Barbara and had children:

    (1) Bruce Allen Watkins, born March 30, 1948, and married to Deborah Lynn Lewis.

    (2) Bradford Lee Watkins, born February 7, 1955, adopted

    (3) Marsha Lynn Watkins, born October 22, 1958

    (4) Stacy Elizabeth Watkins, born September 5, 1964

9. Paul R. Watkins, probably the same who was married February 3, 1921 at Laytonsville, to Helen L. Higgins, daughter of Charles E. Higgins. If so, he was born June 22, 1897 and died March 30, 1952.

10. Earl J. Watkins, born c.1899

11. May Grace Watkins; married Richard T. Schaeffer.

12. Lodge Watkins, died in Washington, D. C., February 7, 1973. Married December 11, 1913 at the Bethesda United Methodist Church parsonage near Browningsville, to Rosa C. Thompson, and had children:

a. John D. Watkins

b. Ollie L. Watkins

13. Avie C. Watkins; married James Paul Warfield.

14. Willis B. Watkins, born September 19, 1901, and married to Marjorie B., born October 7, 1904. Damascus Methodist Church cemetery. At least one son:

a. Willis B. Watkins, Jr., infant death March 25, 1938

15. Otto Watkins, born March 7, 1905; died July 17, 1906. Buried at Upper Seneca Baptist church cemetery.

CHILD 6

Lorenzo Dallas Watkins
1835-1920

This son of Alpha Watkins (1803) and Harriet Ann Lewis (1805) was born August 28, 1835, and died November 26, 1920. Married October 11, 1859 to Jane Dorsey Purdum, born May 12, 1840, died July 14, 1916, daughter of Charles Riggs Purdum (1807) and Mary Shaw (1803), (or Margaret Hobbs). Lorenzo and his wife are buried at Upper Seneca Baptist Church in Cedar Grove. They appear alone in the 1860 census for Damascus District of Montgomery County. In the 1880 census for Clarksburg District, they have seven children in the household. In the 1900 census for Damascus, the couple are living alone. Accounting of the estate of Jane D. Watkins was made by her husband, Lorenzo D., dated November 22, 1916 and recorded in liber HCA 2 at folio 184 in the wills office of Montgomery County. Her husband receives one third of the estate, and the remainder is divided between the eight children then living, all listed by name. There is also a small bequest to Russell B. Lewis and Elva Lewis. The will of Lorenzo Dallas Watkins was dated August 22, 1819 and filed for probate December 21, 1920 in liber HCA 22 at folio 442 of the will records of Montgomery County, Maryland. He makes a specific bequest of his watch and chain to his son, Joseph Dallas Watkins. He then provides that seven eighths of his estate is to be divided between his seven children, all named. The other one eighth is divided into two parts: one part goes to his grandson, Russell V. Lewis, and the other half in trust to his great granddaughter Elva Lewis, daughter of his late grandson, Grover Lewis. Joseph Dallas Watkins is named executor. They had children, not necessarily in this order:

1. Mary B. Watkins, born c.1861, apparently died young; not mentioned in the division of estate of her mother.
2. Margaret Florence Watkins, born December 7, 1862, of whom more following.
3. Charles Lee Watkins, in his father's will, Charles J. L. Watkins; born c.1865. Married February 20, 1889 Minnie A. King, born c.1870. In other records, he is found as Charles

Jefferson Lee Watkins, which appears to be correct. She is also found in some records as Amanda Cornelius King, born February 17, 1870; died November 4, 1946, the daughter of Edward J. King (1821) and Mary Jane Burdette (1825). She is buried at Upper Seneca Baptist Church, at Cedar Grove, Montgomery County. Her father's will lists her as Minnie; church records list her as Minnie A. In the 1900 census for Damascus, she is listed as Minnie A.; he is Charley L.; and they have eight children in the household. Her will, dated April 10, 1942, was probated December 18, 1946 and filed in Liber OWR 21 at folio 135 in Montgomery County. She there lists eleven children, and three of her grandchildren, all following. Charles Lee is also buried at Upper Seneca Baptist, born 1864 and died 1937. They had at least these children:

a.   Clayton K. Watkins, born September 1, 1890. He was, for many years, Clerk of the Circuit Court for Montgomery County. As such, there are hundreds of land record books bearing the initials, CKW, with a following numeral. That is the system of book numbering used by the county, rather than starting from book one and running into the thousands. Each clerk of the court during his tenure begins the next set of books with his initials, and continues that series during his term of office. Clayton was born August 30, 1890, and married January 31, 1917 at Upper Seneca Baptist Church at Cedar Grove, to Addie Belle Hawkins, daughter of James B. Hawkins of Woodfield. She was born October 25, 1898 and died October 12, 1961. Buried in Forest Oak Cemetery, Gaithersburg.

b.   Talmadge Lodge Watkins, born 1891, died 1975; married Myrtle Bryan Burns, born June 25, 1896, and died 1979; daughter of Nicholas Edward Burns (1865) and Laura Gertrude King (1873). Talmadge and his wife are buried in the cemetery of Upper Seneca Baptist Church at Cedar Grove. Nearby are the graves of two of their sons:

(1)   Charles Edward Watkins, born May 24, 1914 and died March 2, 1975. Married Mary Belle Hawkins, born May 6, 1915, daughter of James Bradley

Hawkins (1886) and Hattie Mae King (1893).
Children:
    (a) Joanne Marie Watkins, born 1939. Married
James Edward Musson, born 1936. A son:
      1. Larry Edward Musson; June 22, 1966
    (b) Charles Edward Watkins, Jr., born 1940, and
known as Bucky. Married to Barbara Joan
Beall, born 1943. One daughter:
      1. Cynthia Elaine Watkins: November 5,
1962. Married to Dexter Gordon Mathis
and had children:
        a. Sarah Diane Mathis, born 1984
        b. Jason Kyle Mathis, born 1987
    (c) Carol Lee Watkins, born 1953, and married
Richard Harold Collins, born 1945.
(2) Royce T. Watkins, born 1918, died March, 1972.
Buried Upper Seneca Baptist Church. Married to
Agnes S., born 1919. Children:
    (a) Mary Jo Watkins, married Mayer; a child:
      1. John Talmadge Mayer.
    (b) Jane A. Watkins, married to Robert Ernest
Gartner, Jr., born June 11, 1942, son of Robert Ernest Gartner (1918) and Harriet Catherine Wachter Perry (1917). They had a child:
      1. David Wayne Gartner: June 31, 1968
(3) Gertrude Watkins, married Duvall.
c. Margaret J. Watkins, born c.1893; married Howes.
d. Gladys D. Watkins, born 1894, died 1897.
e. Claudia Lucille Watkins, born August 20, 1894. Married
to Howard.
f. Belle P. Watkins, born c.1896; married Hawkins.
g. Charles Jefferson Lee Watkins, Jr., born c.1898; married
September 14, 1916 at Upper Seneca Baptist Church,
Cedar Grove, to Rose Mae Johnson, daughter of James
W. Johnson of Clarksburg. At least one daughter:
(1) Margaret E. Watkins, born April 18, 1917; died
December 27, 1995. She is perhaps Margaret Ellen
Watkins, who was married June 19, 1943 to Sam-

uel Sylvester Gloyd, born October 12, 1914, son of Henry Dorsey Gloyd (1879) and Margaret Lavina Arnold (1876).

h. Bessie K. Watkins, born c.1899; married Howes.

i. Minnie Hazel Watkins, born c.1900; married Allnutt.

j. Mary E. Watkins, married to Johnson, and had children:
    (1) Bettie Bell Johnson.
    (2) Charles Thomas Johnson.
    (3) Paul Curtis Johnson.

k. Celeste P. Watkins, married Beall.

l. Lorraine E. Watkins, born September 30, 1906, died March 19, 1972. Married William Ralph Walker, born September 16, 1905, died February 13, 1995, the son of McKendree Walker (1870) and Rachel Corrine Holland (1878). No children.

4. Lizzie J. Watkins, born c.1867; married Charles W. Johnson (or Charles T. Johnson). Listed as Jennie E. Johnson in the settlement of estate of her mother.

5. Joseph Dallas Watkins, born c.1870 and died June 20, 1935 in Johns Hopkins University Hospital, Baltimore. Married at the Upper Seneca Baptist Church at Cedar Grove, November 16, 1893 to Ida V. Day, born 1872, died 1934; both are buried there. They appear in the 1900 census of Damascus with their first daughter, and an unnamed son, both of whom may have died young, since they are not mentioned in obituaries. They had two sons and a daughter who survived, and the first two found in the 1900 census:

a. Sallie B. Watkins, born c.1895

b. Son Watkins, born c.1900

c. Guy D. Watkins, born c.1908 at Cedar Grove, Maryland, and died May 30, 1988 at the Friends Nursing Home in Sandy Spring, Maryland. Buried at Upper Seneca Baptist Church, Cedar Grove. He served for 45 years as chief judge in the 12th Election District, and was a member of the Lions Club since 1947. He was a player and a coach of baseball. He was survived by his wife, Fannie E., born 1913, a niece and a nephew.

d. Wilbur Day Watkins, born January 23, 1900 at Cedar Grove, of whom more following.

e. Blanche Watkins married Carson Nicholson.

6. Henry L. Watkins, born 1872, died October 30, 1950. Called Harry L. in his father's will, in the division of his mother's estate, and in the 1880 census. In the 1900 census, he is again called Harry L., listed with his wife. Also in the household at that time is Sarah A. Purdum, born c.1834, listed as an aunt. Henry (or Harry) was married August 27, 1897 in Montgomery County to Annie E. Hall, born 1873, died 1943. Harry's will, dated January 18, 1950, was probated November 8, 1950, and filed in Liber WCC 18 at folio 408 in the will records of the county. He identifies his father as being Lorenzo D. Watkins, providing funds for the maintenance of his father's grave, as well as his own. He also menions one son. Harry and his wife are buried at Upper Seneca Baptist Church cemetery, Cedar Grove, with stone marked "father" and "mother." Also in the cemetery is the grave of another individual who is probably their son, based on his name:

a. Harold Hall Watkins, born 1901, died August 6, 1920 by drowning at Great Falls on the Potomac River.

b. Philip Charles Watkins, born 1905, died January 2, 1966; who received the family farm at Cedar Grove. Married July 1, 1931 in Friendship, Anne Arundel County, Maryland, to Nettie Dorsey Etchison, born 1913. She was a daughter of Dr. and Mrs. Garnett Waters Etchison of Gaithersburg. Philip and his wife are also buried at the Upper Seneca Baptist Church in Cedar Grove. His will, dated November 8, 1950, was probated January 28, 1966 and filed in will book VMB 199 at folio 504 in Montgomery County. He names his wife, and provides that after her death, his estate is to be divided between his six children, who are not named.

7. Cornelius A. Watkins; apparently the same who is buried at the Upper Seneca Baptist Church cemetery, in Cedar Grove, Maryland. He was born May 15, 1875, and died December 20, 1946. Marriage records of the county, and the *Sentinel* newspaper, report his marriage April 12, 1905 at the Upper

Seneca Baptist Church, Cedar Grove, to Rebecca Woodfield, daughter of J. R. Woodfield; and that the couple plan to reside at 1927 Edmondson Avenue, Baltimore. She is perhaps Laura Rebecca Woodfield; and the mother of his children:

    a.   Alfred Woodfield Watkins, born June 18, 1906 and died November 22, 1907, buried with his parents.

    b.   Cornelius R. Watkins.

8.   Pearl B. Watkins, who was married to George Otis Henderson of Germantown.

9.   May Watkins, not mentioned in the will, nor the division of the estate of her mother.

10.   Jennie Watkins, not mentioned in the will, nor the division of the estate of her mother.

Wilbur Day Watkins
1900-1969

This son of Joseph Dallas Watkins (1870) was born January 23, 1900 at Cedar Grove, and died March 21, 1969 in Sebring Ridge, Florida. He was a brother of Guy D. Watkins (1908) and Mrs. Blanche Nicholson. He owned and operated Watkins Sheet Metal before retiring and moving to Florida. Buried at Upper Seneca Baptist Church, Cedar Grove. Married December 26, 1922 in Kemptown to Ruth Selby King, born there June 6, 1904, daughter of Reginald Windsor King (1878) and Ida Mae Grimes (1876). They had children:

1.   Wilbur Day Watkins, Jr., known as Buster, born September 27, 1923 at Cedar Grove, owned Watkins Cabinet Company at Barnesville. Married June 23, 1948 to Agnes Jeanette Walter, born January 2, 1930 at Redland. Seven children:

    a.   Joan Marie Watkins, born December 26, 1949 in Frederick. Married first June 5, 1969 to Mark Harman Schendledecker, born March 8, 1947 in Baltimore; two daughters. Married second June 29, 1985 in Frederick to Gilmore Wayne House, born April 30, 1942, who had two children by a prior marriage. Joan's daughters were:

        (1)   Judith Marie Schendledecker, born April 10, 1970 in Boston, Massachusetts

(2) Joy Marie Schendledecker, born April 19, 1975 in Framingham, Massachusetts
b. Kenneth Leroy Watkins, born December 13, 1950; married December 12, 1970 to Kathryn Ann Vandorf, born May 15, 1951 in Watertown, Wisconsin. Children:
(1) Stephanie Ann Watkins, born July 11, 1971 at the Andrews Air Force Hospital, Camp Springs, Md.
(2) Kristina Marie Watkins, born December 8, 1973 in Olney, Maryland
c. Nancy Louise Watkins, born October 1, 1952 in Olney; married February 28, 1976 Michael Walter Lloyd, born September 28, 1952 in Leonardtown, Maryland, a cabinetmaker. They had four children, the first three born in Olney; the last in Frederick, Maryland:
(1) Emilie Auge Lloyd, born March 10, 1978
(2) Martin Webster Lloyd, born March 20, 1979
(3) Erich William Lloyd, born October 24, 1980
(4) Karin Reine Lloyd, born September 2, 1982
d. Sue Ann Watkins, born July 4, 1955 in Olney; married April 6, 1973 Eben LaMonte Conner, III, born February 15, 1955 in Yakima, Washington. He is a cabinetmaker, owner of the Maugansville Planing Mill. They have children, the first born in Olney, the second in Washington, D. C., and the last four in Hagerstown, Maryland:
(1) AnnaMaria Conner, born January 21, 1974
(2) Elisabeth Marie Conner: September 26, 1975
(3) Deborah Sue Conner, born February 5, 1978
(4) Joanna Ruth Conner, born July 18, 1980
(5) Sarah Grace Conner, born February 21, 1982
(6) Rachel Jeannette Conner, born July 3, 1984
e. Georgia May Watkins, born May 13, 1957 in Olney; married June 24, 1976 Arby Ryan Ray, born June 29, 1957 at Jordan, New York. Children, born at Fayetteville, North Carolina:
(1) Jennifer Marie Ray, born October 4, 1977
(2) Andrew Ryan Ray, born October 15, 1978
f. Franklin Wilbur Watkins, born February 16, 1959 in Olney, Maryland; married first March 18, 1978 to Teresa

Ann Jackson, and had three children; divorced. Married second April 26, 1985 to Marie Frances Eaton, born January 18, 1959 in Washington, D. C. Children were:

    (1)   Franklin Wilbur Watkins, Jr., born August 15, 1978 in Takoma Park

    (2)   Nicholas O'Bryan Watkins, born September 14, 1979 in Silver Spring; lived eleven days; buried in St. Mary's Cemetery, Barnesville, Maryland

    (3)   Joshua Stephen Watkins, born October 21, 1980 in Johns Hopkins Hospital, Baltimore

g.   Gerrianne Watkins, born December 28, 1961 in Olney; married October 6, 1979 to James Owen Conway, born December 15, 1960 in Philadelphia, and had children:

    (1)   Mathew Brian Conway, born September 1, 1980 in Olney, Maryland

    (2)   James Paul Conway, born March 23, 1982 in Martinsburg, West Virginia

    (3)   Amanda Margaret Conway, born July 16, 1984 in Frederick, Maryland

2.   Ida Louise Watkins, born January 22, 1925 at Cedar Grove; married December 11, 1944 in Frederick, Maryland, Charles Franklin Bartgis, born June 4, 1921. Divorced December 22, 1950. No children; moved to Florida.

Margaret Florence Watkins
1862-1924

This daughter of Lorenzo Dallas Watkins (1835) and Jane Dorsey Purdum (1840) was born December 7, 1862 and died January 11, 1924. Married April 24, 1882 to Crittenden King, born August 31, 1857 near Damascus, and died January 13, 1918, at his home near Cedar Grove, son of Charles Miles King (1814). Crittenden and his wife are buried at the Upper Seneca Baptist Church, at Cedar Grove, Maryland. The will of Crittenden King is found in Liber HCA 19 at folio 421 in the will records of Montgomery County, Maryland. Dated March 12, 1917, it was entered for record February 12, 1918. He leaves his farm and personal property to his wife for her lifetime, so long as she remains single, and names four of his children. Final accounts in his estate are filed in Liber HCA 17 at folio 482, dated January 14, 1919, in which division is made equally between the four children:

1. Leslie Crittenden King, born May 24, 1896 at Kings Valley; died December 2, 1974 at his home called Kingstead Farms, near Damascus. Buried Upper Seneca Baptist Church at Cedar Grove, Maryland. Married October 28, 1920 at Cedar Grove his second cousin, Bertha Marie Beall, born September 12, 1901, died September 23, 1968, daughter of Edward Maurice Beall (born September 30, 1870; died November 24, 1938) and Mary Jane Purdum (1882). Leslie Crittenden and his wife are buried at Upper Seneca Baptist Church at Cedar Grove. Four sons are buried there with them, and there were other children:

    a. Maurice Crittenden King, born February 21, 1922, and married February 21, 1952 to Anne Riggs White, born August 13, 1931. They had children:
        (1) Maurice Crittenden King, Jr.; November 27, 1957
        (2) Ann Lyn King, born August 8, 1959. Married to Steven Palmer, and had children:
            (a) Amy Nichole Palmer: January 4, 1986
            (b) Stephen Joseph Palmer: October 29, 1987
        (3) Jane Marie King, born June 14, 1963. Married to Bertali Rojas, born April 24, 1954. Child:
            (a) Mauricio Rojas, born January 29, 1996
    b. Leslie Irving King, born June 26, 1924; died October 27, 1995.
    c. Harold Rufus King, born September 10, 1927, and died August 30, 1994. Served in the 101st Airborne, Army.
    d. Douglas Edward King, born March 16, 1929
    e. Robert Lee King, born April 4, 1931; died 1934
    f. Charles Carroll King, born March 27, 1933; died 1935
    g. Bertha Jane King, born January 18, 1935
    h. James Franklin King, born January 2, 1937; died January 1, 1996 at Frederick, Maryland. Married October 20, 1966 Dorothea Moran, born October 5, 1931. A son:
        (1) James Franklin King, Jr., born May 12, 1968

i. Paul Richard King, born May 22, 1938 at Cedar Grove. Married October 9, 1960 to Kathleen Ann Beall, born March 8, 1942, and had children:
   (1) Peter Brandon King, born May 17, 1963. Married May 22, 1983 to Tracey Marie Copp, born July 3, 1963. Children:
      (a) Krista Lyn King, born January 6, 1984
      (b) Josiah Brandon King, born July 29, 1996
   (2) David Andrew King, born March 13, 1966, and married November 26, 1994 to Susan Marie Hockenberry, born December 6, 1974. Children:
      (a) Amber Nichole King: September 12, 1996
   (3) Leslie Lyn King, born October 28, 1968. Married August 20, 1988 Richard Wager Bailey, born July 24, 1964, and had children:
      (a) Richard Wager Bailey, Jr.: July 24, 1989
      (b) Christian Paul Bailey: September 10, 1991
      (c) Luke Henry Bailey: October 4, 1993
j. Gloria Elaine King, born December 22, 1942. Married to John Joseph Daly, born August 31, 1944. Children:
   (1) John Joseph Daly, Jr., born November 3, 1966 and married to Mary Bodden, born July 9, 1967. They have a daughter:
      (a) Brittany Christian Daly: June 25, 1990
   (2) Christopher Edward Daly: August 13, 1972
k. Mary Florence King, born October 10, 1945
2. Orida Jane King, born c.1883, married April 25, 1907 at Kings Valley to J. Garnet Ward.
3. Beulah Hattie King, born c.1887; married April 25, 1907 at Kings Valley to Harry L. Nicholson.
4. Charles Dow King, born January 13, 1890 in King's Valley, near Damascus, Maryland, and died August 26, 1962. Married December 29, 1911 at Rockville to Augusta Ward, born November 10, 1888; died April 2, 1922, daughter of Harrison Gilmore Ward (1853) and Ara Matilda Thrift (1857) of Travilah. Charles Dow King was married second June 20, 1923 at Darnestown, to Albertis Ward, born December 20, 1883 and died March 24, 1970, sister of his deceased wife. Buried at

Upper Seneca Baptist Church at Cedar Grove. At least one son, born to his first marriage:

a. Harrison Crittenden King, born October 1, 1912, of whom more.

Harrison Crittenden King
1912- 1995

This son of Charles Dow King (1890) and Augusta Ward (1888), was born October 1, 1912 at Kings Valley, near Damascus, Montgomery County, Maryland; died February 17, 1995. Married March 25, 1933 at the Methodist Parsonage in Laytonsville, to Gladys Louise Allnutt, born January 28, 1915 at Etchison, Maryland, and died March 11, 1988; daughter of Walter and Ida Allnutt. She was a member of Montgomery County Fair Board, and numerous other agricultural and home-maker related organizations. He was a farmer, charter, and founding member of the Laytonsville Fire Department and the Laytonsville Lions Club; member of the Agricultural Center, the Farm Bureau, and Montgomery County School Board. They were survived by three children, eight grandchildren, and six great grandchildren. Children:

1. Augusta Mae King, born March 30, 1936; married to Donald Wayne and had children:
   a. Cynthia Louise Wayne, born October 9, 1957, married to David Bowman. Children:
      (1) Stephanie Ann Bowman: November 15, 1988.
      (2) Andrew Bowman, February 15, 1992
      (3) Amy Bowman, December 23, 1993
   b. Donna Marie Wayne, born November 27, 1960; married August 1982 to Michael Hill and adopted two children from Korea:
      (1) Scott O. Sung Hill, June 23, 1989
      (2) Kathryn Won Hill, December 21, 1991
   c. Mary Beth Wayne, born June 9, 1968, married May, 1994 Brian Grant. No children.
2. John Dow King, married and had children:
   a. Michael Harrison King, born April 20, 1968 and married to Teresa Start. No children.

b. Susan Lynn King, born February 28, 1970
c. David Henry King, born June 1, 1975
3. Thomas Gilmore King, married and had children:
   a. Patrice Marie King, born March 6, 1967, and married to Scott Brickman. One daughter:
      (1) Anna Brickman.
   b. Joel Thomas King, born April 30, 1969, and married to Tierney. One daughter:
      (1) Adelain King.

CHILD 7

Edward King Watkins
1837-1913

This son of Alpha Watkins (1803) and Harriet Ann Lewis (1805), was born May 31, 1837, and died January 21, 1913. Married September 19, 1861 in Ellicott City, Maryland, Sophronia R. Phelps, born October 1, 1846 and died January 9, 1924; who became fifteen years of age just two weeks after her marriage; daughter of a neighbor, Sarah Phelps. They are buried at Salem United Methodist Church cemetery in Cedar Grove. The will of Sophronia, dated July 23, 1918, was probated February 20, 1924 and filed in Liber PEW 2 at folio 141, will records of Montgomery County. It is quite detailed, naming their six surviving children, and grandchildren and great grandchildren. The family appears in the 1870 census with four of their children, and in the 1880 census for Clarksburg District, with six. The 1900 census, on Soundex cards and film at the National Archives, lists Edward with two children, although the transcriber has spelled his name incorrectly as Edwin. His two eldest sons filed final accounts relative to his estate, on December 10, 1913, recorded in liber HCA 13 at folio 371 in the wills office of the county. His widow is named, as well as six children; three having died young. The nine children were:
1. George Orlando Watkins, born March 19, 1864, and died November 15, 1940, single.
2. Walter Wilson Watkins, born June 2, 1866, and died May 21, 1927. Married on November 11, 1891 to Rosa L. Mathews,

(or Mathers) at Upper Seneca Baptist Church, Cedar Grove, Maryland. She was born July 21, 1870, according to the stone at Salem United Methodist Church, Cedar Grove, where both are buried. They had at least one daughter:

a. Marie Columbia Watkins, died January 15, 1951. Married to Felty and had at least one son:

    (1) Walter Thomas Felty.

3. Alonzo Claggett Watkins, born July 28, 1867, and died January 25, 1946. Married July 27, 1893 to Mary Luana Boyer, born March 9, 1870, died June 28, 1945, daughter of Milton Boyer (1834) and Elizabeth Washington Purdum (1840). Alonzo and Mary are buried in the cemetery of the Damascus Methodist Church. Alonzo and his wife appear in the 1900 census for Damascus with first three children. They had six:

a. Faye Huntington Watkins, born July 18, 1894, died May 14, 1962. Married October 28, 1915 to Oliver Morgan Duvall, born March 22, 1889, died June 12, 1964 at Damascus. Children:

    (1) Mary Virginia Duvall, born 1917; married Ray Deitz, and had one daughter:

        (a) Rae Dietz.

    (2) Paul Burton Duvall, born 1920; married to Margaret Louise Musgrove, and had four children:

        (a) Richard Burton Duvall.

        (b) Paul Wayne Duvall.

        (c) Robin Duvall.

        (d) Carol Duvall.

    (3) Robert Morgan Duvall, born January 19, 1923. Married to Lois and had six children:

        (a) Pamela Duvall.

        (b) Robert Morgan Duvall, Jr.

        (c) Wendy Duvall.

        (d) Nancy Duvall.

        (e) Julie Duvall.

        (f) James Duvall.

    (4) Edward Boyer Duvall, born December 11, 1925 in Damascus, died January 4, 1996, and buried in Damscus Methodist Church cemetery. He was a

Navy veteran of the second world war, and active in numerous organizations in his retirement. For many years he was customer service manager for Kettler Brothers, Inc., builders of Montgomery Village and other communities. Married Ruth Irene Oland, and was the father of six children:

(a) Linda Lou Duvall, born May 5, 1948; married Barry Phelps of Frederick.

(b) Edwin Allen Duvall, born December 19, 1950; married Hilda, of Myersville.

(c) Stephen Leigh Duvall, born July 30, 1952, of Damascus.

(d) Deborah Kay Duvall, born March 26, 1955; married to James Popp of Monrovia.

(e) Karen Jean Duvall, born March 7, 1957 and married John Jordan of Adamstown.

(f) Timothy Edward Duvall, born December 9, 1958; married Kim, of Mount Airy.

(5) Gerald Leigh Duvall, born June 27, 1927. Married Miriam and had four children.

(6) Rodney H. Duvall, married Margaret Wygant.

(7) Shirley Jane Duvall, who was married to John Trega Zimmerman and had six children.

(8) William C. Duvall, married Shirley Johnson.

(9) Rose Eleanor Duvall, born May 23, 1935, died February 3, 1939.

b. Paul Winstead Watkins, born November 22, 1897, died August 6, 1979. Married June 2, 1920 to Rose Ethel Mullinix, daughter of Granville and Mary Mullinix. They had children:

(1) Kenneth Watkins.

(2) Walter Lee Watkins.

c. Dorothy Elizabeth Watkins, born April 28, 1900 and died September 28, 1970. Buried in the Damascus Methodist Church cemetery. Married July 14, 1932 Raymond Lafayette Warfield, son of Basil T. Warfield (1859) and Alice Flavilla Mullinix (1867). He was first married to

Bessie Allnutt, by whom he had two children. Children born to Dorothy Elizabeth included:
  (1)   Raymond Lafayette Warfield, Jr.
  (2)   Dorothy Warfield.
  (3)   Ellis Warfield, died at six months.
d.   Ralph W. Watkins, born 1901, died 1948, and married to Nona M. Burdette, born 1904, died July 24, 1974. Both are buried at Damascus Methodist Church cemetery. Two children:
  (1)   Lula Mae Watkins, married Edward Coolidge.
  (2)   Clara Watkins, married Gerald Johnson.
e.   Irma Watkins, born March 29, 1903. This may be the granddaughter, Erma Sophronia Watkins, mention is her grandmother's will. Married to Miel Wright Linthicum, son of Miel E. Linthicum (1865) and Mary L. Purdum (1866). They had children:
  (1)   Miel Wright Linthicum, Jr., born April 10, 1928, married Mary Emma Johnson, and had children:
      (a)   James Miel Linthicum, born 1952
      (b)   Robert Earl Linthicum, born 1954
      (c)   John Monroe Linthicum, born 1961
      (d)   Jill Suzanne Linthicum, born 1962
  (2)   George Morsell Linthicum, born April 4, 1926, married Jeanne Marie Brown, and had children:
      (a)   Mary Martha Linthicum.
      (b)   Beverly Jeanne Linthicum.
      (c)   Donna Joan Linthicum.
      (d)   George Morsell Linthicum, Jr.
      (e)   Ann Marie Linthicum, born 1962
  (3)   Joseph Linthicum, born April 21, 1930, married Gay Elizabeth Harding. No children.
  (4)   Bernard Lee Linthicum, born November 21, 1934. He married Martha Hooper and had children:
      (a)   Irma Jane Linthicum.
      (b)   Amanda Jean Linthicum.
f.   Annie Loree Watkins, born June 11, 1906, died May 20, 1975. Married William Kenneth Layton, born July 28,

1908 and died December 28, 1959 at Damascus. They had children:

    (1)   William Kenneth Layton, Jr.; married Emma.

4. Fannie Frank Watkins, born February 16, 1869; died April 18, 1869.

5. Florence Edward Watkins, born April 29, 1870, and married January 26, 1888 to Reuben M. Nicholson. The 1870 census lists her name as Frances E. Watkins, one month old at the time the census was taken. She and Reuben had children:

    a.   Clifford Newman Nicholson, born November 13, 1888, apparently the father of:

        (1)   Dorothy Beatrice Nicholson.

    b.   Carson Edward Nicholson.

    c.   Jessie Randolph Nicholson.

    d.   Walter Wilson Nicholson.

6. Harriet Roberta Watkins, born March 3, 1872; died October 2, 1944. Married October 26, 1898 Franklin Waters. The 1880 census reports a child born c.1872, named Alberta, which is probably this child, improperly reported by the census taker.

7. Addie Sophronia Watkins, born October 15, 1875, died December 21, 1970. Married to Jones. The 1880 census record for this child, while hard to read, appears to report Ada L. Watkins, again probably poorly read or reported. Final accounts of her father's estate clearly read Addie S. Jones, confirming the name we report here.

8. Samuel Watkins, born March 6, 1877; infant death

9. Nellie Watkins, born November 5, 1878; infant death

CHILD 11

Benjamin Franklin Watkins
1844-1929

This son of Alpha Watkins (1803) and Harriet Ann Lewis (1805) was born December 20, 1844 in Cedar Grove, Montgomery County, and died January 23, 1929, perhaps in Carroll County. Married November 11, 1868 Sarah Jane Benson, born March 2,

1849, and died January 7, 1931; the daughter of William H. Benson and Catherine Crawford. Buried with her husband in Forest Oak Cemetery at Gaithersburg. They appear in the 1880 census for Clarksburg District of the county, with five of their children. Children, perhaps all born near Middlebrook, Montgomery County; many are buried at Forest Oak:

1. Wesley W. Watkins, born May 2, 1871; died January 24, 1893 at Middlebrook, Montgomery County. Single.
2. William Clarence Watkins, born April 26, 1873, died December 27, 1899, single.
3. Lillian May Watkins, born April 23, 1875; died July 3, 1963 in Montgomery County, Maryland. Married there December 10, 1894 to James E. L. Sibley, born April 18, 1866; died June 4, 1949. Both buried Forest Oak cemetery, Gaithersburg. Children:
   a. Joseph Russell Sibley, born August 9, 1901, married Flora Elizabeth Watkins, born May 1, 1900, daughter of Maurice Watkins (1867) and Martha Rebecca King (1874). Married second Hettie. One child each marriage:
      (1) Flora Elizabeth Sibley, born February 2, 1935, and married first to Vickroy, by whom she had a child. Married second to Martin Alexander Case, born October 18, 1932, and had a son. Children:
         (a) Donna Lynn Vickroy, born August 1, 1958
         (b) David Martin Case, born May 4, 1964
      (2) Mary Sibley; married Norton. At least a son:
         (a) Wayne Norton.
   b. Irene Sibley; married Roy Arnold.
   c. Edward Arnold Montgomery Sibley, born April 3, 1897 at Germantown, Montgomery County. Died November 19, 1991; single.
4. Bradley G. (or C.) Watkins, born March 26, 1877, died November 24, 1899 at Middlebrooke, Montgomery County, Maryland.
5. Walter Howard Watkins, born May 5, 1879, died February 8, 1881.

6.	Harvey C. Watkins, born March 1, 1881; died November 30, 1916. Married March 29, 1904 at Germantown, Grace Violet Diffenderffer, daughter of Mrs. Jennie Diffenderffer.

7.	Virgie Lee Watkins, born January 9, 1882, and died November 8, 1931 in Montgomery County, Maryland. Married December 14, 1905 in Grace Methodist Church, Albert Franklin Thompson, born May 24, 1877; died February 5, 1951; son of John Thompson and Eliza Virginia Rabbitt. Husband and wife are buried in Forest Oak cemetery, Gaithersburg, Maryland. Children, born in Montgomery County:

a.	Mabel Jane Thompson, born September 12, 1906, and married to James Stephen Frendach, and had a son:

(1)	Paul Franklin Frendach, born July 28, 1941, married February 20, 1965 in Washington to Teresa Catherine Barnard, and had children:

(a)	Eric Barnard Frendach, born October 2, 1965

(b)	Angela Christine Frendach, born December 27, 1966

(c)	Stephen Frank Frendach, born February 1, 1973

(d)	Katy Frendach, born after 1974

b.	John Franklin Thompson, born January 17, 1909, of whom more following.

c.	Myrtle Lee Thompson, born May 10, 1911

d.	Albert Thompson, born January 13, 1918; died January 17, 1918

e.	Judson Collins Thompson, born September 11, 1923; married November 18, 1945 to Miriam Groves Groves. One child:

(1)	Collins Groves Thompson, born October 12, 1946; married before 1973 Janet, and second before 1976 Mary Elizabeth Mack, and had two children:

(a)	Ann Marie Thompson, born August 18, 1976

(b)	Sarah Elizabeth Thompson; July 18, 1978

8.	Clara Blanche Watkins, born November 11, 1886. Married April 30, 1913 Thomas G. Hilton. Children:

a. Thomas Stinson Hilton, born March 31, 1914, and died February 7, 1955. Married February 28, 1933 to Annie Phillips.
b. Elizabeth Jane Hilton, born January 14, 1918; married October 10, 1947 Arthur John Lear.
9. Bessie Myrtle Watkins, born September 8, 1888; died August 13, 1889. Single.

John Franklin Thompson
1909-1993

This son of Albert Franklin Thompson (1877) and Virgie Lee Watkins (1882), was born January 17, 1909, and died March 14, 1993 in Washington Grove, Maryland. Married June 17, 1932 at Friendship, Anne Arundel County, Maryland, to Gladys Mae Fraley, born May 17, 1911 at Claysville, and died February 2, 1995; daughter of Ernest Lee Fenton Fraley and Daisy Belle Allnutt. Both are buried at Forest Oak cemetery, Gaithersburg. John Franklin was a farmer and a horseman; he and his wife were members of the Goshen and Redland Hunt Clubs, and won a number of trophies for their show horses. They owned the horse named "Black Caddy" which later became a world champion show horse, breaking several jumping records. Four children, first three born in Montgomery County, the fourth in Washington, D. C.:

1. Janet Dale Thompson, born October 3, 1935; married October 15, 1955 Lovie Lee "Buck" Manuel, born September 14, 1930 Compton, Virginia, son of John Thomas Manuel and Linda Mae Hill. Two children:
   a. Donna Lee Manuel, born April 11, 1957; married June 27, 1987 in Frederick, Maryland, David Allen Schultz, born there June 17, 1956, who was the son of David Kieffer Schultz and Avis Bondena Kepler. Children, born in Frederick:
      (1) Megan Elizabeth Schultz, born March 1, 1989
      (2) Matthew David Schultz, born December 16, 1991
   b. Darin Thomas Manuel, born October 16, 1963, single, a musician and composer.

2. Beverly Ann Thompson, born November 23, 1936, and married first November 26, 1951 at Rockville, John Michael Eader, Jr., born May 20, 1931, son of John Michael Eader and Alice E. Whalen; three children. Married second at Grace Church in Gaithersburg, Joseph Mackin Ganley, born February 12, 1927. The children were:
   a. Brenda Kay Eader, born September 22, 1951, married first March 8, 1977 in Rockville, to Edward Franklin Knight, born October 24, 1948 in Charlestown, West Virginia, the son of Edward Franklin Knight and Daphne Carson Lawson; one son. She married second October 22, 1994 in Howard County, Maryland, David Richards.
      (1) Steven Carson Knight, born December 23, 1979.
   b. John Michael Eader, born February 10, 1960, married October 14, 1989 at Germantown, to Brenda Lee Whitworth, born October 1, 1964, daughter of George Irwin Whitworth and Wilma Elizabeth Fitzwater.
   c. Carol Ann Eader, born February 8, 1962. Married first June 22, 1985 Edward Stephen Caglione, born June 20, 1963, son of Edward S. and Valeta Caglione. Married second September 7, 1991 Clark Matthew Wagner, born April 30, 1961 in Casper, Wyoming, son of James Francis Wagner and Kathryn Jo Atwood. Two children, born to the second marriage; Montgomery County:
      (1) Shannon Wagner; September 6, 1993
      (2) Matthew Wagner: March 12, 1995
3. Nancy Jeanne Thompson, born May 2, 1940; married first June 8, 1957 at Rockville to Louis William Carr, the son of William Harold and Helen Carr. Married second May 25, 1961 in Ellicott City, Maryland, to William Stone, born May 15, 1938 Rainelle, West Virginia, the son of William Stone and Dolly Mae Brown. She had two children from the first marriage, and one from the second:
   a. William Dean Carr, born October 8, 1957
   b. Kenneth Paul Carr, born August 17, 1959; married January 21, 1989 Boyds, Maryland, Robin Kathleen Arnold, born September 2, 1964 at Silver City, New Mexico,

daughter of Walter Claude Arnold and Mary Lee Wilson. One child:

   (1)   Krysten Daniele Carr; April 20, 1991

c.   Robert Jay Stone, born March 19, 1962; married June 11, 1988 Rockville, Maryland, to Holly Joy Lebowitz, born February 13, 1962 Bridgeville, Pa., the daughter of Alan Harvey Lebowitz and Shirley Cohen. Two children, born in Montgomery County:

   (1)   Daniel Evan Stone: April 6, 1990
   (2)   Jena Renee Stone: March 6, 1993

4.   Joseph Franklin Thompson, born May 16, 1946; married first December 28, 1968 in Silver Spring, Maryland, to Kathleen McGuire, born May 17, 1947 in Takoma Park, Maryland, daughter of Martin Duane McGuire and Annetta Maline. Married second May 18, 1991 in Frederick, to Sarah Jane Tipton, born March 16, 1959 in Washington, daughter of Wellstood White Tipton and Elizabeth Ann Field. Two children, from the first marriage, Montgomery County:

a.   Jeffrey Thompson, born June 27, 1969
b.   Katrina Lynn Thompson, born July 8, 1973

CHILD 12

Noah Watkins
1846-1929

This son of Alpha Watkins (1803) and Harriet Ann Lewis (1805) was born August 23, 1846, and died December 8, 1929. Married November 28, 1871 to Julia Ann Linthicum of Frederick County, born October 21, 1850, and died December 27, 1931, daughter of John Hamilton Smith Linthicum (1812) and Julia Ann Garrett (1810). Noah and wife are buried at Salem United Methodist Church at Cedar Grove, Montgomery County, Maryland. They appear in the 1880 census for Clarksburg District, with the first six of their children, and in the 1900 census for Damascus with seven. There were a total of thirteen:

1.   Garrett Webster Watkins, born 1872; died 1947. Married to Vertie A. Mullinix, born 1873, and died 1959. Both buried at

Salem United Methodist Church in Cedar Grove, Maryland. He and his wife appear in the 1900 census for Clarksburg, with their first son. They had at least these children:

a.   Roy W. Watkins, born c.1897. Married Bessie King, daughter of Holady Hix King (1857). Children:
  (1)   Lois Watkins, married to Charles King Burdette, born December 10, 1917, the son of Claude H. Burdette (1872) and Sarah Rebecca Boyer (1874).
  (2)   Grace Watkins.
  (3)   William Watkins, who married a daughter of Joe Abrams.
  (4)   Infant death, March 7, 1920. Cemetery of Salem United Methodist Church, Cedar Grove.

b.   Wilbur Noah Watkins, born December 4, 1900, died October 13, 1989 at Frederick Hospital. Married May 18, 1940 to Nora Belle King, born July 7, 1907, daughter of Edward Walter King (1869). No children, and both are buried at Salem United Methodist Church, Cedar Grove.

c.   Granville W. Watkins, born 1906, died 1968. Buried at Salem United Methodist Church, Cedar Grove. Married to Dorothy L., and the father of:
  (1)   William E. Watkins.
  (2)   Agnes Watkins, married Moxley.
  (3)   Linda L. Watkins, married Cordell.

d.   Julia Elizabeth Watkins, married May 10, 1923 Maurice E. Purdum. She shot and killed him July 3, 1925.

e.   Mabel A. Watkins, born April 8, 1909 at Cedar Grove and died July 6, 1996 at Shady Grove Hospital. Married John M. Tregoning; four grand-children, five great grandchildren, and one son:
  (1)   Robert Tregoning.

2.   Leah Jane Watkins, born 1874; married April 30, 1895 to William G. Iglehart.

3.   Herbert Hamilton Watkins, born April, 1876; died October 6, 1880.

4.   Mary Avondale Watkins, born February 25, 1878, and of whom more following.

5. Nora Watkins, twin, born January 9, 1880; married April 6, 1898 Charles H. Barber.
6. Bessie Watkins, twin, January 9, 1880 to June 10, 1880.
7. John Lester Clark Watkins, born December 25, 1881; died March 25, 1966. Married to Bessie T. Wallach, born May 13, 1892; died April 20, 1967. Buried at Salem United Methodist Church, Cedar Grove. They had children:
   a. Ernest C. Watkins, born August 18, 1927 at Cedar Grove in Montgomery County, Maryland; died of cancer on December 15, 1982 at Shady Grove Hospital. Survived by wife, Virginia M., seventeen grandchildren, and children:
      (1) Karen Watkins, married Eppley.
      (2) Richard Watkins.
      (3) Sally Watkins, married Lorence; moved to Texas.
      (4) Pauline Watkins, married Offenstein, and moved to Leesburg, Virginia
      (5) Linda Watkins, married Golliday.
      (6) Clara Watkins, married Rugg; moved to Colorado.
   b. Jack Watkins, moved to West Virginia.
   c. Janet Watkins, married to Marsh of Rockville.
8. Clinton Cleveland Watkins, born October 29, 1883; died December 12, 1911. Buried Salem Methodist, Cedar Grove.
9. Arthur Linthicum Watkins, born April 5, 1885; died March 16, 1957. Married April 28, 1909 in Rockville to Esther Pearl Luhn, born June 7, 1885, died May 18, 1981, daughter of Randolph and Sarah Elizabeth Luhn. Arthur and Esther are buried at Salem United Methodist Church, Cedar Grove, Maryland. His will, dated September 23, 1953, was probated April 9, 1957 and filed in will record book EA 75 at folio 424. He names his wife, and six children. His property consisted of the Noah Watkins farm, the John Oliver Thomas Watkins farm, and the Joshua L. Riggs farm purchased from William Lawson King, all located near Cedar Grove. They had seven children:
   a. Oliver R. Watkins.
   b. Herbert W. Watkins; married Mary Mae Barnes.
   c. L. Elizabeth Watkins, married Davidson.
   d. Virginia Watkins, married Souder.

e. Lillian Maybelle Watkins, born October 18, 1922. Married December 29, 1942 to James Francis Perry, born June 12, 1921, son of Harry Clay Perry (1896) and Nannia Frances Bentz (1896). A daughter:
  (1) Lynn Diane Perry, born March 17, 1944. Married September 14, 1963 to James L. Colpo, Jr., born June 14, 1944, and had two children:
    (a) Michael James Colpo, born August 9, 1964
    (b) Sandra Lynn Colpo, born April 28, 1969
f. Noah Luhn Watkins, born March 4, 1910; died July 25, 1910; buried at Salem Methodist Church, Cedar Grove.
g. Arthur Linthicum Watkins, Jr., born March 22, 1912 at Cedar Grove, Montgomery County, died May 16, 1992 at Frederick Memorial Hospital. Together with his partner, John M. Burdette, he established the Watkins-Burdette Motor Company. Married first Ethel B. Gue, born March 2, 1912, and died December 4, 1964, while living in Frederick, having had a child. She and her husband are buried at Salem United Methodist Church cemetery, in Cedar Grove, Maryland. He was married second to Hilda Mae Hyatt Roekle. The one known child was:
  (1) Daughter, married David H. Patten; three children.
10. Maude Ethel Watkins, born 1886; married Edgar W. Davis. In the 1900 census, this child is listed as Ethel M., reversing the given names shown here from other sources.
11. Raymond Ridgely Watkins, born December 26, 1888; died August 16, 1913. Buried at Salem Methodist Church in Cedar Grove, Maryland. Married February 8, 1911 Nellie Virginia Musgrove, daughter of Wampler Musgrove of Brunswick, Maryland. Raymond's death notice in the *Sentinel* newspaper mentions two children, one of whom was:
  a. N. Evelyn Watkins, born c.1912, died January 22, 1918 and buried with her father.
12. Grace Louise Watkins, born 1891; married Ralph Butterwick or Butterick, and lived in Fargo, North Dakota.
13. Frances Marian Watkins, born 1895 Cedar Grove, Maryland. Married July 20, 1914 to Filmore Cleveland Brown, born October 12, 1893 near Purdum, Maryland, son of John Wesley

Brown (1850) and Frances American Cornelia Burdette
(1857). In some reports, his first name is said to be Philip.
They had children:
a.   Francis Earl Brown, born February 9, 1915. Married
     August 18, 1937 to Glenrose Mary Flair, born May 12,
     1916 in Frederick. Children:
     (1)   Allen Wayne Brown, born October 27, 1938, and
           married Mach 18, 1959 to Margaret Klug, born
           July 12, 1941 in Germany.
     (2)   Francis Earl Brown, Jr., born October 5, 1941,
           and married November 6, 1959 Evelyn Jeanette
           Lawson, born August 4, 1942. They had a son,
           born in Frederick:
           (a)   Ricky Allen Brown: September 20, 1960
     (3)   David Anthony Brown, born March 27, 1950, and
           married May 29, 1969 to Nancy Jo Nash, born
           September 10, 1950. One son:
           (a)   David Anthony Brown, Jr.
b.   Julian Wilson Brown, born April 14, 1918, and married
     September 2, 1937 to Mary Virginia Purdum, born Au-
     gust 28, 1919, and had one child. Married second Octo-
     ber 14, 1946 to Violet Marie Jessee, born July 18, 1927,
     and had three children. Four children, first born Shady
     Grove, second at Frederick, last two at Olney:
     (1)   James Richard Brown, born October 19, 1940.
           Married April 11, 1966 to Carolyn Delores David-
           son, born April 30, 1948 at Saltville, Virginia. One
           son, born at Olney, Maryland:
           (a)   Steven Gary Brown, born October 18, 1971
     (2)   Julia Wilhelmina Brown, born November 2, 1947.
     (3)   Benita Lee Brown, born September 30, 1949.
     (4)   Kay Arlene Brown, born January 18, 1959.
c.   Doris Virginia Brown, born April 9, 1925, and married
     November 18, 1945 to Forrest Chipman Beane, born
     March 16, 1927 in Washington, D. C. No children.
d.   Ruth Evelyn Brown, born March 25, 1931, and married
     to Leon Hladchuk. One son:
     (1)   Craig Sheldon Hladchuk, born February 18, 1958.

Mary Avondale Watkins
1878-1958

This daughter of Noah Watkins and Julia Ann Linthicum was born February 25, 1878 and died February 15, 1958. Married June 8, 1898 at Cedar Grove Methodist Church to Franklin Monroe King, born January 5, 1876 and died June 8, 1935, son of Singleton Lewis King (1843) and Mary Rachel Elizabeth Burdette (1852). The couple are buried at Wesley Grove Methodist Church cemetery, and had children:

1. William Oliver King, born April 29, 1899, and died April 5, 1974 at Damascus. Married to Dorothy Craft, born 1912, and at the time of his death, there were twenty-seven grandchildren. Their children were:
   (a) Roberta Olivia King, born 1931
   (b) Herbert Charles King, born April 5, 1932 and died May 31, 1951
   (c) Pearle Avondale King, born 1933, married John Malcomb Clarke, and had children:
      (1) Patricia Jean Clarke, born 1956. Married to Grover and had a son:
         (a) Benjamin John Grover, born 1974
      (2) Wade Malcolm Clarke, born 1958
      (3) Barry Kevin Clarke, born 1962, died September 29, 1962
      (4) Kimberly Ann Clarke, born February 29, 1964
      (5) Gary Barton Clarke, born August 2, 1966
   (d) Earl Raymond King, born 1934, married Esther Lucille Hargett, and had children:
      (1) Katherine Ann King, born September 9, 1959. Married to William Gregory Miller; children:
         (a) Kathleen Michelle Miller, born 1981
         (b) Stephen Andrew Miller, born 1985
      (2) Susan Elizabeth King, born May 9, 1961 and married John Wandishin.
      (3) Sandra Jean King, born January 28, 1964
   (e) Henry Franklin King, born 1936, married Eleanor Marie Weber, born 1939, and had children:

(1)   Lorena Marie King, born July 29, 1961, and married 1984 at Woodfield, Maryland, to Harold Kenzel. One child:

       (a)   Dustin Robert Kenzel, born April 30, 1987

(2)   Wayne Allen King, born 1963. Married 1985 to Dawn Fountain and had children:

       (a)   Sarah King, born May 12, 1990

       (b)   Hannah King, born November 1, 1991

(3)   Neil Herbert King, born 1965. Married May 12, 1990 to Teri Kline, and had a child:

       (a)   Tayler Lynn King, born March 23, 1992

(4)   Dale Edward King, born February 12, 1969

(5)   Kari Lynn King, born 1971. Married July, 1992 to Andrew Mitchell.

f.   Margaret Ann King, born 1937, married 1958 at Woodfield, Maryland, James Boyette, born 1934 at Pensacola, Florida, son of Green Lester Boyette and Eva Boutwell. Children, the first child born at Riverdale, Maryland; the rest Frederick, Maryland:

(1)   Teresa Ann Boyette, born 1958. Married 1981 at Tallahassee, Florida, Timothy Mullen born 1956 at Baltimore, Maryland.

(2)   Deborah Faye Boyette, born June 17, 1961 and married 1984 at Tallahassee, Florida, to Eugene Borovsky, born 1954.

(3)   Gretchen Noel Boyette: December 17, 1964 and married 1989 at Lake Wales, Florida, to Jesse Pennington.

(4)   Renee Lynn Boyette, born January 24, 1968. Married 1991 at Orlando, Florida, Edward Grubb.

g.   Dorothy Olivia King, born 1939 at Woodfield, Maryland. Married April, 1961 to Carrol Don Hunter, born 1936 at Abilene, Texas, son of John Hunter and Velma Huchingson, and had children, born at Lubbock, Texas:

(1)   Donna Yvonne Hunter, born November, 1961

(2)   Jennifer Jean Hunter, born January 16, 1963. Married November, 1987 at Monterey, California, to Christopher Harrison. Children:

          (a)   Daniel Harrison, born 1989 in Germany

          (b)   Amanda Harrison, born 1992, Germany

    (3)   Gwynn Ellen Hunter, born April 2, 1965 and married June, 1988 at Midland, Texas, to Kevin Albright.

h.   Opal Elena King, born 1940 at Woodfield, Maryland. Married 1961 to Eugene Wilson Brown, Jr., born 1935 at Rich Square, North Carolina, the son of Eugene Wilson Brown and Hollie Parker, and had children, born at Ahoskie, North Carolina:

    (1)   Elena Rene' Brown, born November 24, 1963

    (2)   Eugene Wilson Brown, III, born July 20, 1966. Married 1993 Kathryn Ann Jones.

i.   William Oliver King, Jr., born 1942, married Joan Marie Watkins, born 1943 and had children:

    (1)   William Oliver King, III, born 1964

    (2)   Karen Marie King, born 1972

    (3)   Brian Charles King, born 1974

j.   James Thomas King, born 1943, married Martha Maelou Miller, born 1946, and had children:

    (1)   Shannon Sherelle King, born March 25, 1968

    (2)   Herbert Thomas King, born 1971

    (3)   James Thomas King, Jr., born 1973

2.   Mary Frances King, born December 9, 1900. Married August 27, 1919 to James Raymond Kemp, born August 14, 1898 at Clarksburg, died August 7, 1970, son of James Monroe Kemp and Sarah Elizabeth Duvall. Mary Frances and James Raymond had children:

a.   Julia Louise Kemp, born July 18, 1920 at Woodfield, Maryland, and died October 18, 1990. Married October 10, 1946 to Donald Elisha Warfield, born August 19, 1918 at Damascus, died September 3, 1985; son of Elisha S. and Ethel P. V. Warfield. Julia had two children:

    (1)   James Harvey Warfield, born August 25, 1947 Frederick. Married November 29, 1974 Jennifer Lynn Hamm, born May 13, 1954 at Fairfield, Alabama, daughter of James Hamm and Florence Y. Anthony. Children:

        (a)   Sarah Elizabeth Warfield: November 5, 1981.

        (b)   Jennifer Lynn Warfield: November 11, 1987.

    (2)   Diane Louise Warfield, born October 2, 1948.

b.   Mary Elizabeth Kemp, born October 20, 1921, died December 27, 1921.

c.   Edith Roberta Kemp, born March 25, 1925. She was married September 19, 1946 at Wesley Grove Presbyterian Church in Woodfield, Maryland, to Charles Oscar Baker, born June 25, 1922 at Mt. Airy, Maryland, son of Oscar Lee Baker and Bessie Clay Beshears (or Brashears). He was Fire Chief at National Bureau of Standards. Children, born at Frederick Hospital:

    (1)   Glenn Charles Baker, born February 20, 1948. He was married September 26, 1976 at Damascus Methodist Church to Beryl Alta Andrews, born May 23, 1947 at Bethlehem, Pennsylvania, the daughter of Richard and Aileen Andrews. They divorced after having children, two of whom died young. He married second to Kimberly Cuthbert, born May 1, 1958. His children were:

        (a)   Matthew Aaron Baker, born January 25, 1973 and died February 18, 1973

        (b)   Aimee Elizabeth Baker, died December 27, 1974

        (c)   Seth Ashley Baker, born June 7, 1977

    (2)   Jerry Wayne Baker: January 27, 1951, and married August 7, 1984 Carson City, Nevada, to Ada Katherine Poole, born February 27, 1952 Frederick, Maryland, daughter of Harry and Doris Poole. A son, born Frederick:

        (a)   Carson Remington Baker; October 12, 1985.

    (3)   Dennis Raymond Baker, born March 17, 1955 and married October 26, 1985 in the Catholic Church at Sykesville, Maryland, to Sherry Harrison, born 1959.

3.   Julian Pearre King, born December 5, 1903, and died January 18, 1973. Married June 17, 1925 in Methodist Church at Damascus to Sarah Elizabeth Burdette, born March 15, 1904 in

Damascus, Maryland, died August 15, 1982, the daughter of Claude H. Burdette (1872) and Sarah Rebecca Boyer (1874). Julian and his wife are buried at Salem United Methodist Church in Cedar Grove. For a time, Julian operated the garage and service station at Cedar Grove, and was a member of the Damascus Lions Club. Elected to the Maryland House of Delegates 1946, he served two four-year terms. Children:

a.　Elizabeth Jean King, born September 10, 1927 at Woodfield, Maryland. Married February 7, 1948 to Oliver Lee Baker of Mt. Airy, born June 5, 1927. Children, born at Frederick:

   (1)　Terry Lee Baker, born February 6, 1949. Married January 24, 1970 to Lucinda Louise Lare, born there August 20, 1950. At least two children:

      (a)　Valerie Jill Baker: February 2, 1973

      (b)　Jeffrey Lee Baker, born 1975

   (2)　Marilyn Jean Baker, born March 28, 1951. Lived at Berryville, Arkansas. Married to Patrick Ronald Salisbury, Jr., born 1950.

   (3)　Darlene Dee Baker, born October 29, 1952. Married May 19, 1973 Michael David Wilt, born July 1, 1950 at Leesburg, Virginia, and had at least one daughter:

      (a)　Veronica Rae Wilt, born 1981

b.　Julian Pearre King, Jr., born February 26, 1932 at Cedar Grove, Maryland. Married June 26, 1954 to Gloria Thomisina Reichard, born August 15, 1933 at York, Pennsylvania; divorced. Three children born in Los Angeles, California:

   (1)　Susan Burdette King, born April 27, 1956

   (2)　John Brian King, born January 19, 1962

   (3)　Jay Michael King, born June 28, 1963

c.　Patricia Ann King, born December 1, 1933 at Cedar Grove. Married April 24, 1954 to Elmer Dale Allgood, born May 26, 1931 at Sasakwa, Seminole County, Oklahoma, son of Charles H. Allgood and Carrie Hardesty. He was a Montgomery County police officer; they had four children, born Montgomery County, Maryland:

(1)   Brooks Dale Allgood, born October 20, 1954. Married August 3, 1974 at Salem United Methodist Church, Cedar Grove, to Bina Sue Miller, born October 23, 1954 at Baltimore, daughter of Richard Miller and Dorothy Heil. They had children, born at Carroll Hospital, Westminster, Carroll County, Maryland:

    (a) Blake Dale Allgood: March 12, 1985

    (b) Brent Denning Allgood: May 26, 1987

(2)   Gilbert Blake Allgood, born April 15, 1956 and died October 13, 1956

(3)   Nita Ann Allgood, born September 8, 1957. Married October 1, 1988 at Salem Methodist Church, Cedar Grove, to Mark Lawson, born November 27, 1957, son of Richard Lawson and Kay Gladhill.

(4)   Stacy Ann Allgood, born September 12, 1968 and married February 14, 1993 at Salem United Methodist Church, Cedar Grove, John Patrick Calloway

4. Marjorie Roberta King, born September 3, 1908. Married Marvin Louis Spooner, and divorced. One daughter:

a. Margaret Louise Spooner, born May 30, 1936 and married November 12, 1955 in Washington, D. C., to Kenneth Allen Hughes, born July 17, 1935 in Washington, son of Arnold Victor Hughes (1894) and Helen Cecilia Dove (1904). Children, born Washington:

(1)   Donna Lee Hughes, born August 15, 1956. Married December 29, 1977 in Bloomsburg, Pennsylvania, to Raymond Eugene Goodwin, born March 28, 1952, and had children, born in Bloomsburg (Note: the source of this information lists the children with the surname of Phillips; possible error):

    (a) Christopher Eugene Goodwin; July 10, 1979.

    (b) Adam Lee Goodwin, born June 16, 1980

(2)   Kenneth Allen Hughes, Jr., born October 29, 1957. Married September 4, 1982 at East Riverdale, Maryland, to Joan Carol Evans, born February 18, 1961. Children, all born in Houston, Texas:

       (a)   Alexander Evans Hughes; April 21, 1986

       (b)   Kelsey Victoria Hughes, a twin, born February 10, 1989

       (c)   William Kenneth Hughes, a twin, born February 10, 1989.

    (3)   Robin Marie Hughes, born April 6, 1960 and married June 15, 1981 to Christopher Honeycutt, and divorced. They had a son:

       (a)   Jason Tanner Honeycutt: July 1, 1983

    (4)   David Arnold Hughes, born October 24, 1964

5.   Noah Franklin King, born December 16, 1912. Married first December 23, 1933 to Cecil Lawson; second Martha Hillery, born April 4, 1916 at Kemptown, Maryland, daughter of John Hillery and Gertrude Estelle Purdum. No children.

6.   Jeremiah Lewis King, born November, 1915 Woodfield, Maryland. Also reported as Jeremiah Louis King; neither spelling as yet positively confirmed. Married at Delmar, Maryland, to Lillian Estelle Jones, born October 3, 1914 at Kemptown, Maryland; the daughter of Louis L. Jones and Bessie Bellison; and had twin girls, born Washington:

a.   Janet Louise King, born November 24, 1937. Married 1961 to David Wesley McCloughan, born 1934 at Clarksummit, Pennsylvania; son of Donald C. McCloughan and Elizabeth Gose. Children:

    (1)   Dwight David McCloughan, born May 17, 1963; married August, 1991 in St. Louis, Missouri, to Laura Turpin.

    (2)   Stephen Wayne McCloughan, born August 21, 1965 at Annapolis, Maryland.

b.   Nancy Roberta King, born November 24, 1937. Married December 16, 1967 in Washington to James Henry Coonrod, born September 1, 1923 at Waterloo, Iowa.

7.   Calvin Lee King, born April, 1925. Married first Delora Simonds; second Millie Ikner. Three children second marriage:

a.   Charles Lee King, born 1946, and married Marilyn Kornegay, born 1947; one child. Married second to Tamara Rasner, and had a second child:

    (1)   Calvin Edward King, born 1969

      (2)   Tegan King, born 1979

b.   David Franklin King, born 1947; married Karen Hook; one son. Married second Suzanne Marie Hack; a son:

      (1)   Christian King, born 1971

      (2)   Brian David King, born 1982

c.   Linda Marie King, born 1949, and married Jerry Burriss. Two children. She married second Bruce Butler, and had a child. Her three children were:

      (1)   Nikki Burriss, born 1972

      (2)   Barbara Burriss, born 1973

      (3)   Kimberly Butler, born 1979

CHILD 13

James Willard Watkins
1848-1928

This son of Alpha Watkins (1803) and Harriet Ann Lewis (1805) was born September 26, 1848, and died November 29, 1928 at Cedar Grove, Maryland. Married December 19, 1872 Charlotte J. Williams, born September 23, 1850 and died February 10, 1923. Both buried at Salem United Methodist Church at Cedar Grove, in Montgomery County, Maryland. His will, dated December 11, 1927, was probated December 18, 1928 and filed in Liber PEW 14 at folio 124 in Montgomery County records. He lists his children, and a grandson. Final accounts in his estate were filed by his son, Maynard D. Watkins, dated September 18, 1929 and recorded in liber PEW 17, at folio 203 in the wills office of the county. He appears as head of household in the 1880 census for the Clarksburg District,, with his wife and three of their children. His mother is also living with them at the time, at the age of 75 years. They also appear in the 1900 census for Damascus, with six of their children. There was a total of at least eight:

1.   Manona E. Watkins, born 1873 to 1875, and died 1958. She is called Nonie in the will. Married April 16, 1896 to Harry J. King, born 1867 and died 1949. Both are buried at Salem United Methodist Church at Cedar Grove, Maryland.

2. Jessie P. Watkins, born c.1877, and married April 30, 1901 at the Upper Seneca Baptist Church, Cedar Grove, Maryland, to Charles R. Tabler. His occupation is listed as carpenter; hers as a lady. At least one child:
    a. Milton Tabler, named in his grandfather's will.
3. William A. Watkins, born c.1879
4. Della C. Watkins, born c.1883 married Charles Barber. She predeceased her father, and he included her children in his will, although they were not named. The final accounts provide the names:
    a. Gaynell Barber, married Kendall.
    b. Roberta Barber.
    c. Malcolm Barber.
    d. Geneva Barber.
    e. Eldridge Barber.
    f. Garner Barber.
    g. Catherine Barber.
    h. Maud Barber.
    i. Margaret Barber, married Iglehart.
5. Ola G. Watkins, born c.1887 married Englehart (or Iglehart) and McAtee
6. James Haller Watkins, born December 2, 1888, died December 20, 1965. Called Haller in the will. Married Annie Ellen, born June 3, 1889, died September 13, 1926. Both are buried at Salem United Methodist Church, Cedar Grove.
7. Maynard D. Watkins, born May 30, 1891 at Cedar Grove, and died January 13, 1981. Married November 22, 1911 to Laura Jane Soper, born c.1893; died 1967, the daughter of William Wooten Soper (1850) and Catherine Jemima King (1854) of Clarksburg. Maynard and his wife are buried at Upper Seneca Baptist Church at Cedar Grove, in Montgomery County, Maryland, and had children:
    a. Charlotte Watkins, born 1912; married Elroy Kaufman.
    b. William D. Watkins, born 1914; married Julia Norwood and had a child. Married second Frances Chandler. His child was:
        (1) Shirley Watkins.

c. Earl Wheeler Watkins, born 1921. Married August 3, 1944 at Methodist parsonage in Clarksburg, Maryland, to Marian Phyllis Thompson, born 1923, the daughter of William H. Thompson of Rockville, and had children:

    (1)   Dianne K. Watkins, born 1947

    (2)   Gail M. Watkins, born 1951

d. Maynard D. Watkins, Jr., born April 7, 1928. Married May 30, 1959 to Mary Jane Mullinix, born December 23, 1937, daughter of James F. Mullinix (1910). A son:

    (1)   Craig Stephen Watkins, born May 4, 1961

8. Olive R. Watkins, born c.1895; married Windsor.

CHAPTER 6

Samuel B. Watkins
1807-1885

Appearing as head of household in the 1850 census for the Clarksburg District of Montgomery County, Samuel was born c.1807. He is listed with a wife, Sarah J. Watkins, born c.1819, and what appears to be six of his children at that time. In the house, there is also one Josiah W. Watkins, born c.1832, a laborer, and one John H. Harwood, a black laborer, born c.1843. Josiah W. Watkins is probably the son of John W. Watkins (1782) and Eleanor C. Hitchcock (1797). He is listed again in the census of 1870 for Damascus, with his wife and six children. He appears again in the 1880 census, apparently as a widower, with three of his daughters still at home. Samuel died April 29, 1885 and his wife Sarah died March 24, 1879. Both are buried in the cemetery of the Bethesda United Methodist Church at Browningsville. His eldest son filed final accounts of his estate, and obtained receipts from the heirs, dated August 18, 1886 and recorded in liber RWC 16 at folio 50, Montgomery County wills office. The children were:

1. William Thomas Watkins, born c.1837, of whom more
2. Matilda R. Watkins, born c.1838. Married Norwood.
3. Amanda Watkins, born c.1841
4. Amy C. Watkins, born about February 24, 1844, died January 16, 1886 at the age of 41 years, 10 months and 22 days. Buried at Bethesda United Methodist Church, Browningsville. The date of death and her age at death appeared on her stone, but the 1880 census would calculate her birth as c.1853. Her estate was reported by her eldest brother, William Thomas, in liber RWC 15 at folio 123, with her brothers and sisters named, excepting Julius.
5. Margaret L. Watkins, born c.1844; married Beall.
6. Isabella Virginia Watkins, born March 24, 1848. Married November 8, 1870 at her father's home in Hyattstown to Joseph McKendree Burdette, born June 12, 1845, died January 21,

1922, son of James William Burdette (1813) and Cassandra Purdum (1804). Joseph's will was dated May 28, 1921 and probated February 7, 1922 and recorded in liber HCA 26 at folio 204 in Montgomery County, Maryland. He died January 21, 1922 and left to his son, Moody M. Burdette, property located in Barnesville, where Moody kept a store. Joseph and Isabella are both buried at Bethesda United Methodist Church cemetery. An infant stone is there also, with no name or dates. There were three other children, also mentioned in the will:

a. Moody M. Burdette, born 1884, died 1945. Married to Ellen G., born 1891, died 1977. Both buried at Bethesda United Methodist Church near Browningsville. They had at least two sons:

    (1) Merle M. Burdette, died October 1, 1968. Married M. Hazel Williams, born May 18, 1914 at Damascus, daughter of Downey M. Williams and Frances Elizabeth Bolton. Children:

        (a) Daughter, apparently married twice; first to Philip Springirth, and second to Lee Leathery.

        (b) Michael M. Burdette.

    (2) Irving M. Burdette.

b. Willis B. Burdette, probably the same Willis who was born October 26, 1871 and died February 21, 1930, a teacher. If so, he was married to Lula B. Walker, born November 23, 1870, died December 24, 1942, the daughter of John Wesley Walker (1849). One son:

    (1) Aubrey Wilson Burdette, born March 2, 1897 and died May 26, 1943. Buried at Forest Oak cemetery in Gaithersburg, Maryland. Married March 1, 1915 to Ruby Adelaide Gloyd, born July 16, 1898, daughter of Edmund Alexander Gloyd (1863). They had children, including:

        (a) Audrey Marie Burdette, born November 24, 1915; married August 25, 1934 James Robert Millan and had children:

            1. Robert Lawrence Millan, born November 21, 1937

2. William Bradford Millan, born October 4, 1939, and died October 30, 1940
3. David Lewis Millan; September 25, 1942
4. Dale Alexander Millan; July 12, 1948
   (b) Vera Regina Burdette, born April 8, 1919; married May 17, 1941 Robert Ford Sheffield.
   c. Prudence V. Burdette, married Dorsey W. Day.
   d. Lilly May Burdette, married to Umberger.
7. Sebastian W. Watkins, born c.1853, died September 18, 1877 at age 24 years, 11 months and 3 days. Buried with parents.
8. Harriett A. Watkins, born c.1857 (1870 census)
9. Laura Dorcas Watkins, born February 22, 1858. Married October 16, 1885 to Titus Granville Day, born September 16, 1850, died November 23, 1931, son of Rufus King Day (1827) and Ann Priscilla Brandenburg (1831). No children.
10. Antonia C. Watkins, born 1860 (1880 census). Included in the estate of her father. Probably the same individual married June 15, 1897 to Charles L. Housen at Browningsville.
11. Ann Dorcas Watkins, born 1862 (1880 census)
12. Julius Watkins, included in the estate of his father in 1886, but not in the estate of Amy C. Watkins.

<h3 style="text-align:center">William Thomas Watkins
1837-1891</h3>

This son of Samuel B. Watkins (1807), was born about September, 1837 on his father's farm in Montgomery County, Maryland, and died May 20, 1891 on his own farm near Urbana, Frederick County, Maryland, aged 53 years, 8 months and twenty days. Buried at Bethesda United Methodist Church at Browningsville, Maryland. He was married to Sarah E. Williams, of the Clarksburg community, in Montgomery County, born June 2, 1844 and died February 17, 1928, daughter of Samuel Williams. She is buried with her husband. He is found listed only by his first name in the 1880 census of Frederick County, with his wife and four children. Also in the household is Tobias C. Watkins, born c.1860, a cousin. His will, dated May 20, 1891, was probated June 9, 1891 and filed in Liber HCA 4 at folio 351 in Montgomery County. There, he names only his wife, and his son, Maurice, spelled Morris in the will. In the 1900 census for Frederick County, Sarah appears as head of household, with William Ernest still at home; and Vernon T. is living there with his wife and first child. Also in the household at that time is Mary Browning, born c.1880, listed as a niece. William Thomas and Sarah had five children:

1. Olive M. Watkins, born c.1866, of Browningsville.
2. Maurice Watkins, born December 15, 1867, of whom more
3. Bradley Watkins, born February 14, 1870, of whom more
4. Vernon T. Watkins, born August 18, 1871, of whom more
5. William Ernest Watkins, born September 14, 1881 and died January 6, 1915. Buried Bethesda United Methodist Church cemetery near Browningsville, Maryland. Married at his bride's home, February 3, 1909 to Myrtle Estelle King, born May 13, 1883, died January 6, 1964, daughter of John Edward Howard King (1845) and Martha Elizabeth Linthicum (1844). Myrtle Estelle is buried with her husband. They had three children, two of whom were:
   a. William Ernest Watkins, Jr., born December 20, 1909 at Kemptown
   b. Margaret Elizabeth Watkins, born July 5, 1911

Maurice Watkins
1867-1940

Maurice was born December 15, 1867 and died March 31, 1940, the eldest son of William Thomas Watkins (1837) and Sarah E. Williams (1844). He was married January 9, 1894 at Wesley Grove Church to Martha Rebecca King, born December 4, 1874, died January 4, 1950. She was a daughter of Singleton Lewis King (1843-1909) and Mary Rachel Elizabeth Burdette (1852-1923). Maurice and Martha Rebecca (Mattie) are buried at Bethesda United Methodist Church near Browningsville. They appear in the 1900 census for Damascus with three children. The will of Maurice, dated March 1, 1927, was probated April 23, 1940 and filed in Liber HGC 33 at folio 113 in Montgomery County. He leaves to his wife, Mattie R. Watkins, the property on the north side of the road leading from Browningsville to Lewisdale, for her life-time, and then to be divided equally between his children, not named. The only names appearing are two of his sons (Otis L. and William M.) as executors. Children:

1. Otis Lewis Watkins, born June 22, 1895, died September 15, 1958. Married Byrd Butler Kidd, born March 4, 1889, died November 6, 1977, daughter of Jesse and Martha Jane Butler. She had a daughter born to her first marriage: Madlyn Kidd, married Hyatt of Damascus. Buried together at the Bethesda United Methodist Church, Browningsville. No children
2. Infant Watkins daughter, August, 1897
3. Iva May Watkins, or Ivy May Watkins, born December 13, 1897, died May 15, 1960. Married Ray Hilton, who died 1966. They had children:
   a. Catherine Hilton, born August 23, 1928; married Jesse Lee Riggs, born January 25, 1925. Children:
      (1) Charles Larry Riggs, born December 1, 1948. Married Patricia Kirchgassner. Children:
         (a) Andrew Hilton Riggs: December 13, 1973
         (b) Carolyn Patricia Riggs: March 19, 1975.
      (2) James Bryan Riggs, born September 10, 1950 and married Linda Ann Driskill, born April 12, 1953, and had children:
         (a) James Bryan Riggs, Jr.; May 6, 1972
         (b) Jessica Christine Riggs; November 6, 1975.
      (3) Julie Marie Riggs, born August 8, 1957, and married C. Wayne Frum. A child:
         (a) Kelly Marie Frum, born April 20, 1979
   (b) Robert Maurice Hilton, born November 29, 1932. Married Evelyn May Day, born March 30, 1930, daughter of James Day and Edna Beall. Children:
      (1) Gwendolyn Mae Hilton, born September 1, 1955. Married to Terry Lee Brown, born July 21, 1955, son of Delaney Pearl Brown (1919) Children:
         (a) Scott Delaney Brown: March 14, 1980
         (b) Kevin Robert Brown: October 19, 1984

(2)   Gail Dianne Hilton, born December 21, 1957. Married Joel Thomas Hudlow, born September 23, 1955. A son:
       (a) Jesse Thomas Hudlow: April 20, 1984
(3)   Suzanne Marie Hilton, born August 13, 1959. Married Jefferson Donald Federmeyer; a child:
       (a) Lindsay Marie Federmeyer, born September 12, 1984.
(4)   Sharon Lynn Hilton, born April 21, 1961
(5)   Robert Ray Hilton, born August 31, 1963

4. Flora Elizabeth Watkins, born May 1, 1900; married Joseph Russell Sibley, born August 9, 1901. A child:
    a. Flora Elizabeth Sibley, born February 2, 1935, and married first to Vickroy, by whom she had a child. Married second to Martin Alexander Case, born October 18, 1932, and had a son. Children:
       (1) Donna Lynn Vickroy, born August 1, 1958
       (2) David Martin Case, born May 4, 1964

5. William Maurice Watkins, born April 17, 1902, died November 14, 1971; buried at Bethesda United Methodist Church cemetery, Browningsville. Married November 11, 1922 to Fannie Wagner McElfresh, born August 4, 1903. Children, born Browningsville:
    a. Dorothy Janice Watkins, born May 6, 1924, and married to Edward Warfield Mullinix, born December 11, 1921, and had children:
       (1) Everett Wayne Mullinix, born October 29, 1946. Married Sharon Williams, born March 21, 1952, and had children:
          (a) Angelique Mullinix: December 2, 1969
          (b) Jessica Amy Mullinix: July 3, 1976
       (2) Thomas William Mullinix, married Brenda Jane Gadow. Married second Margaret Palozi and had children:
          (a) Megan Ruth Mullinix; September 18, 1980
          (b) Noah Warfield Mullinix; October 3, 1983.

(3) Stephen Earl Mullinix, born November 6, 1952. Married Carol Williams, born April 5, 1953, and had children:
  (a) Jason Robert Mullinix: March 7, 1977
  (b) David Ryan Mullinix: April 11, 1980
  (c) Lindsay Michelle Mullinix; August 29, 1984.
(4) Kevin Patrick Mullinix, born April 9, 1958. Married Deanna Dawn Watson, born October 16, 1962, and had a child:
  (a) Brooks Grayson Mullinix: July 4, 1985
b. Ruth Evelyn Watkins, born October 25, 1926. Married John Cronin Beall, son of Barry Beall and Edith Burdette, and had five children. Married second Rudell C. Beall; no children. The children were:
(1) Carolyn Ann Beall, married to Glenn Kenneth Shriver, Jr., and had children:
  (a) Sarah Kathryn Shriver.
  (b) Carolyn Ann Shriver.
  (c) Glenn Kenneth Shriver, III.
  (d) Susan Lynn Shriver.
(2) Sandra Ruth Beall, married Randall Allen Grear. Children:
  (a) Jennifer Ann Grear.
  (b) John Robert Grear.
  (c) Matthew David Grear.
  (d) Aaron Ray Grear.
(3) John Cronin Beall, Jr., born December 14, 1949, died in Vietnam, October 31, 1971 and buried at Browningsville, Maryland.
(4) Patsy Lee Beall, married to Robert Wayne Pickett, and had children:
  (a) Lisa Ann Pickett.
  (b) Rachel Marie Pickett.
  (c) Nathan Robert Pickett.
(5) Barry William Beall, born April 14, 1959 and married Melissa Martin, born December 27, 1963. They had children:
  (a) Teresa Elizabeth Beall; September 14, 1983

        (b)   Heather Marie Beall: June 21, 1986

c.   Robert Lee Watkins, born October 29, 1932 at Brown-ingsville, and married Ardis Mae Hanson, born July 17, 1932. Two children:

    (1)   Sharon Lynn Watkins, born June 13, 1958, and married to Larry E. Hunt, born December 27, 1956. They had children, and she married second James Fraley. Her children were:

        (a)   Robin Marie Hunt: August 20, 1974

        (b)   Katherine Hunt: November 21, 1978

        (c)   Erin Michelle Hunt: October 27, 1980

        (d)   Daniel Robert Hunt: October 28, 1982

    (2)   Robin Leigh Watkins, born July 2, 1960, and married Charles E. Cole, Jr., born September 22, 1961.

6.   Mary Rebecca Watkins, born April 12, 1905, married November 27, 1924 at the Bethesda United Methodist Church parsonage at Browningsville, Maryland, Milton W. Burdette, born 1900, the son of Willie H. Burdette and Mamie Pugh. At least one daughter:

a.   Ann Burdette, born 1932, married to Alfred Freysz and had children:

    (1)   Alfred Freysz, Jr., born October 7, 1953, married Brenda McDonald. Children:

        (a)   Michelle Freysz, born July 11, 1977

        (b)   Richard Allen Freysz, born 1989

    (2)   Sandra Kay Freysz, born January 26, 1957, and married Wayne Johnson, born September 30, 1954. Children:

        (a)   Courtney Elizabeth Johnson, born December 22, 1984.

        (b)   Merridith Ann Johnson, born 1988

        (c)   Jeremiah Paul Johnson, born 1990

7.   Grace Alice Watkins, also found as Grace Olive Watkins and Olive Grace Watkins, born May 6, 1907. Married to David Irvin Ward, born February 4, 1907, and had children:

a.   Lloyd Irvin Ward, born July 2, 1931. Married to Mary Helen Talbot, born June 23, 1932, and had a one son:

    (1)   David Lloyd Ward, born November 5, 1957 and married Robyn Barklay. One son:
        (a) Robert Christopher Ward; March 22, 1983
  b. Carleton Wendell Ward, born October 7, 1935. Married Sandra Norson, born October 30, 1936. Children:
    (1)   Thomas Carleton Ward, born August 6, 1958 and married Jo Ann Wilkes. A daughter:
        (a) Jennifer Ward: October 13, 1986
    (2)   Steven Craig Ward, born May 12, 1967
    (3)   Boy Ward, stillbirth July 25, 1960
    (4)   Boy Ward, stillbirth March 16, 1961
8. Carlton T. Watkins, born May 8, 1914, died January 15, 1915; buried with his parents
9. Harold Willard Watkins, born October 31, 1919, and married January 3, 1946 to Catherine Sally Beall, born December 15, 1925, daughter of Barry Ranson Beall (1886) and Edith Elizabeth Burdette. Children:
  a. Martha Joanne Watkins, born July 16, 1947, and married to Ted Hawk, born September 7, 1944 in Ohio. They were missionaries, serving in Honduras, and had children:
    (1)   Donald Harold Hawk, born December 28, 1969 in Indiana.
    (2)   Jody Theodore Hawk, born July 9, 1971, born in Honduras, Central America, as were the next two children.
    (3)   Travis Lavern Hawk, born March 26, 1973.
    (4)   Catherine Jean Hawk, born October 30, 1974.
    (5)   Angela Marie Hawk, born January 13, 1982, born in Ohio.
  b. Beverly Elizabeth Watkins, born December 1, 1956, and served as a missionary in Medellin, Columbia. Married July 10, 1982 to the Reverend Paul Dean Duerksen, born 1953, and had children:
    (1)   Benjamin Harold Duerksen, born January 11, 1984 in Texas.
    (2)   Joseph Michael Duerksen, born April 8, 1987 in New Jersey.
    (3)   Emilee Grace Duerksen, born 1988

c. Dwayne Maurice Watkins, born March 26, 1960, and married to Dorothy Louise Staton, born August 12, 1961. Children:
    (1) Wesley Willard Watkins, born May 1, 1984
    (2) Christopher Dwayne Watkins, born June 10, 1987

Bradley Watkins
1870-1941

Bradley was born February 14, 1870 and died March 11, 1941, the son of William Thomas Watkins (1837) and Sarah E. Williams (1844). Married October 14, 1896 at Browningsville in Montgomery County to Rebecca Zerah Burdette, born October 14, 1877 and died June 24, 1945, daughter of the Reverend Caleb Joshua Burdette (1849) and Roberta King (1855). Bradley and Rebecca are buried in the cemetery of Bethesda United Methodist Church, Browningsville, Maryland. Children, born in Montgomery County:

1. Lena Elizabeth Watkins, born February 22, 1898 at Lewisdale and died March 23, 1982. Married June 6, 1917 at Bethesda United Methodist Church parsonage to Floyd Sims Moxley, born July 19, 1895, died July 23, 1974, the son of Cornelius Edward Moxley and Florence E. Poole. At least one son:
    a. Floyd Keen Maloy Moxley, born August 16, 1926. Married June 28, 1951 to Ruby Jo Garland, born June 6, 1930 in Tennessee, daughter of Dave W. Garland and Nora Ledford. Two children:
        (1) Glenn Floyd Moxley, born April 4, 1953, and married April 19, 1985 Barbara Ann Peterson born December 19, 1964, the daughter of Roger J. Peterson, Sr.
        (2) Nancy Lee Moxley, born February 7, 1957. She was married May 20, 1978 to Denis Rex Hood, born September 26, 1952, son of Clarence Ellis Hood and Lillian Mae King (1921). Children:
            (a) Andrea Lee Hood: September 1, 1982
            (b) Daryl Ellis Hood: January 7, 1986

2. Roberta Eveline Watkins, born 1901, died 1961. Married at the home of her parents October 20, 1917 to George Lincoln Burdette, born July 9, 1897, died January 25, 1918, son of Abraham Lincoln Burdette (1864) and Georgia Ellen Waters King (1867). No children. She married second to Charles F. Burdette, born 1898, died 1947, son of Willie H. Burdette and Mamie Pugh, and had two children. Married third to Tightus E. Brown, born 1880, died June 11, 1966, son of Thomas Ephraim Brown and Sarah E. Hilton. No issue. Her two children, born to the second marriage, were:

   a. Wallace Franklin Burdette, born January 5, 1924 and died October 6, 1994. Buried at the Bethesda United Methodist Church, Browningsville. Married Dolly May Keeney and had children:

      (1) Robert Franklin Burdette, born 1947, married February 19, 1966 to Barbara Ann Schaffer.
      (2) Stephen W. Burdette.
      (3) Teresa Ann Burdette, born 1960. Married to Huff and had children:
      (a) Mathew P. Huff.
      (b) Charity Huff.
      (c) Rebecca Huff.

   b. Ella Irene Burdette, married Gordon Hall; children:
      (1) Lawrence Hall.
      (2) Beverly Hall.
      (3) Judy Hall.
      (4) Patti Hall.
      (5) Donald Hall.

3. Howard Raymond Watkins, born December 19, 1903, died October 30, 1954; buried at the Bethesda United Methodist Church cemetery, at Browningsville, Maryland. Married early August, 1928 at Clarksburg Methodist Church, to Lois Lillian Davis, born May 23, 1911, daughter of Clarence Davis, all of Damascus, and had children:

   a. Marjorie Ann Watkins, married Charles J. Green, Jr., born September 5, 1925, died August 10, 1984, son of Charles J. and Helen E. Green. At least two children:
      (1) Charles Raymond Green.

(2)   Rita Lynn Green.
b.   Bradley Parker Watkins, born October 14, 1931 at Damascus. Married Patricia Rae Smith and had children:
(1)   Jay Bradley Watkins.
(2)   Patti Gail Watkins, born 1956
(3)   Jan Parker Watkins, born 1960

Vernon T. Watkins
1871-1943

This son of William Thomas Watkins (1837) and Sarah E. Williams (1844) was born August 18, 1871 on the family farm near Urbana, Frederick County, Maryland and died 1943. Buried in cemetery of Bethesda United Methodist Church at Browningsville. He received his early education in the Frederick county public schools. In the 1900 census for Damascus, he and his wife, with their first child, were living in the household of his widowed mother. As late as 1910, he owned 137 acres of farmland; part of the tract called *William and Elizabeth*, on the road from Price's distillery to Ijamsville; which he purchased from R. H. Magruder. Married June 1, 1898 at Providence Church to Edith P. Mount, of Kemptown, Maryland, daughter of William Mount and Alice Duvall. Edith was born 1878, died 1941, and is buried with her husband. They had five children, probably all born at or near Browningsville, Maryland:
1.   Mazie Noreen Watkins, born c.1899
2.   William Thomas Watkins, christened September 16, 1919 at home at Browningsville. He is probably the same individual of that name who is buried in the cemetery of the Bethesda United Methodist Church. His stone indicates that he was born December 14, 1900 and died April 13, 1943.
3.   Alice Olivia Watkins, christened September 16, 1919 at home at Browningsville.
4.   Sally Virginia Watkins.
5.   Ray Mount Watkins, born February 8, 1908. He probably married Edna V., and had at least one son:

a. Charles V. Watkins, born August 1, 1935, died January 27, 1937. Buried at Bethesda United Methodist Church, Browningsville.
6. Edith Pearl Watkins, born November 29, 1912
7. Mildred Eveline Watkins, born September 21, 1914

CHAPTER 7

Denton Watkins
1795-1864

Various references to the family of this individual have been found in card files at the library of the Montgomery County Historical Society, and elsewhere. We have not placed him within the principal family now under study, but assume a relationship. Born c.1795, died 1864; married Mahala Brandenburg, and had children:

1. Matilda Watkins, born c.1820. Married Loren Todd.
2. Jepe Watkins, born c.1821 and died at about nine months.
3. Priscilla Watkins, born c.1824. Married Robert Farnsworth.
4. Edward Taylor Watkins, married and had children, including:
   a. Clarence E. Watkins, who had children:
      (1) Lois Allene Watkins, born December 27, 1915
      (2) Dorothy Watkins, born September 22, 1917 and married to William Newton.
      (3) Kenneth Watkins.
      (4) Marjorie Nell Watkins, born either January 12 or March, 1922. Married to Kenneth Rupp.
   b. William Henry Watkins, born January 25, 1867, of whom more following.
   c. George Washington Watkins, born June 24, 1869 and died 1945. Married three times: first to Dora Waldron; second November 26, 1900 to Bertha Gunther; third in 1927 to Anna Hart. He had children:
      (1) George Victor Watkins, born July 17, 1904, and married to Frances.
      (2) Winifred Lenore Watkins, born November 26, 1906 and married to Cochran.
      (3) Herbert Taylor Watkins, born December 7, 1910
      (4) William Edward Watkins, born August 3, 1916 and married to Mary.
   d. Stella Florence Watkins, born September 9, 1872, died October 10, 1954. Married James Ira Sellers.

e. Mary Winifred Watkins, born September 29, 1876, died
    November 23, 1963. Married George Washington Jones.
5. Miranda Watkins, born April 6, 1828. Married twice: first to
    George McVey and second to Jesse Miracle.
6. Mary Watkins, born c.1830. Married to Jacob Farnsworth.
7. McKendree Watkins, born c.1833
8. Milton B. Watkins, born c.1845. Married Rachel A. Miracle.
    Children, including:
    a. Wannie Blanche Watkins, born 1879. Married to Allen
        Whetstone.
9. Hamilton Watkins, born February 18, 1847, died January 12,
    1937, and had children:
    a. Ernest Watkins, who had children:
        (1) Lawrence Watkins, born 1893, an infant death
        (2) Opal Watkins, born July 15, 1907
    b. Jesse Watkins, born May 1, 1872. He had children:
        (1) Joyce Watkins.
        (2) Merhle Watkins, born October 10, 1896 and died
             October 19, 1971.
        (3) Paul Watkins.
        (4) Ralph Watkins.
    c. Hattie Watkins, born August 13, 1873, died July 5, 1956.
        Married to Reese Ingle. These may be their children:
        (1) Iva Ingle, born May 24, 1891
        (2) Lawrence Ingle, born 1893, an infant death
        (3) Vera Ingle, born May 24, 1895, and married to
             McGavern.
    d. Laura Blanche Watkins, born September 3, 1884; died
        May 21, 1963. Married May 22, 1907 to John Roscoe
        Lieurance.
    e. Edward Evan Watkins, born May 10, 1906, and died July
        24, 1965. Married 1929 to Vera Dempsey. Children:
        (1) Dorothy Watkins, who married Pierce.
        (2) Harold Watkins, who had children:
             (a) Jack Watkins.
             (b) Kenneth Watkins.
             (c) Norma Watkins.

f. Inza Isidore Watkins, married twice: to Will Branaman, and to Summer Crumpacker.
g. Pearl Watkins, married May 9, 1906 Elbert L. Maxedon.
10. Evan R. Watkins, who had children:
  a. William T. Watkins, born 1863
  b. Harriet Watkins, a twin, born 1874. Married Rhodes.
  c. Harry Watkins, a twin, born 1874

William Henry Watkins
1867-1947

This son of Edward Taylor Watkins, was born January 25, 1867, and died 1947. Married Lillian May Hutchings; children:
1. John Alva Watkins, born July 4, 1893 and died February 23, 1965. Married twice: first October 2, 1915 to Margaret Miller; second November 25, 1926 to Golda May Parker. He had children:
  a. Leroy Alva Watkins, born March 2, 1916 and died August 10, 1963. Married June 21, 1936 to Genevieve Arline Hicks and had children:
    (1) Judith Arlene Watkins, born October 13, 1938. Married Paul Leroy Latchaw.
    (2) Jerauld Alva Watkins, born May 21, 1940, and married to Nadine Peterson.
    (3) Jeanette Alvene Watkins, born September 26, 1942. Married twice: first November 11, 1960 Eldon Edward Markes; and second November 28, 1967 Robert Lee Hatfield.
    (4) James Alan Watkins, born September 23, 1946. Married May 28, 1964 Mary Luella Maddon.
    (5) Kim Allen Watkins, born February 13, 1955
  b. Mildred Lolita Watkins, born December 24, 1917. Married February, 1936 to Leland Lee Lingle.
  c. John Alva Watkins, Jr., born July 12, 1929 and married twice: first to Nadine Goetz and second to Peggy Brown. Children, including:
    (1) John Alva Watkins, III
    (2) Marsha Ann Watkins.

      (3)   Sheila Marie Watkins.

      (4)   William Lewis Watkins.

   d. William Lewis Watkins, born June 13, 1931. Married Delores Ann Bozarth. Children:

      (1)   Wanda Jean Watkins, born October 9, 1952. Married to Archie Douglas Simmons.

      (2)   Robert Eugene Watkins, born November 13, 1958

      (3)   Michael James Watkins, born August 11, 1962

2. Virgil Lloyd Watkins, born September 1, 1895 and died May 23, 1944. Married to Retta.

3. Vernon Edward Watkins, born January 29, 1898, died August 14, 1972. Married Glenora Frances Boldrey.

CHAPTER 8

Miscellaneous Watkins Families
of
Montgomery County

Several families have been found in Montgomery County records who have not been yet located within the framework of the principal groups under study. They appear here for further research and information.

Nathan B. Watkins
1826-

This individual is shown as head of household in the 1870 census for Damascus, then Clarksburg District, Montgomery County. He is listed as being 44 years old, thus born c.1826. It does not appear that there is a female of the age to be his wife, so he is assumed to be widowed, with nine children in the household. We have yet to identify any member of this family from any other record. The children were:

1. Fannie H. Watkins, born c.1848
2. George W. Watkins, born c.1851
3. Jason P. Watkins, born c.1852
4. Cornelius V. Watkins, born c.1856
5. Nathan B. Watkins, Jr., born c.1857
6. William E. Watkins, born c.1859
7. Alfred C. Watkins, born c.1862
8. Annie L. Watkins, born c.1863
9. Mary E. Watkins, born c.1865

Joseph Watkins

This individual lived in Montgomery County, and was married to Matilda Norwood. They had at least two sons and a daughter, and perhaps other children as well:

1. Richard Watkins, born c.1816. Richard appears as head of household in the 1850 census of the Clarksburg District, Montgomery County, Maryland; and in the 1860 census of Damascus District. His age indicates birth between 1812 and 1816. His wife is listed as Ellen Watkins, born c.1818 to 1821, and there are five children in 1850 and eight in 1860. He is listed also in the 1870 census, apparently widowed, with five of his children. In the 1880 census, he appears at age 62, with only two sons, Luther and Burton, still at home. As is typical of census records, Luther is shown as born c.1849 and Burton at c.1857, somewhat different from that reported elsewhere. Richard is reported in *Ancestral Colonial Families*, by Luther W. Welsh as being a son of Joseph Watkins and Matilda Norwood. His wife is Eleanor Norwood, who died 1866, daughter of Ralph Norwood and Mary Ann Hyatt (1800). Their children were:

    a. James Edward Watkins, born c.1842
    b. Eugenia Elizabeth Watkins, born c.1843 to 1845. Married to John W. Bodine, and had children:
        (1) Elizabeth Bodine.
        (2) Minnie Bodine.
    c. Luther Watkins, born c.1845 to 1847. This is probably Luther M. Watkins, born February 19, 1845, died April 10, 1908. Buried at Hyattstown Christian Church, Montgomery County. He was married January 20, 1885 to Alta Lee Davis of Frederick County, born October 31, 1866, and died June 16, 1939 and buried with her husband. The estate of Luther M. Watkins was administered by his widow, Alta Lee, and reported to the court March 23, 1909, recorded in liber HCA 7 at folio 352 in the wills office of the county. His widow received the customary one third, and his only surviving child, Luther L. Watkins, received the remainder. Children, including:
        (1) Luther L. Watkins.
        (2) Maude G. Watkins, born April 11, 1890, died January 1, 1896
        (3) Lena Watkins, born February 12, 1892, died February 19, 1892.

d. Laura V. Watkins, born c.1847 to 1849, married Daniel Price.
e. Charles A. Watkins, born July 15, 1849 and died March 24, 1932. Buried at Boyds Presbyterian cemetery, with a double stone bearing his name and that of Susan G. Watkins, who is apparently his wife, born November 7, 1855, died December 24, 1915. She was Susan G. Williams. They had one son, buried same cemetery. The couple appear in the 1880 census, Clarksburg District, Montgomery County, with two young children, and in the 1900 census of Barnesville with the two youngest daughters. Report of the death of Susan, appearing in the Sentinel newspaper of December 31, 1915, reports that she was survived by three daughters, giving the husband's names. From all sources, we can identify the children:

(1) Claude E. Watkins, born May 22, 1874, and died April 26, 1900. The *Sentinel* newspaper of May 4, 1900, reports that he committed suicide at North Branch, Allegany County, Maryland, and that his body was returned to Boyds Station, Montgomery County, his former home. Married one week prior to his death to Lillian Lewis of Ithica, New York.

(2) Ella May Watkins, born 1879; married to Smith Hoyle.

(3) Edith Maude Watkins, born 1882 and died 1951; married to Oscar Fernando Fulks, born June 10, 1876 and died September 24, 1952, son of Ignatius Thomas Fulks (1832) and Elizabeth Matilda Gloyd (1840). Administration of his estate is found in Book WCC 41, folio 308, in Montgomery County, Maryland, by his daughter, Blanche F. Peter, in which his two daughters are named. The will of Edith Maude is found in Book WCC 23, folio 416, dated September 14, 1948 and probated October 17, 1951. She names her two sisters as being Laura V. Hicks and Ella May Hoyle, and her two daughters:

167

(a) Blanche Vinton Fulks, born August 26, 1903, and married August 1, 1936 to George Peter, born October 9, 1894 and died January, 1954. A son, although her mother's will states that she has no children, suggesting that the son had died prior to 1948. He was:
1. George L. Peter, born September 29, 1941
(b) Lillian Frances Fulks, married Lloyd Berkner. Children:
1. Patricia Ann Berkner, married Charles Booth.
2. Phyllis Jean Berkner, married James Ashley.
(4) Laura V. Watkins, born c.1884; married to Joseph W. Hicks.
f. Burton Watkins, born c.1851 to 1857.
g. Eleanor Watkins, born c.1853. Married Edward Darby, who was a miller in Hyattstown. Children:
(1) William Darby.
(2) Elizabeth Darby.
h. Francis Watkins, born c.1857 to 1860
2. Matilda Watkins, married Ralph Norwood, Jr., who died November 2, 1866, son of Ralph Norwood and Mary Ann Hyatt (1800). Three children:
a. William Norwood.
b. Mary Ann Norwood.
c. Alice Norwood.
3. Rizpah Norwood Watkins, born October 31, 1802. Married in 1822 to Philip Hyatt, born October 1, 1795, son of Jesse Hyatt. They had twelve children:
a. Luther Lingan Hyatt, born May 21, 1823. Served as 1st sergeant, Co. A, 142nd Regt. Lived in Ohio, married first March 31, 1853 to Fannie M. Smith, and second Catherine Davis Wolfe, daughter of Eli and Caroline Ann Wolfe. Lived in Ohio, and had children only from the first marriage:

(1) Charles Hamilton Hyatt, born January 17, 1854. Married Civita Magness.

(2) Luella Hyatt, born July 14, 1855, married Alonzo Rock in Lima, Ohio.

(3) Carrie Josephine Hyatt, born May 18, 1859, married Frank McFadden.

(4) John Henry Hyatt, born December 15, 1865.

b. Ann Riggs Hyatt, born October 30, 1824, married the Reverend William J. Holland.

c. Susan Matilda Hyatt, born January 21, 1826, married May 3, 1849 William Wells Chapin, born March 27, 1824 in New York state, son of Asher Chapin and Mary Look. Four children:

(1) Charles Hamilton Chapin, born April 20, 1850. Married October 31, 1873 Ada Winifred Millett. Four children:

    (a) Archie Bertrand Chapin, born June 22, 1875. Married Lydia Hall and had three children.

    (b) Carl Kenneth Chapin, born July 4, 1883 and married Anabel Frayne. Two children.

    (c) Alice Chapin.

    (d) Helen Chapin.

(2) William Franklin Chapin, born September 10, 1851. Married November 1, 1877 to Mary Miller, and had children:

    (a) Earl Chapin.

    (b) Bertha Chapin.

    (c) Charles Chapin.

    (d) William Chapin.

    (e) Franklin Chapin.

(3) Florence Chapin, infant death April 28, 1857

(4) Jennie Maria Chapin, born April 4, 1866. Married 1885 to Edward C. Denny, a jeweler in Kansas City, Missouri. One daughter:

    (a) Erma Chapin Denny, born November 18, 1888. Married George S. Coleman.

d. Philip Hammond Hyatt, born August 18, 1828, served in the Civil War, died single over the age of 86 years.

e. Joseph Hamilton Hyatt, born February 19, 1830. Married Victorine Seymour and had five children:
    (1) William Philip Hyatt, born 1860, died 1861
    (2) John Francis Hyatt, born 1862, died 1888 single
    (3) Henry Holly Hyatt, born May 25, 1864
    (4) Edwin Hamilton Hyatt, born April 27, 1870
    (5) Fletcher Seymour Hyatt, born October 20, 1872
f. Elizabeth Sarah Hyatt, born March 1, 1832, married the Honorable T. E. Cunningham, and had children.
g. John Thomas Hyatt, born April 14, 1834, served as 3nd Lieutenant, Co. D, 65th Regt. Died in camp Mansfield, Ohio, single.
h. Columbia Anna Hyatt, born Ap[ril 19, 1836, died single
i. Caroline Hyatt, born April 25, 1838. Married Henry Cassell; no children.
j. Olive Hyatt, born March 30, 1840, married Charles G. Smith and had children:
    (1) Philip Smith, died young
    (2) Florence Smith, died young
    (3) Willie Smith.
    (4) Lesley Smith.
    (5) Oliver Smith.
    (6) Sinclair Smith.
k. Maria Hyatt, born August 4, 1842, married Alexander B. Tarr, of Mt. Vernon, Ohio, and had children:
    (1) Alexander Percy Tarr, born September 7, 1871
    (2) Rizpah Norwood Tarr, born June 21, 1876
    (3) Philip Hyatt Tarr, born June 15, 1878
    (4) Howard Sterling Tarr, born July 14, 1882
l. Columbus Delano Hyatt, born June 8, 1845, a merchant of Lincoln, Nebraska.

John T. Watkins
1814-

John appears alone in the 1850 census for Clarksburg District of Montgomery County, Maryland, born c.1814, a farmer. He may be the same individual who is buried at Bethesda United Methodist

Church cemetery at Browningsville; born 1814, died 1879. There is a John T. Watkins, born c.1816, in the 1860 census for Damascus District, living in the household of Sarah A. Poole (1817), with what appears to be her two young children: Hester A. Poole (1845) and Sarah E. Poole (1855). This could be the same individual.

Thomas Watkins
1769-

The 1850 census of Clarksburg District, Montgomery County, Maryland, lists Thomas as head of household, living with Mary Watkins, born c.1783, presumably his wife. There are no others in the household at the time.

Joseph S. Watkins
1808-

The 1850 census of Clarksburg District, Montgomery County, Maryland, includes a household headed by Joseph, a farmer. In his household, there is only one other person, Jeremiah Watkins, born c.1814, a laborer, and perhaps his brother. They appear together again in the 1860 census of the Damascus District. In the 1870 census, Joseph appears, this time with John T. Watkins, born c.1814 (above), who may also be a brother. We have not identified the family to which they perhaps all belong. There is a Joseph Watkins buried at Bethesda United Methodist Church cemetery at Brown-ingsville, who is probably this individual. Born April, 1808, and died April, 1873.

Gassaway Watkins
1807-

Found in the 1850 census of Cracklin District, in Montgomery County, Maryland, this Gassaway was born c.1807, and had a wife Lucy S. Watkins, born c.1823 in the District of Columbia, with one small child:
1.   Elizabeth B. Watkins, born c.1848

Richard Watkins
died 1842

The parentage of this individual is not yet established, but he lived in Montgomery County, Maryland, and had children there. His will, dated January 5, 1837, was probated June 14, 1842, and originally filed in Liber X at folio 479 in the will records of the county. Some time later, a zerox copy was rerecorded in Liber VMB 4 at folio 267. He mentions only a few members of his family including one son, a daughter-in-law, a grandson, a daughter, and a number of slaves. He provided that his slaves, Daniel, Peter, Medley and John are to be set free in a given number of years after his death. The mulatto girls and boys; Ann, Charlotte, Perry and William had previously been set free, and each of them is to receive thirty dollars from the estate. He writes at some length about his faithful slave, Eliza, who had paid great attention to him during his illness, and she is to have immediate freedom; one hundred and fifty dollars; all his loom and tackle; second choice of his cows; one hundred pounds of bacon; two barrels of corn; five bushels of wheat; and her daughter, Evaline, commonly called Becky. The rest of his estate goes to his son, Gassaway, the only one mentioned by name. It appears that he probably had these children:

1. Gassaway Watkins, father of:
   a. Richard Gassaway Watkins.
2. Juliet Watkins, a twin, born May 20, 1802
3. Julius Watkins, a twin, born May 20, 1802, and married to Caroline Watkins, born c.1804, the daughter of Colonel Gassaway Watkins (1752).

Rudolph Lewis Watkins
1844-1909

Rudolph was born c.1844, and reared in Georgetown, D. C., but lived in Montgomery County, along present-day Route 355, opposite the intersection with Redland Road. His middle name may have been Lewis. Married January 21, 1868 to Mary (or Maria) Catherine Hunter, born 1844 and died January 25, 1933, daughter of Thomas Hunter and Susannah Key Scott. Witnesses to the mar-

riage were Charles J. Maddox and Susan Hunter, and it was recorded in the records of St. Mary's Catholic Church in Rockville, as "mixtae religionis" or mixed religions. The *Sentinel* newspaper carried a death notice for Mary Catherine Hunter, there calling her Molly, dated February 2, 1933. The Derwood Post Office opened in April, 1883, with Rudolph as its first postmaster, who held the post until 1885, when he was succeeded by his wife. He died November 8, 1909, having had six sons and three daughters. Four of his sons predeceased their father, and none of the family stayed in the Derwood area. The following records of the children were taken from records of St. Mary's Catholic Church in Rockville, and from the 1880 census of Rockville District. In the census, the first five children listed following included, as well as one more child, indicated in the census to have been a girl, although it is reasonably apparent that the child was a son. The Montgomery County *Sentinel* carried a notice dated November 12, 1909, citing the death of Rudolph. On July 28, 1911, it also commented that Mrs. Rudolph Watkins was visiting her son, Ramsey, in South Dakota. The death notice of Rudolph's wife, mentioned above, also states that she is survived by three daughters and two sons, one of them being Ramsey, of North Dakota. That we believe to be the child now discussed; the spelling in the census is not easily read, but could clearly be Ramsey. The three daughters are said to be Mrs. J. R. Durette of Denver; Mrs. Joseph C. Shatard of Los Angeles; and Mrs. Wilson of Bethesda; although we do not now know which of the three daughters below married which of these gentlemen. The census also included three other children, described as nieces and a nephew of Rudolph. They are not yet identified, but were: Lucy Watkins, born c.1866; George Watkins, born c.1868; and Rebecca Watkins, born c.1870. All the children now known were:
1.   George Simpson Watkins, born October 23, 1868, died April 21, 1888
2.   Susanna Ashton Watkins, born March 27, 1870
3.   Mary Julia Watkins, born March 31, 1872; in 1902 living in Denver, Colorado.
4.   Rudolph Lewis Watkins, Jr., born March 6, 1874, died November 8, 1893 of typhoid. Buried St. Mary's old Catholic cemetery, Rockville. The name of this child was recorded in

church records in Latin, reading Rudolphum Ludovicum Watkins.
5. Maria L. A. Watkins, born December 27, 1875; baptized January 20, 1876
6. Ramsey Watkins, born c.1878.
7. Joseph Henry Watkins, born June 15, 1879.
8. Louis Watkins, born September 7, 1880, died February 24, 1886 of brain fever.
9. Thomas Hunter Watkins, born March 15, 1882, died August 4, 1936. Married March 1, 1905 Mary E. Kelley of Valentine, Nebraska, where they lived following the wedding.
10. Ogden Blackson Watkins, born October 24, 1884, baptized November 21, 1884, and died March 3, 1892 of measles. At least one record reports his middle name as Blackfan.

Richard Watkins
1812-

Information relative to this family was found in a transcript of the family Bible, in the folder files of the Montgomery County Historical Society library in Rockville. The family also appears in the 1850 census for the Clarksburg District of Montgomery County, with Richard as head of household, born c.1812. He appears again in the 1860 census for Damascus District, with wife Jane, and seven children. He married January 30, 1837 to Jane E. Thompson, born c.1822, died October 23, 1869. By 1850, she was the mother of six children, and there was one William Cost, black, born c.1840 also in the household. In the 1870 census, he appears with four of his children, without a wife, who was apparently deceased between 1860 and 1870. Richard apparently married second November 14, 1876 to Harriet A. H. Burdette. He appears in the 1880 census for Clarksburg District, with Harriet A. H. as his wife, born c.1850, less than half the age of her husband. Richard had a number of children, if all those in the Bible are his, and they appear to be. We have entered the spellings here as we believe they were intended, although it appears obvious to the author that some of them are poorly spelled by the original author:

1. Survila Catherine Watkins, born May 8, 1839; died May 30, 1856
2. Survila Vilora Washington Watkins, born January 8, 1841, died May 16, 1875. The 1850 census lists Viola W. Watkins, born c.1841, which is probably this child, there listed as being deaf and dumb. The 1860 census does not list the first name, Survila. The 1870 census lists her as Vilora W., and again classifies her as deaf and dumb, so we appear to be dealing with the same child in each case.
3. Susannah Margaret Watkins, born December 9, 1843, and died August 9, 1938. Married February 9, 1861 to George W. H. Mount. At least one son, who was living in the home of his grandfather during the census of 1880:
   a. George W. Mount, born c.1865
5. Rodolphus Grafton Watkins, born May 4, 1846, and died March 3, 1885. Buried at Montgomery Chapel cemetery in Claggettsville. Guardianship bond was posted November 7, 1887 by Mrs. Eudolphia Watkins, and others, and recorded in liber RWC 16 at folio 128 in the office of the Register of Wills for Montgomery County. It names seven children of the couple, who are minors. Married November 5, 1868 to Eudolphia Clagett, born c.1840 and died late September, 1929. The *Sentinel* report of her death states that she died at the home of her daughter, Mrs. George H. Lilly at Mt. Rainier, although we do not now know which of her daughters married Lilly. The same stone carries another name; Reuben E. Watkins, died February 4, 1905 at age 40 years, 4 months and 4 days (thus born c.1864). It appears that, after the death of her first husband, Eudolphia married second February 12, 1889 to the younger man, Reuben E. Watkins. Rodolphus and his wife appear in the 1870 census of Damascus with one child, and in the 1880 census for Clarksburg District, Montgomery County, Maryland, with five children:
   a. William C. Watkins, born c.1869 and died February 22, 1935 in Montgomery County. Sentinel abstracts report the marriage of William C. Watkins on October 18, 1893 to Carrie B. Ward, born November 3, 1873 and died December 16, 1952, daughter of William English Ward. The

couple appear in the 1900 census for Rockville, with their first two children. The will of William C. Watkins, dated September 24, 1934, was probated February 27, 1935 and filed in Liber HGC 11 at folio 10, in will records of Montgomery County, Maryland. He names his wife and children. Her will, dated April 20, 1945, was probated December 19, 1952 and filed in Liber WCC 31 at folio 484; also naming her children. William C. and his wife are buried in the Rockville cemetery. Children:

(1)   A. Guy Watkins, the eldest child, born c.1897. For many years, he operated the business known as A. G. Watkins and Son, Furniture, in old Rockville, prior to urban renewal in that section. His will, dated 1943, was probated May 27, 1949, and filed in Liber WCC 13 at folio 240 in the will records of Montgomery County. He lists only his wife, Rachel H. Watkins as an heir. She was Rachel Hansen, died March 20, 1969, and her will, dated July 11, 1949, was probated April 8, 1969 and filed in will book WES 108 at folio 707. Her son is the sole heir:
     (a)   Guy Hansen Watkins.
(2)   Henry Clay Watkins, born c.1898, died September 22, 1971 at his home in Silver Spring. Buried in the Union Cemetery at Burtonsville, Maryland. Married Eva Lethbridge, and had children:
     (a)   Mary E. Watkins, married Hawthorne.
     (b)   Darlene E. Watkins, married Crowder.
     (c)   William C. Watkins.
(3)   Gladys Watkins, married Kailer.
(4)   Otis W. Watkins, born 1905, died June 19, 1982. He was married to Marjorie Jolley and had seven children:
     (a)   Barbara Ann Watkins.
     (b)   Joanne Watkins, married Weicht.
     (c)   Betty Jane Watkins, married Snowburger.
     (d)   Judy Watkins, married Williams.
     (e)   Jeannie Watkins, married Bolton.

(f)   Wendy Watkins, married Young.
(g)   Otis W. Watkins, Jr.
(5)   Dorothy I. Watkins, married to Williams. Her father's will, written before her mother's, lists her married name as Ingalls, perhaps a first marriage.
(6)   William C. Watkins, Jr.
b.   Carrie G. Watkins, born c.1873. In the guardianship papers, this child is spelled Cary G. Watkins, suggesting a male, rather than female, as reported in other records.
c.   Edith M. Watkins, born c.1875
d.   Arthur Watkins, born c.1876
e.   Dora E. Watkins, born c.1878
f.   Edward E. Watkins.
g.   Mary L. Watkins.
6.   Rosetta F. Watkins, twin, born January 3, 1849; died October 28, 1866
7.   Henrietta V. Watkins, twin, born January 3, 1849, and died December 3, 1941. Married December 24, 1874 to William F. L. Clagett.
8.   Uriah Thomas Watkins, born August 23, 1851, died June 20, 1926. Married November 26, 1884 to Margaret A. Brown, born July 10, 1853, died August 9, 1838. They are buried in the cemetery of Montgomery Chapel at Claggettsville. Uriah appears in the 1900 census for Damascus, with his wife, and three children:
a.   Ira D. Watkins, born c.1885
b.   Marshall T. Watkins, born April 3, 1886; died March 23, 1962. His wife, Mattie E. was born September 19, 1891 and died February 12, 1972. They are buried at Montgomery Chapel, Claggettsville.
c.   Rhoda J. Watkins, born c.1888
9.   Silas Franklin Watkins, born April 17, 1853; died November 4, 1855.
10.   Marshall Crittenden Watkins, born February 1, 1857, died March 16, 1923. Buried at Montgomery Chapel cemetery in Claggettsville, with his third wife. Appears to have been married three times: May 29, 1884 to Olivia J. Brown; December 8, 1897 to Mary E. Watkins, from whom he filed divorce pro-

ceedings in October, 1901; and April 30, 1902 to Rosalie V. Duvall, born January 1, 1885, died October 4, 1971. There was at least one daughter from the third marriage:
a. Alta Viola Watkins, born October 1, 1907
11. Elizabeth J. Watkins, born January 16, 1880

Arthur Leonard Watkins, Jr.
1912-

This individual was born March 22, 1912 near Damascus, and was an auto dealer. Married October 8, 1966 to Hilda Mae Hyatt, born March 28, 1920, daughter of Herbert Hyatt (1888) and Beulah Souder (1889). He was her third husband; no children.

Donald Watkins

Donald was married to Barbara Wright, and had at least one son, born in Montgomery County, Maryland:
1. Michael Craig Watkins, born June 17, 1964; married in Clarksburg, Maryland, to Alethia Kae Woodfield, born March 9, 1961, daughter of Thomas Leslie Woodfield (1939) and Mary Eloise Haney (1940). One child:
a. Kelsey Lynn Watkins, born May 17, 1992

Iris Rebecca Watkins
1914-1984

Iris Rebecca Watkins was born at Lewisdale, November 16, 1914, and died May 24, 1984, daughter of James and Addie E. Watkins. She was christened November 18, 1917 at the parsonage of Bethesda United Methodist Church near Browningsville, Maryland. Married to Ora Henning King, born July 18, 1910; died September 26, 1968, son of Jemima Elizabeth Purdum (1874) and Elias Vinson King (1869). Iris and her husband are buried at Clarksburg United Methodist Church cemetery. One child:
1. Oliver Henry King, born August 12, 1941

Lucinda A. Watkins
1842-1923

We do not now know her parentage, but Lucinda was born c.1842 and died December 25, 1923 in Montgomery County. Married February 21, 1862 to John Duckett King, born c.1836, died August 22, 1905, son of John A. King (1808). John Duckett and Lucinda are buried at Salem United Methodist Church in Cedar Grove. The 1880 census carries the family, this time with five children listed. This appears to be John Duckett King, whose death on August 22, 1905 was reported in the Montgomery County *Sentinel* "in his 69th year." His wife is not reported there by name, but his five sons were:

1. Hiram G. King, born January 10, 1863; died September 11, 1936
2. Thomas O. King, born c.1864, perhaps died 1927 and buried in Damascus Methodist cemetery. May be the same individual married November 15, 1888 to Ida E. Burns, born 1867, died 1945, and also buried there. Two sons are buried with them; there were more:
   a. Barry J. King, born 1889. The obituary of this individual appeared in the *Frederick Post* of November 7, 1970. It stated that he died November 5, 1970 at the age of eighty-one, a retired B. & O. Railroad employee. He had a brother, Howard T. King, of Halethorpe, and two sons:
      (1) Richard B. King, of Park Forest, Illinois
      (2) Thomas M. King, of Baltimore
   b. Howard T. King.
   c. Clinton C. King, born 1898; died 1936
3. Henry J. King, born c.1867, died 1949; buried at Salem Methodist Church in Cedar Grove. Married Manona E., born 1873, died 1958; also buried there.
4. Edward Carlton King, born c.1872, and died 1934. Married February 5, 1895 to Harriet M. Dutrow, born March 7, 1876, died May 11, 1899. Married second March 11, 1901 at Clarksburg, Maryland, to Nonie M. Lydard, born 1881, died about September 23, 1968, daughter of John C. Liddard and Mary Ella Hobbs. Marriage license records list him as a wid-

ower, 28 years of age. Buried Salem United Methodist Church, Cedar Grove. They had children:
a. Carlton King, born 1902, died 1955; buried Salem United Methodist Church, Cedar Grove
b. Mildred King, married John Thompson. A son:
    (1) Fulton Perry Thompson.
c. Mary Norene King, born July 21, 1909. Married to William Windsor. At least one daughter:
    (1) Ann Windsor, married Frank Thompson, and had at least two children:
        (a) Sally Thompson: January 12, 1945
        (b) William Thompson.
4. R. Delaney King, born June 30, 1874; died February 15, 1946, buried at the Damascus Methodist Church cemetery, with his wife, Mary Sybil (or Sybell) Ward, born April 3, 1880; died January 28, 1961. They were married September 3, 1896, at Rockville, and had at least these children:
a. Archie C. King, born May 20, 1897; died young
b. Ida Landella King, born November 22, 1902, died July 4, 1903
c. Maude Alverta King, married September 21, 1921 at Grace Methodist Church in Gaithersburg, to Walter M. Magruder.
d. Glenwood Dawson King, born c.1918 in Cedar Grove, died May 6, 1996 in Damascus. He was, for many years, chief of employee services for the Montgomery County government, prior to his retirement. He was also a Nationwide Insurance agent for 44 years, and chairman of the board of the Bethesda United Methodist Church, where he and his wife are buried. Married September 2, 1939 Olive Virginia Burdette, born January 3, 1919, died April 16, 1995 at home in Damascus, the daughter of Ira Lansdale Burdette (1900) and Fannie C. Cutsail. The children of Glenwood were:
    (1) Bonnie Elaine King, born June 16, 1940 at Browningsville, and married Delmas Foster of Damascus. Two daughters:
        (a) Penny Sue Foster, born 1961

(b) Tammy Lynn Foster, born May 21, 1964
(2) Judy N. King, and married to Thomas Knoll, of Mt. Airy.

John S. Watkins
1881-1960

A resident of Montgomery County, John was born 1881 and died in 1960. Married at Providence Church June 17, 1908 to Melissa B. Day, born c.1883, daughter of Lattimer W. Day (1852) and Venia W. Browning (1857). Two children:
1. John Latimer Watkins, born August 13, 1909; married Mary. No children.
2. Roland Eugene Watkins, born October 9, 1917 at Kemptown; Married Ruth, no information.

Richard Jefferson Watkins

Richard Jefferson was married to Harriet Ann Burdette, born c.1850, died September 21, 1931, daughter of Elmon G. Burdette (1823) and Elizabeth J. Day (1826). Her obituary states that she died in Baltimore at the home of her granddaughter, Mrs. James Dayhoff, and was buried at the Pine Grove Cemetery, in Mt. Airy, Maryland. Children:
1. Elizabeth Watkins, married Hahn; lived in Ridgeville.
2. Mary Laura Watkins, married James Davis Windsor; a child:
   a. Elaine Virginia Windsor, born May 11, 1924 at Mt. Airy, and married November 25, 1950 to Guy Kenneth Howes, born July 5, 1916 at Etchison. A daughter:
      (1) Connie Dianne Howes, born October 2, 1955 at Frederick. Married December 28, 1974 to Richard Sheldon English.

Richard A. Watkins
1866-1961

Born c.1866 and died c.1961, Richard is buried in Mountain View Methodist Church cemetery, Montgomery County. His wife is buried with him, Bertie Belle Hawes, born 1879 and died 1954. Church card files at the Historical Society library in Rockville, list her date of birth as July 24, 1871, and her parents as Columbus and Lucinda Hawes. Children:

1. Melia May, born March 24, 1903. (Could be Amelia).
1. Alexandria Florida Watkins, born January 17, 1906, died February 12, 1972; buried Mountain View Methodist Church cemetery. The name also appears as Alexander F. Watkins on card files at the Historical Society library in Rockville.
2. Cora Lucinda Watkins, born June 12, 1908.

Fillmore C. Watkins
1852-1924

Born August 12, 1852, Fillmore died February 16, 1924 and is buried at Howard Chapel cemetery in Howard County, Maryland. Married May 11, 1876 in Montgomery County, to Louisa E. Lyddard, born c.1858 and died June 22, 1916 at the age of 58 years, 9 months and 5 days. Buried with her husband. They appear in the 1880 census of Clarksburg District, Montgomery County, with three children. Also in the household is Matilda Lyddard, born c.1860, sister of Louisa E. In the 1900 census of Damascus, Fillmore appears with his wife, and nine children, including the triplet daughters. Final accounts in the estate of Fillmore C. Watkins were filed by Emory T. Watkins and Louis F. Watkins, Administrators, October 8, 1924, recorded in liber HCA 4 at folio 127 in the wills office of Montgomery County. Distribution of the estate indicates that ten children survived their father:

1. Minnie E. Watkins, born c.1878, and died before 1924. First married January 31, 1893 to William B. Brandenburg, and second to Brown, with children from both marriages, all named in the estate:
   a. Lela Brandenburg, married to Justice.
   b. Pearl Brandenburg, married to Layton.
   c. Dewey Brandenburg.
   d. Claude Brandenburg.
   e. Alvin Brandenburg.
   f. John Brown.

g. Madeliene Brown.

2. Emory Thomas Watkins, born c.1879, and died February 19, 1927, in a fire at his home near Damascus, leaving a wife and three children, according to the *Sentinel* newspaper report; buried in the Damascus Methodist Church cemetery. His mother, Mamie Elizabeth Watkins Ridgley, is buried there also. Her son's obituary lists her name as Browning; card files of cemetery records found at the Montgomery County Historical society list her name as Ridgley. The will of Mamie E. Watkins Ridgley of Mt. Airy, dated November 18, 1947, was probated August 17, 1955 and filed in will book EA 58 at folio 192 in Montgomery County. She died July 12, 1955. She mentions in the will that her husband is James Ridgley, and that she has two daughters and a son, Emory T. Watkins. The two daughters are Mary Elizabeth Watkins, married to Martz; and Irene Watkins, married to Grimes. Obviously, all this report creates a number of questions about the family of Fillmore C. Watkins; was he married twice? Final accounts of his estate clearly include Emory T. Watkins as one of his administrators, and a son. And, Fillmore's wife, Louisa E. Lyddard (1858) lived until 1916, several years after the birth of Emory Thomas, and was therefore probably his mother; not Mamie E. Watkins Ridgely. We have reported here what was found in the records. Emory Thomas Watkins had children, including:

a. Emory William Watkins, born August 20, 1911 and died June 17, 1977 at Montgomery General Hospital at Olney. Library card files list his name as William Emory; the obituary as we have shown it here.

3. Louis Fillmore Watkins, born December 5, 1879, died June 3, 1955, Louis was buried at Mt. Lebanon cemetery. His wife was Katie Lee Johnson, born November 26, 1878 and died August 13, 1982, daughter of Smith Johnson and Octavia Redman of Virginia. She died at the Wilson Health Care Center in Gaithersburg, Montgomery County, at the age of one hundred and three years. At the time of her death, there were five grandchildren, eleven great grandchildren, and five great great grandchildren. The children, with their place of residence in 1982, were:

a. Louis Fillmore Watkins, Jr., died August 24, 1970 at his home in Gaithersburg, buried at Park Lawn Cemetery, Rockville. Married Janet Plummer, and had children:
   (1) J. Anita Watkins, married Dunn, and had a son:
       (a) Scott Alan Dunn.
   (2) Judith A. Watkins, married Wegener.
b. Nelly Watkins, married Beall, of Damascus.
c. Alma O. Watkins, married Fleming, of Sykesville.
d. Madeline Watkins, married Windsor, of Gaithersburg.
e. Thelma Watkins, married Gordon, of Harpers Ferry, West Virginia.
4. Ernest C. Watkins, born April 17, 1885 and died April 15, 1934. Ernest was buried at Howard Chapel cemetery, in Howard County. His wife, Susie A., is buried there also, born February 17, 1881 and died December 6, 1951. A son and daughter, both of whom died young, are also buried there:
   a. William Crawford Watkins, born August 30, 1909, and died March 9, 1910.
   b. Hilda Estell Watkins, born July 11, 1911, died May 29, 1912.
5. Harry B.Watkins, born c.1888
6. Hilda W. Watkins, born c.1892; married Williams.
7. Edna C. Watkins, born c.1897 married Pearce.
8. Louise Watkins, a triplet, born June 3, 1899, died February 25, 1978. Married Clay.
9. Lucille Watkins, a triplet, born June 3, 1899, died February 25, 1978. Married Eli Thomas Molesworth, born January 29, 1898, died Ocober 30, 1980. At least two children:
   a. Olin L. Molesworth, born June 5, 1920, owner of the Molesworth Funeral Home in Damascus.
   b. Loretta Estelle Molesworth, born August 31, 1926, and married February 8, 1947 to Albert Lewellys Watkins, born February 9, 1922, which see.
10. Lucinda Watkins, a triplet, born June 3, 1899, died February 25, 1978. Married Windsor.

Whitney Watkins
died 1989

Whitney Watkins lived in Montgomery County, where he died October 15, 1989. Just one month later, his wife, the former Edna E. Bailey of Washington, born c.1911, died on November 7, 1989 at Suburban Hospital. She was buried at Parklawn Cemetery near Rockville. They had at least one son:
1. Gerald W. Watkins, of Kensington, Maryland. Children:
   a. Carrie Watkins.
   b. Julie Watkins.

Howard R. Watkins
died 1960

The will of Howard R. Watkins, dated May 18, 1948, was probated August 23, 1960 and filed in will book VMB 127 at folio 543, Montgomery County, Maryland. He died May 14, 1960, and names his wife as Nina C. Watkins. There are three daughters:
1. Mary Lee Watkins, married Schumaker.
2. Elizabeth Hope Watkins, married Allen.
3. Louise Stewart Watkins, married Moore.

Howard H. Watkins

Howard lived in the Kemptown area, and his name has been found as Howard K. in church records reporting his marriage of December 27, 1916 to Willie Lewis. They had children:
1. William Howard Watkins, born April 1, 1918
2. India Marie Watkins, born June 28, 1921.

Herbert A. Watkins
died 1957

The estate of Herbert A. Watkins was filed in Case Number 10712, in the Register of Wills Office of Montgomery County. He died June 13, 1957, intestate, single, leaving as his only heirs his three sisters: Regina C. Watkins; Elizabeth Watkins Nolte; and Helen Watkins Stevens.

Arthur Leroy Watkins
1945-

Born May 17, 1945, Arthur Leroy was married June 5, 1965 Sandra Lee Hurley, born May 18, 1946, daughter of Joseph Arthur Hurley (1899) and Esther Mae Thompson (1909). Two children:
1. Tammy Sue Watkins, born May 31, 1967. Married April 22, 1989 to Dennis Ray Mullican, born March 10, 1965, son of Oscar Ray Mullican and Olive Elizabeth Rice.
2. Timothy Lee Watkins, born January 17, 1972.

CHAPTER 9

Miscellaneous Watkins Family Members

During the course of research, several groups of Watkins family members, and a number of individual references, have been found, but not identified within the main body now under study. They are included here for future reference and research.

Nicholas Watkins
m/1782

We have not identified this Nicholas, but he is probably the same individual who was married in Anne Arundel County, Maryland, February 1, 1782 to Sarah Disney. Their children included:
1. James Watkins, born January 20, 1783. Married to Mary Ann Chatterton, June 9, 1807
2. Nicholas J. Watkins, a minister, born 1784, married January 25, 1806 in Anne Arundel County, Maryland, to Patience Barnes, daughter of James Barnes and Elizabeth Shipley, and had at least these children:
   a. Nicholas J. Watkins, Jr., born c. 1812; died 1831.
   b. James Barnes Watkins, born August 14, 1814 and died April 12, 1859. Married Elizabeth Thomas, November 15, 1841 in Kentucky, and had children:
      (1) Margaret, born October 4, 1842, died November 19, 1862.
      (2) John Dill Watkins, born October 22, 1843; died June 13, 1844.
      (3) Henry Thomas Watkins, born June 27, 1845; died July 28, 1911.
      (4) James Edgar Watkins, born July 30, 1847; died October 14, 1857.
      (5) Ada Weisenfels Watkins, born February 20, 1852, died August 16, 1930. Married Wilfred Carrico.

(6) Martin Spaulding Watkins, born October 7, 1856
     and died October 18, 1858
(7) Lucian Barnes Watkins, born March 29, 1859 and
     died September 4, 1885
   c. Thomas Worthington Watkins, born 1818; married May,
       1845 to Susan Thompson.
   d. James H. Watkins, married Martha Ann Iglehart, who
       was born August 21, 1818 and died July 10, 1855.
   e. Richard Watkins, born c.1821; died September, 1831
   f. Margaret Watkins, married John Selby.
   g. Mary Clare Watkins, married Reverend S. V. Blake.
   h. Sally Disney Watkins, died young.
   i. Patience Rachel Watkins.
   j. Sarah Elizabeth Watkins.
   k. Elvirah Ann Watkins.
   l. William Watkins.
4. Sally Ann Watkins, married Richard Warfield March 9, 1803
   under a Baltimore marriage license.

Benjamin Watkins

References to Benjamin as a parent have been found in various
files, indicating that he was born in North Carolina, married to
Sarah, and had children. The first six were reportedly born either in
Coffee or Warren County, Tennessee; last two in Wayne County,
Tennessee. Certain comparisons can be made between this family
and that of Silas B. Watkins (1814), son of Gassoway Watkins
(1772). Both were married to Sarah, and both had a daughter
named Lucinda, born about the same time. We know that many of
our ancestors in this period migrated south to North Carolina and
Tennessee, and many of them returned. Perhaps this is one of them.
The author has tried to consider that we are here dealing with one
individual, Silas Benjamin Watkins, but leave that question open,
lacking proof. Children of this Benjamin were reported as being:
1. Greenberry Watkins, a twin, born March 22, 1827
2. Samuel Watkins, a twin, born March 22, 1827.
3. James Watkins, born December 11, 1829
4. William Watkins, born c.1834

5. Martha Elizabeth Watkins, born March 14, 1838
6. Thomas H. Watkins, born October 18, 1840.
7. Henry Watkins, born c.1843
8. Lucinda Watkins, born c.1845

Francis Watkins

A number of the family members carried this name; this one appears as father of:
1. Jane Watkins, born November 17, 1743

Thomas Watkins
died c.1814

The will of this individual, dated February 19, 1814, is found in Liber G, at folio 360, in the will records of Rowan County, North Carolina. It is known that a few members of the Maryland Watkins families moved to that area, as did numerous other Marylanders. He names his wife, Elizabeth, six sons and five daughters. His wife is the executrix, and the witnesses were Jesse Etchison and Evan Ellis. The children were:
1. David Watkins.
2. Thomas Watkins.
3. Israel Watkins.
4. Eli Watkins.
5. John Watkins.
6. Samuel Watkins.
7. Catherine Watkins, in her father's will, said to be "married off"
8. Kezia Watkins, also "married off"
9. Judith Watkins.
10. Jean Watkins.
11. Elizabeth Watkins.

Edward G. Watkins
died 1941

The will records of Montgomery County, Maryland, include the will of this individual, dated November 4, 1938 and probated

October 3, 1941. He was living in Gardner County, Massacusetts, when he wrote the will, as were members of his family. However, he mentions his wife, Nellie O. Watkins, who had three daughters by an earlier marriage, and their own children, as well as other members of his family. He names two of his brothers; Royal P. Watkins and Dr. Robert Lincoln Watkins of New York. The bulk of his estate consisted of common and preferred stock in the Simplex Time Recorder Company of Gardner County, which he left in trust to the benefit of his heirs. He had at least these children:

1. Helen Watkins, who received lands in Minnesota.
2. Jessica Watkins, who received lands in Takoma Park, which is apparently the reason for filing the will in Maryland.
3. Curtis G. Watkins, who received a one hundred acre farm in Gardner County, Massachusetts.

Benjamin Watkins, Jr.
m/1870

This individual was the son of Dr. Benjamin Watkins and Mary Hodges, and was married November 22, 1870 in Maryland to Ann Elizabeth Welsh, born October 4, 1840 and died November 5, 1925, daughter of Thomas and Elizabeth Welsh. Three children:

1. Katherine Welsh Watkins, born October 2, 1871
2. Eleanora Evans Watkins, born April 13, 1873
3. Benjamin Watkins, III, born January 29, 1877. He married November 12, 1902 to Lucy Berry Beall, who died April 24, 1910, daughter of Thomas Balsh Beall and Marion Berry of Baltimore. Children:
   a. Benjamin Watkins, IV, born September 11, 1903
   b. Marion Edmonston Berry Watkins, born June 19, 1906

Samuel Watkins
1849-

Samuel was found as head of household in the 1880 census for Frederick County, born c.1849. His wife was Rachel, born c.1853, and they had a niece living in the household, Florence Fox, born c.1865. There were two children:

1. Martha Watkins, born c.1872
2. Lorenzo Watkins, born c.1878

William H. Watkins
1843-

William is found as head of household in the 1880 census for Howard County, born c.1843. His wife, Annie S., was born c.1847 and there were six children listed:
1. Thomas J. Watkins, born c.1868
2. Sarah E. Watkins, born c.1870
3. Charles A. Watkins, born c.1874
4. Anna S. Watkin, born c.1876
5. Laura C. Watkins, born c.1877
6. George W. Watkins, born c.1879

Alfred Watkins
1856-

Alfred appears in the 1900 census for Frederick County, born c.1856. His wife, Gertie, was born c.1873, and they had children:
1. Clara M. Watkins, born c.1892
2. Malcolm Watkins, born c.1900

Charley L. Watkins
1868-

Probably Charles L. Watkins, he is found in the 1900 census of Damascus, born c.1868. His wife, Lydia A., was born c.1870 and they had three children:
1. Florence C. Watkins, born c.1886
2. Harry W. Watkins, born c.1888
3. Frank F. Watkins, born c.1900

Humphrey Watkins
1867-

Humphrey is listed as head of household in the 1900 census for Poolesville, Maryland, born c.1867. His wife, Margaret R., was born c.1870, and they had four children listed:
1. Rosetta Watkins, born c.1888
2. Georgia A. Watkins, born c.1892
3. William F. Watkins, born c.1894
4. Cora B. Watkins, born c.1895

Vernon W. Watkins
1860-1943

Vernon was born August 12, 1860, and died May 6, 1943. He was married July 8, 1886 to Rebecca Unglesbee, born December 19, 1859, died December 3, 1946. Goshen Methodist Church cemetery. He is listed as head of household in the 1900 census for Gaithersburg, with his wife, and a child:
1. Annie C. Watkins, born c.1899

William Watkins
1835-

This William Burdette was found as head of household in the 1900 census for Prince George's County, born c.1835. His wife, Mary, was born c.1842, and they had a number of children:
1. Georgianna Watkins, born c.1873, listed as a daughter, with three children, bearing the Watkins surname:
   a. William A. Watkins, born c.1893
   b. John R. Watkins, born c.1895
   c. Mary A. Watkins, born c.1898
2. Stephen R. Watkins, born c.1878
3. Richard M. Watkins, born c.1881
4. James Watkins, born c.1884
5. Julia M. Watkins, born c.1888
6. Carrie L. Watkins, born c.1892

William A. Watkins
1844-

Found in the 1900 census for Howard County, William was born c.1844. His wife, Annie S., was born c.1847, and they are listed with three children:
1. Mary Watkins, born c.1882
2. John D. Watkins, born c.1885
3. Louisa Watkins, born c.1886

The following listings are one-liner type information gleaned from various records during the course of research. The Maryland county of record is shown at the end of the entry, with initials.

Given Name	Information
A. Broadhurst	Born April 5, 1906, son of A. H. and N. B. Watkins.
Albert B.	Born 1906, died 1954; married March 8, 1924 to Edna Burdette, born 1906. Bethesda United Methodist Church, Browningsville.
Alice V.	Md July 21, 1886 Thomas F. Gardiner. MO
Alton L., Jr.	Born October 9, 1944, died January 2, 1968. Vietnam soldier. Son of Alton L. and Doris E. Watkins.
Amanda J.	Married December 7, to 1912 Lawrence L. Long. MO
Andrew A.	Born April 24, 1882, died October 19, 1948, buried at Rockville cemetery.
Annie E.	Md October 5, 1895 Philip Elfrey. MO
Anny	Buried September 14, 1808. Dau/of Major Leonard Watkins.
Archibald	Md June 27, 1799 Elizabeth Parsons. BA
Arey	Md August 7, 1855 Jeremiah Watkins. MO
Barry Kenneth	Born September 25, 1952, died December 12, 1958, buried Damascus Methodist cemetery.
Benjamin	Born c.1802 in North Carolina; married Sarah.
Carrie E.	Md January 18, 1894 Jesse D. Boyer. MO
Carrie G.	Md November 4, 1889 Andrew J. Brandenburg. MO
Catherine J.	Md November 24, 1861 Amon R. Miles. MO
Cecil V. (fem)	Born c.1884, died December 1, 1964. Buried Rockville cemetery.

Charles L.	Born 1897; wife Rosie J., born 1900. Upper Seneca Baptist Church cemetery.
Cora E.	Md June 16, 1914 Edward W. Kruemmel. MO
Cornelius H.	Md February 21, 1914 Iva E. Snyder. MO
Dallas D.	Born September 10, 1919, killed in action during second world war, April 20, 1944. Bethesda United Methodist Church cemetery, Browningsville.
Daniel Scott	Of Francis, born December 5, 1739; md twice: December 29, 1761 Elizabeth Hatten and second 1770 Josie Biddeston. St. John's Episcopal Parish.
Earl J.	Of Cedar Grove; md July 17, 1920 Edith Thompson, daughter of Douglass Thompson of Hyattstown. MO
Edith M.	Md March 13, 1890 William H. Wright. MO
Edward	Born c.1867. 1900 census for Avondale, in Frederick County. Md. Bertha E., born c.1872. Daughter Rachel V., born c.1897.
Elizabeth	Md December 20, 1807 Jonathan Lewis. MO
Elizabeth	Md April 23, 1866 Eugene V. Walker. PG
Ella May	Md October 29, 1896 Smith Hoyle. MO
Ella May	Md October 25, 1899 George H. Cutsail. MO
Evelyn Eader	Born June 30, 1924, died August 5, 1953. Buried Damascus Methodist Church.
Fannie Z.	Md April 1, 1889 Richard A. Mullinix. MO
Flossie Ivoy	Born January 24, 1892, d/o A. H. and S. G. Watkins. MO
Francis	Of Middle River, md Christina Wrights.
Francis	Of Francis, born September 27, 1741. St. John's Episcopal Parish.
Francis	Md September 25, 1769 Elizabeth Pines. St. John's Episcopal Parish.
Gassaway	Died June 6, 1737
Gassaway	Md April 17, 1784 Mary Loflin. PG
Gassaway	Md April 20, 1826 Catherine Willett. MO
George W.	Born 1864, died 1950. Married Jennie E., born 1864 and died 1953. Potomac Methodist Church cemetery.
Gloria Jean	Born February 13, 1944, died August 26, 1965. New John Wesley Methodist Church cemetery.
Harry Everett	Born March 11, 1910, son of Cora Watkins. MO
Henrietta	Md October 23, 1799 John Wells. AA
Henry Clay	Of Rockville; md in Arlington, Virginia, December 20, 1923, to Mary E. Marvel, the daughter of James J. Marvel of Rockville.

Hester	Md December 14, 1805 to Rezin Iglehart. AA
Ignatius	Md May 18, 1793 Elizabeth Gale. AA
Ida Belle	Md July 25, 1894 Robert E. Clagett. MO
Ida M.	Md July 10, 1884 Henry C. Edwards. MO
Irvin B.	Born May 6, 1912, died December 13, 1979. Married to Mildred V., born December 14, 1913. Montgomery Chapel cemetery, Claggettsville.
Isaiah W.	Born c.1831, died October 7, 1897 at Browningsville. Left 3 sons, 4 daughters, and widowed mother. MO
James	Md May 17, 1788 Rebecca Miller. BA
James	Md March 15, 1757 Mary Johnson. St. Lukes Parish.
Jane	Md November 4, 1714 Samuel Hughs.
Jane	Md August 7, 1766 Joseph White. St. Johns Episcopal Parish
Jeremiah	Md August 7, 1855 Arey Watkins. MO
Jeremiah	Md June 16, 1842 to Mary J. Dorsey. Washington County, Kentucky
John	Md February 10, 1747 Elizabeth Jones. St. Johns Episcopal Parish
John	Md June 25, 1750 Elizabeth James. St. John's Episcopal Parish.
John	Md October 9, 1754 Purify Greenfield. St. John's Episcopal Parish.
John	Md November 11, 1790 Margaret Tydings. AA
John	Born 1755, died 1826, private in Revolutionary War. Md May 31, 1796 Ruth Guyton. BA
John	Of Stephen; died February 14, 1815 at West River
John	Md January 7, 1783 Elizabeth Hall. AA
John	Md October 26, 1791 Ann Rutland. AA
John	Md February 7, 1812 Willy Ann Davis. AA
John S.	Born c.1813; lived near Clarksburg, Maryland. MO
Joseph	Md June 29, 1797 Polly Shaney. BA
Joseph	Colonel, died February 8, 1823 south side of South River
Julia A.	Md December 8, 1891 John H. Bellison. MO
Julianna	Md November 28, 1811 Leonard Iglehart. AA
Laura G.	Md December 9, 1903 to John A. Engel, at Providence Church. MO
Laura V.	Md June 11, 1875 Richard T. Burdette. MO
Lavander W.	Born October 27, 1852, died December 12, 1909. Buried Damascus Methodist Church. Eliza A. Miles on same stone.

Lewis Jones	Of Thomas. Born January 18, 1803, died June 1, 1848. Md April 20, 1843 Ann Hardy.
Leyton	Md November 24, 1841 Mary Grimes. MO
Lorraine	Md William Ralph Walker, no children. MO
Louis J.	Md December 11, 1879 Cornelia Hodges. PG
Lucy B.	Md February 13, 1817 Thomas Pindell. PG
Maggie	Of Lewisdale. Married December 25, 1917 to T. Deets Day of Monrovia, Maryland.
Manelia E.	Md January 1, 1864 Bushrod Gartrell. MO
Marcella K.	Born 1907, died 1973. Buried St. John's, Forest Glen.
Margaret	Md December 21, 1755 Ralph Rench. St. Johns Episcopal Parish.
Margaret	Md April 20, 1789 Benedict Dorsey. AA
Margaret	Md May 7, 1794 Ezekiel Phelps. AA
Margaret	Md December 1, 1795 Edward Disney.
Margaret E.	Md July 3, 1937 at Providence Church to George L. Wilhide. MO
Margaret L.	Md December 3, 1888 Joseph C. Hawkins. MO
Margaret L. V.	Md May 15, 1878 Philip N. Poole. MO
Maria	Md September 1, 1820 Joseph Stewart. PG
Martha	Md October 6, 1737 James Standeford. St. Johns Episcopal Parish.
Mary	Md August 28, 1792 John Barry. AA
Mary	Md December 12, 1794 Henry Bashford.
Mary	Md February 28, 1786 Richard Disney. AA
Mary	Md November 14, 1797 William Ijams Stockett. AA
Mary	Md Marcy 27, 1780 Francis Thompson. AA
Mary J.	Md April 21, 1890 Charles T. Johnson. MO
Matilda	Md March 15, 1809 Gassaway Lyshear. MO
May Belle	Md November 20, 1882 William J. Lewis. MO
Mildred M.	Md December 8, 1943 Edgar L. Bass. MO
Mosehel	Born May 9, 1886, stillbirth. MO
Nancy	Md March 28, 1797 Theodore Sherly. PG
Nancy Raye	Md Mark Lawrence Walker. MO
Naomi	Md July 5, 1806 William Harwood. AA
Nathaniel	Md September 24, 1788 Catherine Ogden. PG
Nicholas	Md February 1, 1782 Sarah Disney. AA
Nicholas	Md April 3, 1786 Elizabeth Walker. PG
Nicholas	Major; died December 14, 1794
Nicholas	Md January 25, 1806 Patience Barnes. BA
Nicholas	Of Thomas, died August 22, 1826
Nicholas Edwin	Annapolis, md December, 1834 Mary Thomas.

Nicholas G.	Md August 31, 1798 Margaret Harwood. AA
Nicholas I.	Md May 7, 1801 Rachel L. Watkins. AA
Nicholas T.	Md Margaret Louisa Howard. AA
Olivia Jane	Born April 2, 1857, died April 12, 1897. Wife of M. C. Watkins. Montgomery Chapel, Claggettsville.
Ollie M.	Born c.1865 Frederick, md January 3, 1884 to William F. Lewis, born c.1852 Montgomery. MO
Ora D.	Md August 3, 1911 to Hiram Dorsey Musgrove. MO
Otis Wilbur	Of near Rockville, md October 10, 1931 to Mary Elizabeth Pugh of Woodmont, daughter of Andrew D. Pugh.
Paul R.	Born June 22, 1897, died March 30, 1952; wife Louisa H., born November 13, 1896, died January 10, 1951. Laytonsville Cemetery.
Peggy	Md February 1, 1787 Joseph Wells. PG
Peter	Private, 3rd Md Regt; died February 10, 1778
Philip	Md November 18, 1884 Tillie Brown. PG
Rachel	Md May 5, 1808 Isaac H. Hopkins. AA
Rachel L.	Md May 7, 1801 Nicholas Watkins. AA
Rebecca	Of Thomas, born April 6, 1815
Rezba	Md June 28, 1822 Philip Hyatt. MO
Rezin	Md January 11, 1798 Amey Meads. AA
Richard	Of Calvert Co. Md Anne, widow of William Oury, 1695.
Richard	Md March 8, 1800 Elizabeth Beddo. MO
Richard	Md October 5, 1778 Ruth Beard. AA
Richard	Md February 28, 1813 Mary Purdy. AA
Richard G.	Md February, 1824 Lucretia Margaret Harwood at West River. AA
Robert	Md August 1, 1736 Margaret Phinnicum. St. Lukes Parish.
Rose A.	Born c.1857, died April, 1924 in Cedar Grove. Wife of Robert Watkins.
Ruth Elizabeth	Md August 15, 1936 Walter E. Haines, Jr. MO
Sallie V.	Of Monrovia; md there February 27, 1925 to George D. Blumenauer of Frederick.
Samuel	Md June 2, 1757 Frances Hardesty. St. Johns Episcopal Parish.
Samuel	Md January 26, 1795 Elizabeth Watkins. AA
Sarah R.	Md December 12, 1834 Arnold T. (or L.) Lewis. MO
Shirley Thames	Died January 2, 1963. Daughter of Mathias and Nellie E. Thames of Charleston, South Carolina. The wife of

	James G. Watkins. Buried cemetery of Upper Seneca Baptist Church, Cedar Grove.
Solomon	Md April 2, 1749 Elizabeth Johnson. St Luke's
Sophia	Md August 20, 1827 Overton Ridgeway. PG
Sophia	Md September 9, 1875 Nathan Simms. MO
Stella A.	Md August 31, 1897 Bryon D. Magers. MO
Stephen	Md May 18, 1784 Frances Hanstep Warman. PG
Stephen	Md September 9, 1793 Alice Woodward, d/o William Woodward, Jr. and Jane Ridgely. AA
Stephen Eugene	Born July 3, 1947, died May 19, 1976. Marine veteran. Howard Chapel Cemetery. HO
Susanna	Md November 11, 1708 Alexander Goodin. St. Peters
Susannah	Md first John Ijams; second Joseph Taylor; and third Captain Marsh Mareen Duvall.
T. C.	Born September 24, 1859, died May 15, 1949. Wife, Catharine P., born February 11, 1857, died April 4, 1924. Bethesda United Methodist, Browningsville.
Thomas	Died by 1680; md Lydia Baldwin, and had children: Lydia Watkins, md c.1680 Brittison; Thomas Watkins, Jr, born 1670s, md September 8, 1698 Mary Wells, had children: Thomas Watkins, III, born April 14, 1699, and Basil Watkins, born December 14, 1701.
Thomas	Md September 8, 1698 Mary Wells. St. James.
Thomas	Md January 19, 1738 Elizabeth Mead. St. Johns Episcopal Parish.
Thomas	Md March 12, 1799 Elizabeth Spurrier. BA
Thomas	Md December 6, 1779 Lucy Belt.
Thomas	Md November 4, 1797 Sarah Disney. AA
Thomas	Of Thomas, born March 21, 1807
Thomas	Born c.1779, died July 9, 1851, md Elizabeth.
Thomas	Md October 18, 1825 Ann Wheeler.
Thomas, Jr.	Elk Ridge. Md February 19, 1835 Amanda Watkins
Thomas W.	Born 1823, died 1829. AA
Tobias	Of Thomas. Born December 12, 1780, died November 14, 1855. Md May 16, 1802 to Mary Simpson.
Violett	Md February 19, 1696 John Walker. All Hallows.
W. Maurice	Md November 15, 1887 Madora H. Cecil. MO
Wilen	Md February 7, 1860 Jonathan Stewart. MO
Willard R.	Md November 28, 1940 Dorothy V. Benson. MO
William	Md December 9, 1741 Ann Barkabee (Blackabee).
William	Md March 29, 1779 Catherine Owings. BA
William	Md November 17, 1791 Margaret Edwards. BA

William	Md May 3, 1792 Susanna Minksey. BA
William	Md January 11, 1799 Peggy McMillan. BA
William	Md February 25, 1805 Eleanor Harwood. AA
William	Md November 2, 1822 Lydia Dorsey, daughter of Lt. Charles Griffith Dorsey (1778) and Catherine Welsh.
William L.	Md September 2, 1878 Jane E. Turner. PG
William O.	Born March 24, 1934, died March 22, 1935. Same stone with John S. Parker. Wildwood Cemetery.
William W.	Of Thomas. Born December 18, 1799, died July 29, 1862. Md June 18, 1846 Elizabeth L. Watkins.
William W.	Md August 13, 1826 Mary Ann Harris. MO
Willy E.	Md February 3, 1860 Jonathan Stewart. MO

BIBLIOGRAPHY

American Genealogical Research Institute. *Walker Family History*, Washington, D. C. 1972.

American Historical Society. *History of Virginia, 1924*

Asplund. *Register of Baptist Churches*

Badger, Matilda R. *Genealogy of the Linthicum and Allied Families*. 1934. Privately published, Baltimore, Md.

Barnes. *Maryland Marriages, 1634-1777*

_____. *Maryland Marriages, 1778-1800*

_____. *Marriages and Deaths From the Maryland Gazette*

Beitzell. *Point Lookout Prison Camp for Confederates*

Block, Maxine, Editor. *Current Biography, Who's News and Why*, New York: H. W. Wilson Company, 1940

Bockstruck, Lloyd DeWitt. *Virginia's Colonial Soldiers*

Bowie. *Across The Years in Prince George's County*

Bowman, Tressie Nash. *Montgomery County Marriages, 1796-1850*

Brown. *Index of Marriage Licenses, Prince George's County, Maryland*

_____. *Index of Church Records, Maryland*

Brumbaugh. *Maryland Records.* 1915 and 1928 issues; Washington County Marriages.

_____. *Maryland Records, Colonial, Revolutionary, County and Church.* Volume 1.

_____. *Census of Maryland, 1776*

Burke. *Burke's Peerage and Baronetage.*

_____. *The General Armory*

Carr, Lois Green; Menard, Russell R.; Peddicord, Louis. *Maryland at the Beginning.*

Chapman. *Portrait and Biographical Record of the Sixth Congressional District, Maryland.* Chapman Publishing Company, New York. 1898

Church of Jesus Christ of Latter Day Saints. *Family group sheets, computerized ancestral files, International Genealogical Index, and other pertinent records.* Family History Center, Silver Spring, Maryland.

Coldham, Peter Wilson. *The Bristol Register of Servants Sent to*

Foreign Plantations 1654-1686, Genealogical Publishing Company, Baltimore. 1988

_____. *The Complete Book of Emigrants, 1607-1660,* Genealogical Publishing Co., Baltimore, 1987

Crozier. *The General Armory*

Day, Jackson H. *The Story of the Maryland Walker Family, Including the Descendants of George Bryan Walker and Elizabeth Walker Beall.* 1957, privately printed manuscript.

Ferrill, Matthew & Gilchrist, Robert. *Maryland Probate Records 1635-1777.* Volume 9.

Filby. *Passenger and Immigration Lists Index.*

Fry, Joshua & Jefferson, Peter. *Map of Virginia, North Carolina, Pennsylvania, Maryland, New Jersey 1751.* Montgomery County, Md Library, Atlas Archives.

Gaithersburg, Maryland, City. *Gaithersburg, The Heart of Montgomery County.* Privately printed. 1978

Gartner Funeral Home, Gaithersburg, Maryland. *Alphabetical computer print-out of funerals and dates.*

Goldsborough. *Maryland Line in the Confederacy.*

Hardy, Stella Pickett. *Colonial Families of the Southern States of America.* Genealogical Publishing Co., Baltimore, 1981

Hinke and Reinecke. *Evangelical Reformed Church, Frederick, Maryland*

Hopkins, G. M. *Atlas of Montgomery County, Maryland.*

Jourdan, Elise Greenup. *The Land Records of Prince George's County, Maryland, 1710-1717*

Malloy, Mary Gordon; Sween, Jane C.; Manuel, Janet D. *Abstract of Wills, Montgomery County, Maryland 1776-1825*

Malloy, Mary Gordon; Jacobs, Marian W. *Genealogical Abstracts, Montgomery County Sentinel, 1855-1899*

Manuel, Janet Thompson. *Montgomery County, Maryland Marriage Licenses, 1798-1898*

Maryland State. *Archives of Maryland,* all volumes.

Maryland Hall of Records. *Wills, estates, inventories, births, deaths, marriages, deeds and other reference works relative to counties of Maryland.*

_____. *Maryland Calendar of Wills.* Eight volumes.

_____. *Maryland Historical Society Magazine.*

_____. *Vestry Book of St. John's Episcopal Parish Church, 1689-1810.* Original.

Montgomery County Court Records. *Wills, inventories of estate, deeds.* Rockville, Maryland.

Montgomery County Historical Society, Rockville, Maryland. *Folder files; correspondence, newspaper records, library, and family records.*

_____. *Queen Anne Parish Records, 1686-1777*

_____. *King George Parish Records 1689 - 1801*

_____. *King George Parish Records 1797-1878*

_____. *St. Paul's at Baden, Parish Records*

_____. *Frederick County Maryland Marriage Licenses*

_____. *Montgomery County Marriages*

_____. *1850 Census, Montgomery County, Maryland*

_____. *1850 Census, Prince George's County, Maryland*

_____. *Pioneers of Old Monocacy*

Mormon Church, Genealogical Library. Archival family group sheets and other records.

_____. *International Genealogical Index.* North Carolina, Tennessee, Maryland, Pennsylvania, Ohio, Kentucky, Alabama, Virginia and other states.

Morrow and Morrow. *Marriages of Washington County, Maryland, An Index, 1799-1866.* DAR library, Washington, D. C.

Newman, Harry Wright. *Mareen Duvall of Middle Plantation.*

_____. *Anne Arundel Gentry, Volumes 1 and 2.* 1971. Privately published at Annapolis, Maryland.

Omans, Donald James and Nancy West. *Montgomery County Marriages 1798-1875.* Maryland.

Preston, Dickson J. *Talbott County, A History*, Centreville, Md., Tidewater Publishers, 1983

Prince George's County, Md Historical Society. *Index to the Probate Records of Prince George's County, Maryland, 1696-1900*

_____. *Prince George's County Land Records, Volume A, 1696-1702.* Bowie, Maryland, 1976

_____. *1850 Census, Prince George's County, Maryland.* Bowie, Maryland, 1978

_____. *1828 Tax List Prince George's County, Maryland.* Bowie, Maryland, 1985.

Reinton, Louise Joyner. *Prince George's County, Md. Piscataway or St. John's Parish (now called King George's Parish. Index to Register, 1689-1878.*

Ridgely. *Historic Graves of Maryland and the District of Columbia*

Sargent. *Stones and Bones, Cemetery Records of Prince George's County, Maryland.*

Scharff. *History of Maryland.* Three volumes. Tradition Press, Hatboro, Pennsylvania. 1967 edition.

Skinner, V. L., Jr. *Abstracts of the Prerogative Court of Maryland, 1726-1729*

Skordas, Gust. *Early Settlers of Maryland*

_____. (Perhaps). *Servants to Foreign Plantations*

Tepper, Michael. *Emigrants to the Middle Colonies.*

_____. *Passengers to America.* Genealogical Publishing Company, Baltimore, 1979

Tombstone Records. Bethesda United Methodist Church, Browningsville, Maryland. Forest Oak Cemetery, Gaithersburg, Maryland. Goshen United Methodist Church (now Goshen Mennonite Church), Laytonsville, Maryland. St. Paul's Methodist Church, Laytonsville, Maryland.

Warfield, J. D. *The Founders of Anne Arundel and Howard Counties, Maryland.* Regional Publishing Company, Baltimore, Maryland 1973. Original edition, Kohn & Pollock, Baltimore. 1905.

Welsh, Luther W. *Ancestral Colonial Families, Genealogy of The Welsh and Hyatt Families of Maryland And Their Kin.* Lambert Moon Printing Co., Independence, Missouri. 1928

Williams, T. J. C. *History of Frederick County, Maryland.* Two volumes. L. R. Titsworth & Co. 1910

_____. *History of Washington County, Maryland*

Wright, F. Edward. *Maryland Militia, War of 1812.*

INDEX

All names appearing in the text appear in the index, with each page on which they can be found. In order to distinguish between family members with the same name, most names in the index will be followed by a date, in most cases the date of birth. Occasionally, a name will be followed by the date of marriage or death, as in m/1876 or d/1923. Entries without dates may be more than one individual; in the case of common names such as James, Sarah and the like, they are nearly always more than one person.

Bailey, Richard Wager, Jr. 1989, 121
Baker, Aimee Elizabeth 1974, 140
Baker, Carson Remington 1985, 140
Baker, Charles Oscar 1922, 140
Baker, Darlene Dee 1952, 141
Baker, Dennis Raymond 1955, 140
Baker, Glenn Charles 1948, 140
Baker, Jeffrey Lee 1975, 141
Baker, Jerry Wayne 1951, 140
Baker, Jesse Lemuel, 13
Baker, Jo Ann 1957, 73
Baker, Marilyn Jean 1951, 141
Baker, Mary Burton 1838, 95, 97
Baker, Matthew Aaron 1973, 140
Baker, Oliver Lee 1927, 141
Baker, Oscar Lee, 140
Baker, Seth Ashley 1977, 140
Baker, Susan S. 1848, 95, 97
Baker, Terry Lee 1949, 141
Baker, Thomas 1800, 95
Baker, Valerie Jill 1973, 141
Baldwin, Lydia, 198
Ball, No given name, 48
Barber, Catherine, 145
Barber, Charles, 145
Barber, Charles H., 134
Barber, Eldridge, 145
Barber, Garner, 145
Barber, Gaynell, 145
Barber, Geneva, 145
Barber, Malcolm, 145
Barber, Margaret, 145
Barber, Maud, 145
Barber, Roberta, 145
Barkabee, Ann, 198
Barklay, Robyn, 155
Barnard, Teresa Catherine, 129
Barnes, James, 187
Barnes, Mary Mae, 134
Barnes, Patience, 187, 196
Barry, John, 196
Bartgis, Charles Franklin 1921, 119
Bashford, Henry, 196

Bass, Edgar L., 196
Batchelor, Lucretia, 36
Bateman, Martha 1709, 17
Batte, Ann Caroline 1797, 6
Batte, Henrietta, 4
Batte, John, Captain, 6
Batte, Lucy, 6
Beale, Mosely, Reverend, 28
Beall, Barbara Joan 1943, 114
Beall, Barry, 153
Beall, Barry Ranson 1886, 155
Beall, Barry William 1959, 153
Beall, Bertha Marie 1901, 120
Beall, Carolyn Ann, 153
Beall, Catherine Sally 1925, 155
Beall, Edna, 151
Beall, Edward Maurice 1870, 120
Beall, Francis C. 1852, 88
Beall, Heather Marie 1986, 154
Beall, John Cronin, 153
Beall, John Cronin, Jr. 1949, 153
Beall, Kathleen Ann 1942, 121
Beall, Mary, 23
Beall, Nettie F. 1872, 49
Beall, Ninian, 23
Beall, Ninian, Colonel, 9
Beall, No given name, 49, 51, 94, 115, 147, 184
Beall, Patsy Lee, 153
Beall, Rudell C. 1918, 153
Beall, Sandra Ruth, 153
Beall, Teresa Elizabeth 1983, 153
Beall, Thomas Balsh, 190
Beane, Forrest Chipman 1927, 136
Beard, Ruth, 197
Beard, Susannah, 15
Becraft, Grafton, 83
Becraft, James, 57
Becraft, Jesse 1879, 83
Becraft, Lucie 1871, 74, 76
Becraft, Mable Watkins 1901, 83
Becraft, Margaret E. 1865, 54
Becraft, Margaret Watkins, 53
Becraft, Martha 1857, 74
Becraft, No given name, 76
Becraft, Richard H., 43

Becraft, Susie 1871, 43
Beddo, Elizabeth, 197
Bell, Lucy Berry, 190
Bellison, Bertie Olivia 1888, 89
Bellison, Bessie, 143
Bellison, Edward Leander, 89
Bellison, Ethel Mae, 89
Bellison, John H., 44, 195
Belt, Benjamin, 12
Belt, Esther, 12
Belt, Lucy, 23, 198
Belt, No given name, 14
Bennett, Burman 1869, 100
Bennett, Elsa Corrine 1901, 100
Bennett, Linda Amelia 1913, 62
Benning, Josephine, 49
Benson, Dorothy V., 198
Benson, Sarah Jane 1849, 127
Benson, William H., 128
Bentz, Nannia Frances 1896, 135
Berkner, Lloyd, 168
Berkner, Patricia Ann, 168
Berkner, Phyllis Jean, 168
Berry, Amelia, 10
Berry, Marion, 190
Beshears, Bessie Clay, 140
Besson, Hester, 9
Biddeson, Josie, 194
Bishop, Ray Edward 1949, 98
Bishop, Seth Edward, 98
Blackabee, Ann, 198
Blake, S. V., Reverend, 188
Blake, Sarah Bond, 12
Bland, Alexandra Connor 1986, 72
Bland, Connor Richard 1988, 72
Bland, Courtney Alcutt 1985, 71
Bland, Jonathan F. 1952, 71
Bland, Lauren Rebecca 1980, 71
Bland, Samuel Connor 1955, 72
Bliss, Allen 1932, 66
Bliss, Dawn 1958, 66
Blumenauer, George D., 197
Bodden, Mary 1967, 121
Bodine, Elizabeth, 166
Bodine, John W., 166
Bodine, Minnie, 166

Bogar, No given name, 97
Boldrey, Glenora Frances, 164
Bolger, James L. 1903, 98
Bolton, Frances Elizabeth, 148
Bolton, No given name, 176
Boone, Carol Ann, 84
Booth, Charles, 168
Borovsky, Eugene 1954, 138
Bortz, Peter, 73
Boscage, 34
Boutwell, Eva, 138
Bowie, Priscilla, 26
Bowman, Amy 1993, 122
Bowman, Andrew 1992, 122
Bowman, David, 122
Bowman, Leah April 1976, 61
Bowman, Mark Preston, 61
Bowman, Stephanie Ann 1988,
    122
Bowman, Terri Marcella 1981, 61
Boyd, Benjamin, 11, 12
Boyd, Eleanor, 11
Boyd, Elizabeth D., 20
Boyd, Peggy, 12
Boyer, Emma Cassandra 1868, 55
Boyer, Harry, 106
Boyer, Henry, 106
Boyer, Jesse D., 193
Boyer, Jesse Darby 1866, 88
Boyer, John, 106
Boyer, John Spencer, 106
Boyer, Mamie, 47
Boyer, Milton 1834, 124
Boyer, Mollie, 106
Boyer, Norman D., 47
Boyer, Ruth L. E. 1896, 88
Boyer, Sarah Rebecca 1874, 133,
    141
Boyette, Deborah Faye 1961, 138
Boyette, Green Lester, 138
Boyette, Gretchen Noel 1964, 138
Boyette, James 1934, 138
Boyette, Renee Lynn 1968, 138
Boyette, Teresa Ann 1958, 138
Bozarth, Delores Ann, 164
Bracco, John, 30

Branaman, Will, 163
Brandenburg, Alvin, 182
Brandenburg, Andrew J., 193
Brandenburg, Ann Priscilla 1831, 149
Brandenburg, Bradley Jefferson 1865, 49, 98
Brandenburg, Charlotte L., 62
Brandenburg, Charlotte Lavinia 1851, 55
Brandenburg, Claude, 182
Brandenburg, Claude Fillmore 1904, 72
Brandenburg, Dewey, 182
Brandenburg, Ezra 1868, 98
Brandenburg, Jesse B. 1824, 54
Brandenburg, Jessie Fay 1892, 98
Brandenburg, Lela, 182
Brandenburg, Mahala, 161
Brandenburg, Mary Roberta 1866, 54
Brandenburg, Mazie N. 1897, 49
Brandenburg, Osca Pearl 1892, 98
Brandenburg, Pearl, 182
Brandenburg, William B., 182
Brashears, Bessie Clay, 140
Brewer, Eleanor Jane, 109
Brewer, Eleanor Jane 1835, 107
Brewer, Vincent, 107
Brickman, Anna, 123
Brickman, Scott, 123
Bridges, Tammy Lynn 1988, 70
Brightwell, Donald C. 1942, 61
Brittison, No given name, 198
Broadhurst, Samuel V. 1866, 51
Brocchus, Mary Tinges, 29
Bromwell, John Edward, 19
Brooke, E. H., General, 35
Brooke, Maria W., 35
Brown's Chance, 26
Brown, Allen Wayne 1938, 136
Brown, Ann, 32
Brown, Anna 1846, 81
Brown, Benita Lee 1949, 136
Brown, Catherine 1854, 81
Brown, Charles, 58

Brown, Christina 1849, 81
Brown, David Anthony 1950, 136
Brown, David Anthony, Jr., 136
Brown, Delaney Pearl 1919, 151
Brown, Dolly Mae, 131
Brown, Doris Virginia 1925, 136
Brown, Elena Rene' 1963, 139
Brown, Elizabeth 1855, 81
Brown, Ephraim 1828, 81
Brown, Eugene Wilson, 139
Brown, Eugene Wilson, III 1966, 139
Brown, Eugene Wilson, Jr. 1935, 139
Brown, Filmore Cleveland 1893, 135
Brown, Francis Earl 1915, 136
Brown, Francis Earl, Jr. 1941, 136
Brown, James Richard 1940, 136
Brown, James T. 1856, 81
Brown, Jeanne Marie, 126
Brown, John, 182
Brown, John Wesley 1850, 136
Brown, Julia Wilhelmina 1947, 136
Brown, Julian Wilson 1918, 136
Brown, Kay Arlene 1959, 136
Brown, Kevin Robert 1984, 151
Brown, Louisa J. 1844, 53, 81
Brown, Lucretia V. 1850, 81
Brown, Madeliene, 183
Brown, Margaret A. 1853, 177
Brown, Margaret E. 1856, 81
Brown, Mary Elizabeth 1844, 81
Brown, No given name, 81, 182
Brown, Olivia J., 177
Brown, Owen, 81
Brown, Owen 1816, 47, 80
Brown, Owen Cornelius 1848, 81
Brown, Peggy, 163
Brown, Philip Cleveland 1893, 136
Brown, Rachel A. 1837, 81
Brown, Rhoda 1827, 81
Brown, Richard G. 1841, 81
Brown, Ricky Allen 1960, 136

Brown, Rosa 1860, 89
Brown, Ruth Evelyn 1931, 136
Brown, Sarah E. 1843, 81
Brown, Scott Delaney 1980, 151
Brown, Steven Gary 1971, 136
Brown, Terry Lee 1955, 151
Brown, Thomas Ephraim, 157
Brown, Thomas G. 1831, 81
Brown, Tightus E. 1880, 157
Brown, Tillie, 197
Brown, William G. 1839, 81
Browning, Mary 1880, 150
Browning, Venia W. 1857, 181
Buckingham, George Walter, 44
Burdette, Abraham Lincoln 1864,
    52, 157
Burdette, Amanda M., 92
Burdette, Anita E. 1879, 93
Burdette, Ann 1932, 154
Burdette, Annie M. 1861, 92
Burdette, Aubrey Wilson 1897,
    148
Burdette, Audrey Marie 1915, 148
Burdette, Benjamin F. 1832, 92
Burdette, Benjamin F. 1876, 92
Burdette, Caleb Joshua, Reverend
    1849, 156
Burdette, Carrie Louise 1908, 69
Burdette, Charles F. 1898, 157
Burdette, Charles King 1917, 133
Burdette, Claude H. 1872, 133,
    141
Burdette, Edith, 153
Burdette, Edith Elizabeth 1888,
    155
Burdette, Edna 1906, 193
Burdette, Ella Irene, 157
Burdette, Ellen G. 1891, 148
Burdette, Elmon G. 1823, 181
Burdette, Fannie M. 1895, 68
Burdette, Frances American
    Cornelia 1857, 136
Burdette, George H. 1870, 50, 67
Burdette, George I. 1908, 92
Burdette, George Lincoln 1897,
    157

Burdette, Harriet A. H., 174
Burdette, Harriet Ann 1850, 181
Burdette, Hezekiah 1800, 88
Burdette, Ira Lansdale 1900, 51,
    180
Burdette, Irving M., 148
Burdette, James W., 92
Burdette, James William 1813,
    148
Burdette, John H., 96
Burdette, John William 1895, 69
Burdette, Joseph McKendree 1845,
    147
Burdette, Lillian Mae 1894, 68
Burdette, Lilly May, 149
Burdette, Martha Ann, 51
Burdette, Mary E. 1873, 55
Burdette, Mary Jane 1825, 109,
    113
Burdette, Mary Rachel Elizabeth
    1852, 137, 150
Burdette, Merle M. d/1968, 148
Burdette, Michael M., 148
Burdette, Milton W. 1900, 154
Burdette, Moody M. 1884, 148
Burdette, Nettie Emily 1911, 50,
    70
Burdette, Nicie, 69
Burdette, No given name, 77
Burdette, Nona M. 1904, 126
Burdette, Olive Virginia 1919, 52,
    180
Burdette, Raymond W. 1892, 68
Burdette, Rebecca Zerah 1877,
    156
Burdette, Richard T., 195
Burdette, Robert Franklin 1947,
    157
Burdette, Sarah Elizabeth 1904,
    140
Burdette, Stephen W., 157
Burdette, Teresa Ann 1960, 157
Burdette, Vera Regina 1919, 149
Burdette, Wallace Franklin 1924,
    157
Burdette, Willie H., 154, 157

Burdette, Willis B. 1871, 148
Burgess, Harriet, 25
Burgess, Ursula, 3
Burgess, Vachel 1756, Captain, 25
Burgess, William, Colonel, 3
Burgess, William, Jr., 3
Burns, Ann Renee' 1958, 72
Burns, Ann Yvonne 1933, 72
Burns, Beverly Jill 1966, 71
Burns, Catherine Jane 1935, 72
Burns, Charles Meredith 1929, 71
Burns, Clifton Webster 1925, 71
Burns, Ida E. 1867, 179
Burns, Karen Kristine 1953, 71
Burns, Lori Gail 1960, 71
Burns, Marcie Lee 1955, 71
Burns, Myrtle Bryan 1896, 113
Burns, Nicholas Edward 1865, 113
Burns, No given name, 52
Burns, Nona Augusta, 63
Burns, Richard Courtney 1932, 71
Burns, Vicki Lynn 1952, 71
Burns, Wendy Sue 1957, 71
Burr, A. D. V., 35
Burrage's End, 17
Burris, Jerry, 144
Burriss, Barbara 1973, 144
Burriss, Nikki 1972, 144
Burton, Anne, 95
Butcher, Hazel, 101
Butler, Bruce, 144
Butler, Jesse, 151
Butler, Kimberly 1979, 144
Butler, Martha Jane, 151
Butt, Donald Eugene, 63
Butt, Donald Eugene, Jr. 1955, 63
Butt, Jacob Watkins 1987, 63
Butt, Kathleen Lee 1984, 63
Butt, Mark Timothy 1958, 63
Butterwick, Ralph, 135
Buxton, Basil F. 1843, 55
Buxton, Basil Francis, 62
Buxton, Delma Viola 1893, 62
Buxton, Elizabeth Jane 1843, 105
Buxton, Emma Rose 1874, 55
Buxton, Helen E. 1880, 61

Buxton, Madeline, 82
Buxton, Upton, 62

—C—

Caglione, Edward S., 131
Caglione, Edward Stephen 1963, 131
Caglione, Valeta, 131
Caldwell, Martha, 25
Callahan, No given name, 4
Calloway, John Patrick, 142
Cantrell, Marsha Lynn 1946, 99
Cantrell, Verdin Smith, 99
Cardwell, J. Albert, 24
Cardwell, John, 25
Cardwell, Robert W., 24
Carr, Helen, 131
Carr, Kenneth Paul 1959, 131
Carr, Krysten Daniele 1991, 132
Carr, Louis William, 131
Carr, William Dean 1957, 131
Carr, William Harold, 131
Carrico, Wilfred, 187
Carter, Nannie, 24
Case, David Martin 1964, 128, 152
Case, Martin Alexander 1932, 128, 152
Cassell, Henry, 170
Cecil, Madora H., 198
Chamberlain, Margaret, 24
Chamberlain, Ninian, 24
Chandler, Frances, 145
Chaney's Adventure, 17, 18
Chaney, Beatrice Bell 1893, 90
Chapin, Alice, 169
Chapin, Archie Bertrand 1875, 169
Chapin, Asher, 169
Chapin, Bertha, 169
Chapin, Carl Kenneth 1883, 169
Chapin, Charles, 169
Chapin, Charles Hamilton 1850, 169
Chapin, Earl, 169
Chapin, Florence 1857, 169

Conway, James Owen 1960, 119
Conway, James Paul 1982, 119
Conway, Mathew Brian 1980, 119
Coolidge, Edward, 126
Coonrod, James Henry 1923, 143
Copp, Tracey Marie 1963, 121
Cordell, Bernard Oscar 1937, 51,
    70
Cordell, No given name, 133
Cordell, Welty, 51, 70
Cost, William 1840, 174
Covington, Charles Wilson, 90
Cowman, Richard Harwood, Dr.,
    6, 38
Cowman, Thomas, 4
Craft, Dorothy 1912, 137
Crapster, Alice, 28
Crapster, Basil, 26, 27
Crapster, Bowie, 29
Crapster, Eleanor, 28
Crapster, Emma, 28
Crapster, Ernest, 28
Crapster, Florence, 28
Crapster, Mary Blanche, 28
Crapster, Mortimer Dorsey, 28
Crapster, Mortimer Dorsey, Jr., 28
Crapster, Rhodolphus, 28
Crapster, Robert Gordon, 29
Crapster, Thaddeus, 27, 28
Crapster, William Channing, 28
Crapster, William, Reverend, 27
Crawford, Catherine, 128
Crawford, No given name, 18
Crockett, Henry W. 1869, 44
Crockett, Ida H. 1877, 44
Crockett, Julius A. 1834, 43
Cromwell, John Hammond, 10
Cromwell, Thomas, 10
Cross, Adam Christian 1985, 71
Cross, Jason Thomas Charles
    1982, 71
Cross, Thomas 1947, 71
Crouch, Alice, 3
Crowder, No given name, 176
Crump, John G., 25
Crump, Mary, 24

Crumpacker, Summer, 163
Crutchley, Lydia M. 1870, 86
Crutchley, William E. 1868, 86
Cunningham, T. E., 170
Cuthbert, Kimberly 1958, 140
Cutsail, Fannie C., 180
Cutsail, Fannie Cochel 1900, 51
Cutsail, George, 51
Cutsail, George H., 194

—D—

Dailey, Douglas Alan, 99
Daly, Brittany Christian 1990, 121
Daly, Christopher Edward 1972,
    121
Daly, John Joseph 1944, 121
Daly, John Joseph, Jr. 1966, 121
Darby, Edward, 168
Darby, Elizabeth, 168
Darby, Mary Catherine, 104
Darby, Rodney H., 80
Darby, William, 168
Davidson, Carolyn Delores 1948,
    136
Davidson, No given name, 134
Davies, Cynthia Anne 1946, 101
Davies, Ronald E., 101
Davis, Alta Lee 1866, 166
Davis, Clarence, 157
Davis, Edgar W., 135
Davis, Florence P. 1859, 95
Davis, Lois Lillian 1911, 157
Davis, Mary J., 96
Davis, Mary J. 1825, 96
Davis, Vachel H., 87
Davis, Willy Ann, 195
Day, Columbus Washington 1859,
    84
Day, Dorsey W., 149
Day, Elizabeth J. 1826, 181
Day, Evelyn Louise 1943, 50
Day, Evelyn May 1930, 151
Day, Hanford Perry 1916, 50
Day, Ida V. 1872, 115
Day, James, 151

Day, Lattimer W. 1852, 181
Day, Leanna, 47
Day, Melissa B. 1883, 181
Day, Rufus King 1827, 149
Day, Sterling Elwood 1891, 84
Day, T. Deets, 196
Day, Titus Granville 1850, 149
DeBan, Jasmine, 100
Degano, Henry, 58
Degano, Henry 1973, 58
DeGrange, Helena Lenora 1906, 58
DeGrange, Thomas F., 58
Deitz, Ray, 124
DeLauter, Amanda Catherine, 100
Dempsey, Vera, 162
Denny, Edward C., 169
Denny, Erma Chapin 1888, 169
Dentz, Carole 1935, 73
Devilbiss, David, 67
Dick, Joseph, 10
Dietrich, Amy Bell 1886, 97
Dietz, Rae, 124
Diffenderffer, Grace Violet, 129
Diffenderffer, Jennie, 129
Dillon, Billie Corby 1919, 90
Dion, Pauline, 101
Dioquino, Fred, 65
Dioquino, Teresa Rene' 1960, 66
Dioquino, Timothy Dean 1958, 65
Disney, Edward, 196
Disney, Richard, 196
Disney, Sarah, 25, 187, 196, 198
Dods, Derek Russell 1987, 72
Dods, Megan Renee' 1984, 72
Dods, Russell, 72
Dodson, Adam Charles 1983, 63
Dodson, Bedford Ashley 1936, 63
Dodson, Norman Bedford 1954, 63
Dornheim, Carl Emile, Dr., 84
Dornheim, Carl Emile, III 1945, 84
Dornheim, Carl Emile, Jr. 1912, 84
Dorsey's Addition to Thomas' Lot, 10
Dorsey, Anna, 23

Dorsey, Anne Maxwell, 11
Dorsey, Benedict, 22, 196
Dorsey, Benjamin, 29
Dorsey, Caleb, 10
Dorsey, Charles Griffith 1778, 199
Dorsey, Eliza, 10
Dorsey, Elizabeth, 28, 30
Dorsey, Elizabeth Ann 1795, 23
Dorsey, Emily, 23
Dorsey, Frances 1756, 11
Dorsey, George Washington, 23
Dorsey, George Washington, Jr., 23
Dorsey, J. Worthington, 29
Dorsey, James Malcolm, 29
Dorsey, James Maxwell, 11
Dorsey, John, 10
Dorsey, John Hammond 1718, 10
Dorsey, John Hammond, Jr. 1744, 10
Dorsey, John Hammond, Jr. 1754, 11
Dorsey, John, Captain, 26
Dorsey, Joshua, 37
Dorsey, Joshua Warfield, 29
Dorsey, Lizzie, 23
Dorsey, Lydia, 199
Dorsey, Mary Hammond 1749, 10
Dorsey, Mary J., 195
Dorsey, Rebecca, 25
Dorsey, Rebecca 1752, 10
Dorsey, Rinaldi W., 5
Dorsey, Robert, 23
Dorsey, Ruth, 26, 38
Dorsey, Sarah, 10
Dorsey, Stephen 1747, 10
Dorsey, Stephen 1758, 11
Dorsey, Tamer, 23
Dorsey, Thomas, 22, 23
Dorsey, Washington, 23
Dorsey, William, 23
Dorsey, William R., 30
Dove, Helen Cecilia 1904, 142
Dowden, Sarah Wilson 1867, 85
Dowden, Zachariah, III 1829, 86
Doyle, Deidre, 56

Doyle, No given name, 56
Doyle, Tina, 56
Driskill, Jack 1924, 84
Driskill, Linda Ann 1953, 151
Dubel, Donna Jean 1963, 101
Dubel, Janet Fay 1956, 101
Dubel, Omar John 1898, 100
Dubel, Robert Ellsworth, 1
Dubel, Robert Ellsworth 1921, 100
Dubel, Robert Ellsworth, Jr. 1941, 101
Dubel, Tyson David, 100
Duckett, Allen Bowie, 21
Duckett, Benjamin M., 20
Duckett, Martha, 20
Duckett, Rebecca 1742, 91
Duckett, Richard, 21
Duerksen, Benjamin Harold 1984, 155
Duerksen, Emilee Grace 1988, 155
Duerksen, Joseph Michael 1987, 155
Duerksen, Paul Dean 1953, 155
Duley, No given name, 106
Dunn, No given name, 184
Dunn, Scott Alan, 184
Durette, J. R., 173
Dutrow, Fannie 1876, 110
Dutrow, Harriet M. 1876, 179
Duvall, Alice, 158
Duvall, Carol, 124
Duvall, Deborah Kay 1955, 125
Duvall, Edward Boyer 1925, 124
Duvall, Edwin Allen 1950, 125
Duvall, Ernest Davis 1883, 84
Duvall, Gerald Leigh, 125
Duvall, Hilda, 125
Duvall, Howard Mareen, Dr., 38
Duvall, Idell Genevieve 1915, 84
Duvall, James, 124
Duvall, Joseph, 84
Duvall, Julie, 124
Duvall, Karen Jean 1957, 125
Duvall, Kim, 125
Duvall, Lewis, 85
Duvall, Linda Lou 1948, 125

Duvall, Lois, 124
Duvall, Margaret Jackson 1828, 34
Duvall, Maria L., 38
Duvall, Marsh Mareen, Captain, 198
Duvall, Mary Virginia 1917, 124
Duvall, Miriam, 125
Duvall, Nancy, 124
Duvall, No given name, 4, 114
Duvall, Oliver Morgan 1889, 124
Duvall, Pamela, 124
Duvall, Paul, 124
Duvall, Paul Wayne, 124
Duvall, Richard Burton, 124
Duvall, Robert Morgan 1923, 124
Duvall, Robert Morgan, Jr., 124
Duvall, Robin, 124
Duvall, Rodney H., 125
Duvall, Rosalie V. 1885, 178
Duvall, Rose Eleanor 1935, 125
Duvall, Sarah Elizabeth, 139
Duvall, Sherwood, 101
Duvall, Shirley Jane, 125
Duvall, Stephen Leigh 1952, 125
Duvall, Timothy Edward 1958, 125
Duvall, Timothy Lee 1954, 101
Duvall, Wendy, 124
Duvall, William C., 125
Dyer, Edward, 46

—E—

Eader, Brenda Kay 1951, 131
Eader, Carol Ann 1962, 131
Eader, John Michael, 131
Eader, John Michael 1960, 131
Eader, John Michael, Jr. 1931, 131
Eaton, Marie Frances 1959, 119
Edge, Allen Clark 1932, 59
Edge, Allen Clark, Jr. 1953, 59
Edge, Nancy Ann 1955, 59
Edmond, Jemima O., 38
Edwards, Henry C., 195
Edwards, Margaret, 198
Elfrey, Philip, 193

Elizabeth's Fancy, 17
Eller, Mary R., 104
Ellerslie, 27
Ellis, Evan, 189
Ellison, W. J., 23
Engel, John A., 195
England, Abram, 28
England, Cordelia, 28
England, Elizabeth, 28
England, George, 28
Englehart, No given name, 145
English, Richard Sheldon, 181
Eppley, No given name, 134
Estapinal, Justin Ray 1983, 62
Estipinal, Gary Ray 1955, 62
Etchison, Blanche, 96
Etchison, Greenbury S., 88
Etchison, Jesse, 189
Etchison, John Osborne, 84
Etchison, Ramona 1929, 84
Etchison, Robert Lee 1898, 83
Etchison, Susanna Ruth 1844, 87
Evans, Joan Carol 1961, 142
Ewing, Rachel, 11

—F—

Faecke, No given name, 56
Fairinholt, James 1954, 73
Farnsworth, Jacob, 162
Farnsworth, Robert, 161
Federmeyer, Jefferson Donald, 152
Federmeyer, Lindsay Marie 1984, 152
Felty, No given name, 124
Felty, Walter Thomas, 124
Field, Elizabeth Ann, 132
Fields, Frank, 36
Fitzwater, Wilma Elizabeth, 131
Flair, Glenrose Mary 1916, 136
Fleming, No given name, 184
Fleming, Sherley Louise 1930, 101
Flemming, No given name, 82
Flinn, Patrick 1833, 34
Flood, Margaret J., 13
Flynn, Thomas H. C., 110

Ford, Richard, 64
Foreland, 20
Foster, Delmas, 52, 180
Foster, Florence, 106
Foster, Penny Sue 1961, 52, 180
Foster, Tammy Lynn 1964, 52, 181
Fountain, Dawn, 138
Fowner, Mary Catherine 1867, 39
Fox, Florence 1865, 190
Fraley, Ernest Lee Fenton, 130
Fraley, Gladys Mae 1911, 130
Fraley, James, 154
Franklin, Doris Ann 1946, 60
Frayne, Anabel, 169
Frendach, Angela Christine 1966, 129
Frendach, Eric Barnard 1965, 129
Frendach, James Stephen, 129
Frendach, Katy, 129
Frendach, Paul Franklin 1941, 129
Frendach, Stephen Frank 1973, 129
Freysz, Alfred, 154
Freysz, Alfred, Jr., 154
Freysz, Michelle 1977, 154
Freysz, Richard Allen 1989, 154
Freysz, Sandra Kay 1957, 154
Frisoli, Georgene Barbara, 60
Frum, C. Wayne, 151
Frum, Kelly Marie 1979, 151
Fulks, Blanche Vinton 1903, 168
Fulks, Ignatius Thomas 1832, 167
Fulks, Lillian Frances, 168
Fulks, Oscar Fernando 1876, 167
Fulton, Mary D. 1953, 73

—G—

Gadow, Brenda Jane, 152
Gaither, Basil, 22
Gaither, Nathan, 23
Gaither, No given name, 23
Galbraith, John Alexander, 24
Gale, Elizabeth, 195
Ganley, Joseph Mackin 1927, 131
Gardiner, Thomas F., 193

Gardner, No given name, 78
Garland, Dave W., 156
Garland, Ruby Jo 1930, 156
Garrett, Julia Ann 1810, 132
Gartner, David Wayne 1968, 114
Gartner, Robert Ernest 1918, 114
Gartner, Robert Ernest, Jr. 1942, 114
Gartrell, Bushrod, 196
Gassaway, Ann, 9, 14, 15, 17
Gassaway, Berry, 10
Gassaway, Hanson, 10
Gassaway, John, 10
Gassaway, Mary, 10
Gassaway, Nicholas, 10
Gassaway, Nicholas, Colonel, 10
Gassaway, Thomas, 10, 15
Gassaway, Thomas, Colonel, 9
Gatton, Helen, 34
Gatton, Kitty Ann, 33
Gatton, Zachariah, 34
Geist, C., 10
Gerhart, Melva 1948, 67
Gibbs, Frances Ann 1945, 69
Gibbs, Kathryn Anne 1975, 69
Gibbs, Milton Paul 1950, 69
Gibbs, Milton Paul, Jr. 1970, 69
Gibbs, Walter Z., 69
Gill, Howard, 31
Gill, M. Gillet, 31
Gill, M. Gillett, Jr., 31
Gill, Mildred, 31
Gill, Royal, 31
Gist, David Thomas 1954, 73
Gist, Kathryn Denise 1957, 73
Gist, Kimberly Ann 1959, 74
Gist, Rodney Thomas 1930, 73
Gladhill, Kay, 142
Glenn, Cynthia 1954, 61
Glenwood, 32
Gloyd, Edmund Alexander 1863, 148
Gloyd, Elizabeth Matilda 1840, 167
Gloyd, Henry Dorsey 1879, 115
Gloyd, Ruby Adelaide 1898, 148

Gloyd, Samuel Sylvester 1914, 115
Goetz, Nadine, 163
Golliday, No given name, 134
Goodin, Alexander, 198
Goodwin, Adam Lee 1980, 142
Goodwin, Christopher Eugene 1979, 142
Goodwin, Raymond Eugene 1952, 142
Gordon, No given name, 184
Gorman, William, 32
Gose, Elizabeth, 143
Gosnell, Joyce Ann 1953, 72
Gosnell, Robert Lincoln 1930, 72
Gosnell, Robin Michelle 1958, 72
Graham, No given name, 64
Granahan, No given name, 65
Grant, Brian, 122
Grason, Ann Matilda, 7
Gray, Ann, 6, 37
Grear, Aaron Ray, 153
Grear, Jennifer Ann, 153
Grear, John Robert, 153
Grear, Matthew David, 153
Grear, Randall Allen, 153
Green, Anne C., 3
Green, Charles J., 157
Green, Charles J., Jr. 1925, 157
Green, Charles Raymond, 157
Green, Helen E., 157
Green, Mary E., 96
Green, Matilda, 7
Green, Rita Lynn, 158
Green, Robert, 96
Green, William S., 4, 7
Greenfield, Purify, 195
Greentree, Ann Rebecca 1830, 32, 39
Gregory, Julia, 28
Grieves, Eleanor, 27
Grieves, Horatio, Doctor, 27
Griffin, Lely, 45
Griffith, Ann d/1815, 18
Griffith, Henry, 18
Griffith, Mary, 27

Grigsby, Christopher Hull 1949, 100
Grigsby, Don Ellsworth 1942, 99
Grigsby, Don Ellsworth, Jr. 1964, 99
Grigsby, Donald Edward 1918, 99
Grigsby, Heather Lea 1973, 99
Grigsby, Heidi 1972, 100
Grigsby, Shane 1973, 100
Grimes, Ida Mae 1876, 117
Grimes, Mary, 196
Grimes, Mary L., 14
Grimes, No given name, 183
Grover, Benjamin John 1974, 137
Grover, No given name, 137
Groves, Miriam, 129
Grubb, Edward, 138
Gue, Anetta 1883, 60
Gue, Ethel B., 135
Gue, Hamilton, 60
Gue, Harry, 60
Gue, Harry Willard 1884, 60
Gunther, Bertha, 161
Guyton, Ruth, 195

—H—

Hack, Suzanne Marie, 144
Hagan, Dave, 89
Hahn, Francis, 98
Hahn, No given name, 181
Haines, Bonnie, 64
Haines, Camrell, 64
Haines, Kenneth, 64
Haines, Maizie H. 1925, 67
Haines, Michael, 64
Haines, Nathaniel, 64
Haines, Sharon, 64
Haines, Walter E., Jr., 197
Haines, Walter Edward 1890, 67
Hall's Delight, 17
Hall, Anne, 21
Hall, Annie E. 1873, 116
Hall, Basil Duckett, 20
Hall, Beverly, 157
Hall, Caroline, 20

Hall, Donald, 157
Hall, Edward, 18
Hall, Effy, 18
Hall, Elizabeth, 11, 18, 20, 21, 195
Hall, Elizabeth Jane, 19
Hall, Elizabeth Watkins, 12
Hall, Ephraim Worthington, 18
Hall, Gordon, 157
Hall, Harriett, 20
Hall, Hazel Viola, 62
Hall, Henry, 5, 17, 18
Hall, Henry 1702, Major, 3, 4, 17
Hall, John 1716, 22
Hall, John Henry, 18, 19
Hall, John Stephen, 20
Hall, John Washington, 18
Hall, Joseph, 18
Hall, Judy, 157
Hall, Julius 1819, 18
Hall, Lawrence, 157
Hall, Lucy, 20
Hall, Lydia, 169
Hall, Margaret, 18, 20, 21
Hall, Margaret 1746, 3
Hall, Margaret 1781, 5
Hall, Martha, 18, 20
Hall, Martha Ann, 19
Hall, Martha Jane, 19
Hall, Mary, 4, 20, 21
Hall, Mary Ann, 18
Hall, Mary Priscilla, 6
Hall, Nancy, 20
Hall, Nicholas, 19
Hall, Nicholas 1757, 18
Hall, Nicholas 1783, 19
Hall, Osborn Sprigg 1797, 18
Hall, Patti, 157
Hall, Richard Henry, 18, 20
Hall, Richard Thomas 1777, Dr., 12
Hall, Sophia, 20
Hall, Sophia Ann 1803, 18
Hall, Thomas Blake, 12
Hall, Thomas Blake, Dr., 11
Hall, Thomas Harwood, 18
Hall, Thomas W., 18

Hall, William, 6, 11
Hall, William 1755, 20
Hall, William Henry 1762, 22
Hamm, James, 139
Hamm, Jennifer Lynn 1954, 139
Hammond, Elizabeth P., 19
Hammond, Ruth, 18
Haney, Mary Eloise 1940, 178
Hansen, Rachel, 176
Hanson, Ardis Mae 1932, 154
Hardesty, Carrie, 141
Hardesty, Frances, 197
Harding, Gay Elizabeth, 126
Harding, John E., 86
Hardy, Ann, 196
Hardy, Annie, 58
Hardy, Arthur R. 1899, 58
Hardy, Joan Lucy, 58
Hardy, John, 32, 49
Hardy, Norman Henry, 58
Hardy, William 1876, 58
Hardy, William A. 1901, 58
Hargett, Esther Lucille, 137
Harne, Alyssa Renee' 1981, 71
Harne, Jacob Daniel 1986, 71
Harne, Nicholas Ryan 1983, 71
Harne, Raymond Franklin 1954, 71
Harris, Mary Ann, 199
Harrison, Amanda 1992, 139
Harrison, Christopher, 138
Harrison, Daniel 1989, 139
Harrison, No given name, 78
Harrison, Sherry 1959, 140
Hart, Anna, 161
Hart, John Walter 1916, 60
Harwood House, 4
Harwood, Ann Elizabeth 1769, 3
Harwood, Benjamin, 7
Harwood, Benjamin 1783, 4
Harwood, Edward 1790, 4
Harwood, Eleanor, 29, 199
Harwood, Elizabeth Ann 1770, 3
Harwood, Henrietta 1780, 4
Harwood, Henry Hall 1773, 4
Harwood, John, 4
Harwood, John H. 1843, 147

Harwood, Joseph 1775, 4
Harwood, Lucretia Margaret, 197
Harwood, Margaret, 6, 11, 197
Harwood, Mary, 4, 7, 18, 38
Harwood, Mary 1778, 4
Harwood, Mary Augustus, 7
Harwood, Matilda, 7
Harwood, Nicholas, 4, 7
Harwood, Osborn, 3
Harwood, Priscilla 1785, 4
Harwood, Rachel 1764, 17
Harwood, Richard, 3, 4
Harwood, Richard 1738, Colonel, 3
Harwood, Richard Hall 1771, 3
Harwood, Samuel, 4
Harwood, Sarah, 4
Harwood, Thomas, 4
Harwood, Thomas 1777, 4
Harwood, Thomas, Captain, 17
Harwood, William, 4, 196
Harwood, William 1788, 4
Hatfield, Robert Lee, 163
Hatten, Elizabeth, 194
Hawes, Bertie Belle 1871/1879, 182
Hawes, Columbus, 182
Hawes, Lucinda, 182
Hawk, Angela Marie 1982, 155
Hawk, Catherine Jean 1974, 155
Hawk, Donald Harold 1969, 155
Hawk, Jody Theodore 1971, 155
Hawk, Ted 1944, 155
Hawk, Travis Lavern 1973, 155
Hawkins, Addie Belle 1898, 113
Hawkins, James B., 113
Hawkins, James Bradley 1886, 114
Hawkins, Joseph C., 196
Hawkins, Mary Belle 1915, 113
Hawkins, No given name, 106, 114
Hawthorne, No given name, 176
Hay, Diane Lynn 1962, 59
Hay, Roxanne Carol 1961, 59
Hay, Wells Clinton, 59
Hayland, 30
Heffner, Erma V., 58

Heil, Dorothy, 142
Henderson, George Otis, 117
Hersche, Elizabeth Ann, 32
Hickory Grove, 34
Hicks, Genevieve Arline, 163
Hicks, Joseph W., 168
Hicks, Laura V., 167
Higdon, Mary Eleanor, 12
Higgins, Charles E., 111
Higgins, Helen L., 111
Higgins, No given name, 106
Higgins, Richard, 20
High, Ann Elizabeth 1930, 39
High, Catherine, 39
High, Dana Alison 1965, 39
High, Deborah Alice 1954, 39
High, Diana Andrea 1957, 39
High, Dorothy Ann 1948, 39
High, Lloyd Horatio 1887, 39
High, Lloyd Robert 1915, 39
High, Margaret Mary 1938, 39
High, Millard Lloyd 1911, 39
High, Paul Arthur 1926, 39
Hill, Kathryn Won 1991, 122
Hill, Linda Mae, 130
Hill, Michael, 122
Hill, Scott O. Sung 1989, 122
Hillery, Martha, 143
Hilton, Brice, 58
Hilton, Catherine 1928, 151
Hilton, Dorothy A. 1828, 87
Hilton, Eldridge Jesse 1847, 46
Hilton, Elizabeth Jane 1918, 130
Hilton, Filmore 1853, 46
Hilton, Gail Dianne 1957, 152
Hilton, George, 58
Hilton, George Earl 1901, 100
Hilton, Gwendolyn Mae 1955, 151
Hilton, Henry Clay 1833, 46
Hilton, Jeanette, 58
Hilton, Lloyd 1798, 45
Hilton, Mary Amelia 1922, 100
Hilton, Ray, 151
Hilton, Richard Washington 1827, 45
Hilton, Robert Maurice 1932, 151

Hilton, Robert Ray 1963, 152
Hilton, Sarah E., 157
Hilton, Sarah E. 1839, 46
Hilton, Sharon Lynn 1961, 152
Hilton, Stanley, 58
Hilton, Susannah Ruth 1842, 46
Hilton, Suzanne Marie 1959, 152
Hilton, Thomas G., 129
Hilton, Thomas Garfield 1880, 58
Hilton, Thomas I., Sr. 1773, 45
Hilton, Thomas Samuel 1831, 46
Hilton, Thomas Stinson 1914, 58, 130
Hilton, William Harrison 1836, 46
Hilton, Willie Elizabeth 1829, 46
Hipano, Alexandro Dillanueva, Jr., 59
Hitchcock, Asael, Jr. 1746, 93
Hitchcock, Eleanor C. 1797, 93, 95, 147
Hladchuk, Craig Sheldon 1958, 136
Hladchuk, Leon, 136
Hoade, Joan Marie 1931, 71
Hobbs, Lena Adelaide, 84
Hobbs, Margaret, 112
Hobbs, Mary Ella, 179
Hobbs, Rachel A. 1830, 105
Hockenberry, Susan Marie 1974, 121
Hodges, Cornelia, 196
Hodges, Mary, 190
Hodges, Thomas, 20
Hogan, George, 66
Holland, Rachel Corrine 1878, 115
Holland, William J., Rev., 169
Holz, Richard G., Dr., 63
Holz, Susan Marie 1959, 63
Honeycutt, Christopher, 143
Honeycutt, Jason Tanner 1983, 143
Hood, Andrea Lee 1982, 156
Hood, Clarence Ellis, 156
Hood, Daryl Ellis 1986, 156
Hood, Denis Rex 1952, 156
Hood, No given name, 81
Hood, Oliver M. 1864, 56

Hook, Karen, 144
Hooper, Martha, 126
Hoopes, Albert W., 31
Hoopes, Edward, 31
Hoopes, Herman, 31
Hoopes, Marian, 31
Hopkins, Isaac H., 197
Hopkins, Samuel G., 20
House, Gilbert Wayne 1942, 117
Housen, Charles L., 149
Howard's Angle, 20
Howard, Benjamin, 21
Howard, Eleanor d/1849, 21
Howard, Elizabeth, 21
Howard, Harriet, 32
Howard, Henry Hall 1772, 21
Howard, Jeremiah, 25
Howard, John Eager, Colonel, 26
Howard, Joseph, 17, 20
Howard, Joseph 1786, 21
Howard, Joseph, Jr. 1749, 20
Howard, Kitty, 21
Howard, Margaret, 21
Howard, Margaret 1752, 5, 17
Howard, Margaret Louisa, 197
Howard, Marjorie d/1857, 21
Howard, Martha, 21
Howard, No given name, 114
Howes, Connie Dianne 1955, 181
Howes, Guy Kenneth 1916, 181
Howes, No given name, 114, 115
Hoyle, Ella May, 167
Hoyle, Smith, 167, 194
Hubble, Kevin Daniel 1986, 72
Hubble, Kevin Richard 1957, 72
Hubble, Marvin W., 72
Hubble, Robert Andrew 1980, 72
Huchingson, Velma, 138
Hudlow, Jesse Thomas 1984, 152
Hudlow, Joel Thomas 1955, 152
Huff, Charity, 157
Huff, Mathew P., 157
Huff, No given name, 157
Huff, Rebecca, 157
Hughes, Alexander Evans 1986, 143

Hughes, Arnold Victor 1894, 142
Hughes, Daniel, Major, 93
Hughes, David Arnold 1964, 143
Hughes, Donna Lee 1956, 142
Hughes, Kelsey Victoria 1989, 143
Hughes, Kenneth Allen 1935, 142
Hughes, Kenneth Allen, Jr. 1957, 142
Hughes, Robin Marie 1960, 143
Hughes, William Kenneth 1989, 143
Hughs, Samuel, 195
Hunt, Daniel Robert 1982, 154
Hunt, Erin Michelle 1980, 154
Hunt, Katherine 1978, 154
Hunt, Larry E. 1956, 154
Hunt, Robin Marie 1974, 154
Hunter, Carrol Don 1936, 138
Hunter, Donna Yvonne 1961, 138
Hunter, Gwynn Ellen 1965, 139
Hunter, Jennifer Jean 1963, 138
Hunter, John, 138
Hunter, Maria Catherine 1844, 172
Hunter, Mary Catherine 1844, 172
Hunter, Susan, 173
Hunter, Thomas, 172
Hurley, Claud C. 1888, 89
Hurley, Harry Mankin 1853, 89
Hurley, Joseph Arthur 1899, 186
Hurley, Sandra Lee 1946, 186
Hutchings, Lillian May, 163
Hutton, Enoch, 31
Hutton, Lucy, 31
Hyatt, Ann Riggs 1824, 169
Hyatt, Caroline 1838, 170
Hyatt, Carrie Josephine 1859, 169
Hyatt, Charles Hamilton 1854, 169
Hyatt, Columbia Ann 1836, 170
Hyatt, Columbus Delano 1845, 170
Hyatt, Edwin Hamilton 1870, 170
Hyatt, Elizabeth Sarah 1832, 170
Hyatt, Fannie Leannah 1861, 83
Hyatt, Fletcher Seymour 1872, 170
Hyatt, Henry Holly 1864, 170
Hyatt, Hilda Mae, 135
Hyatt, Jesse, 168

Hyatt, John Francis 1862, 170
Hyatt, John Henry 1865, 169
Hyatt, John Thomas 1834, 170
Hyatt, Joseph Hamilton 1830, 170
Hyatt, Luella 1855, 169
Hyatt, Luther Lingan 1823, 168
Hyatt, Maria 1842, 170
Hyatt, Mary Ann 1800, 166, 168
Hyatt, No given name, 151
Hyatt, Olive 1840, 170
Hyatt, Philip, 197
Hyatt, Philip 1795, 168
Hyatt, Philip Hammond 1828, 169
Hyatt, Susan Matilda 1826, 169
Hyatt, Thomas A. 1831, 83
Hyatt, Valerie Eveline 1867, 49, 98
Hyatt, William Philip 1860, 170
Hyland, Milicent, 23

—I—

Iglehart, Leonard, 195
Iglehart, Martha Ann 1818, 188
Iglehart, No given name, 145
Iglehart, Rezin, 195
Iglehart, William G., 133
Ijams, John, 22, 198
Ikner, Millie, 143
Ingalls, No given name, 177
Ingle, Iva 1891, 162
Ingle, Lawrence 1893, 162
Ingle, Reese, 162
Ingle, Vera 1895, 162
Ingram, Carla, 66

—J—

Jackson, Samuel, 24
Jackson, Susan W., 24
Jackson, Teresa Ann, 119
James, Elizabeth, 24, 195
Jerdin, Leah Nicole 1983, 59
Jerdin, Perry, 59
Jessee, Violet Marie 1927, 136
Johnson, Bettie Bell, 115

Johnson, Charles T., 196
Johnson, Charles Thomas, 115
Johnson, Charles W., 115
Johnson, Christopher 1836, 53
Johnson, Courtney Elizabeth 1984, 154
Johnson, Elizabeth, 198
Johnson, Gerald, 126
Johnson, James W., 114
Johnson, Jeremiah Paul 1990, 154
Johnson, Julie, 68
Johnson, Katie Lee 1878, 183
Johnson, Mary, 195
Johnson, Mary Emma, 126
Johnson, Merridith Ann 1988, 154
Johnson, No given name, 115
Johnson, Paul Curtis, 115
Johnson, Rose Marie, 114
Johnson, Shirley, 125
Johnson, Smith, 183
Johnson, Wayne 1954, 154
Jolley, Marjorie, 176
Jones, Ann, 25
Jones, Clay F. 1879, 89
Jones, Elizabeth, 23, 195
Jones, Ella R., 108
Jones, George Washington, 162
Jones, Isaac, Colonel, 26
Jones, Kathryn Ann, 139
Jones, Lillian Estelle 1914, 143
Jones, Louis L., 143
Jones, Mary, 23
Jones, No given name, 127
Jones, Richard, Captain, 9
Jones, Samuel C., 108
Jones, Sarah, 26
Jones, Spencer G. 1889, 90
Jordan, John, 125
Justice, No given name, 182

—K—

Kailer, No given name, 176
Kaufman, Elroy, 145
Keene, No given name, 10
Keeney, Dolly May, 157

Keilholtz, Sandra Mae 1941, 90
Kelley, Mary E., 174
Kemp, Edith Roberta 1925, 140
Kemp, James Monroe, 139
Kemp, James Raymond 1898, 139
Kemp, Julia Louise 1920, 139
Kemp, Mary Elizabeth 1921, 140
Kemper, Crystal Lynn 1984, 70
Kemper, John Albert 1961, 70
Kemper, Leonard Martin 1929, 69
Kemper, Leonard Martin, II 1957,
    69
Kemper, Samantha Lynn 1988, 70
Kemper, Sondra Marie 1979, 70
Kemper, Wanda Sue 1962, 70
Kendall, No given name, 145
Kenley, Edna, 28
Kenley, George T., 30
Kenley, John R., 28
Kenley, Nelly, 28
Kent, Jane, 18
Kenzel, Dustin Robert 1987, 138
Kenzel, Harold, 138
Kidd, Byrd Butler 1889, 151
Kidd, Madlyn, 151
Kiefer, Diana, 99
Kiefer, Patricia Dale 1943, 99
Kiefer, William James 1914, 98
Kiefer, William James, Jr. 1947,
    99
Kinder, Amelia A. 1865, 87
King, Adelain, 123
King, Amanda Cornelius 1870,
    113
King, Amanda Marie 1902, 110
King, Amber Nichole 1996, 121
King, Ann Lyn 1959, 120
King, Annie M. 1869, 86
King, Archie C. 1897, 180
King, Augusta Mae 1936, 122
King, Barry J. 1889, 179
King, Bertha Jane 1935, 120
King, Bertie Madeline 1897, 86
King, Bessie, 133
King, Beulah Hattie 1887, 121
King, Bonnie Elaine 1940, 52, 180

King, Bradley T. 1867, 85
King, Brian Charles 1974, 139
King, Brian David 1982, 144
King, Bud, 86
King, Calvin Edward 1969, 143
King, Calvin Lee 1925, 143
King, Carlton 1902, 180
King, Catherine Jemima 1854, 145
King, Charity 1769, 57, 91, 103
King, Charles C. 1846, 85
King, Charles Carroll 1933, 120
King, Charles Dow 1890, 121, 122
King, Charles Lee 1946, 143
King, Charles Miles 1814, 119
King, Christian 1971, 144
King, Clinton C. 1898, 179
King, Crittenden 1857, 119
King, Dale Edward 1969, 138
King, David Andrew 1966, 121
King, David Franklin 1947, 144
King, David Henry 1975, 123
King, Dorothy Olivia 1939, 138
King, Douglas Edward 1929, 120
King, Earl Raymond 1934, 137
King, Edith Pauline 1915, 90
King, Edward 1740, 91
King, Edward Carlton 1872, 179
King, Edward J. 1821, 109, 113
King, Edward Walter 1869, 110,
    133
King, Elias Vinson 1869, 178
King, Elizabeth Jean 1927, 141
King, Eva Lee 1864, 109
King, Eveline Lee 1864, 109
King, Florence G. 1875, 86
King, Franklin Monroe 1876, 137
King, George, 86
King, George G. 1854, 85
King, Georgia Ellen Waters 1867,
    52, 157
King, Glenwood Dawson 1918, 52,
    180
King, Gloria Elaine 1942, 121
King, Hannah 1991, 138
King, Hannah M. 1869, 86
King, Harold Rufus 1927, 120

King, Harrison Crittenden 1912, 122
King, Harry J. 1867, 144
King, Hattie Mae 1893, 114
King, Henry Franklin 1936, 137
King, Henry J. 1872, 179
King, Herbert Charles 1932, 137
King, Herbert Thomas 1971, 139
King, Hiram G. 1863, 179
King, Holady Hix 1857, 133
King, Howard T., 179
King, Ida Landella 1903, 180
King, James Franklin 1937, 120
King, James Franklin, Jr. 1968, 120
King, James Rufus 1871, 90
King, James Thomas 1943, 139
King, James Thomas, Jr. 1973, 139
King, Jane Marie 1963, 120
King, Janet Louise 1937, 143
King, Jay Michael 1963, 141
King, Jeremiah Lewis 1915, 143
King, Jeremiah Louis 1915, 143
King, Joel Thomas 1969, 123
King, John A. 1808, 85, 179
King, John Brian 1962, 141
King, John Dow, 122
King, John Duckett 1836, 179
King, John Edward Howard 1845, 150
King, Josiah Brandon 1996, 121
King, Judy N., 52, 181
King, Julian Pearre 1903, 140
King, Julian Pearre, Jr. 1932, 141
King, Karen Marie 1972, 139
King, Kari Lynn 1971, 138
King, Katherine Ann 1959, 137
King, Krista Lyn 1984, 121
King, Laura Gertrude 1873, 113
King, Leslie Crittenden 1896, 120
King, Leslie Irving 1924, 120
King, Leslie Lyn 1968, 121
King, Lillian Mae 1921, 156
King, Linda Marie 1949, 144
King, Lorena Marie 1961, 138
King, Maggie M. 1877, 86

King, Margaret Ann 1937, 138
King, Marjorie Roberta 1908, 142
King, Martha Rebecca 1874, 128, 150
King, Mary Alverta, 180
King, Mary Ellen 1843, 109
King, Mary Florence 1945, 121
King, Mary Frances 1900, 139
King, Mary Norene 1909, 180
King, Maurice Crittenden 1922, 120
King, Maurice Crittenden, Jr. 1957, 120
King, Michael Harrison 1968, 122
King, Middleton, 92
King, Mildred, 180
King, Minnie A. 1870, 112
King, Myrtle Estelle 1883, 150
King, Nancy Roberta 1937, 143
King, Nannette, 123
King, Neil Herbert 1965, 138
King, Noah Franklin 1912, 143
King, Nora Belle 1907, 133
King, Norris M. 1871, 86
King, Oliver Henry 1941, 178
King, Opal Elena 1940, 139
King, Ora Henning 1910, 178
King, Orida Jane 1883, 121
King, Patrice Marie 1967, 123
King, Patricia Ann 1933, 141
King, Paul Richard 1938, 121
King, Pearle Avondale 1933, 137
King, Peter Brandon 1963, 121
King, R. Delaney 1874, 52, 180
King, Reginald Windsor 1878, 117
King, Richard B., 179
King, Robert Lee 1931, 120
King, Roberta 1855, 156
King, Roberta Olivia 1931, 137
King, Ruth Selby 1904, 117
King, Sandra Jean 1964, 137
King, Sarah 1990, 138
King, Shannon Sherelle 1968, 139
King, Singleton Lewis 1843, 137, 150
King, Susan Burdette 1956, 141

Lewis, Emma Jane 1857, 107
Lewis, Eugene Francis 1910, 62
Lewis, Grover, 112
Lewis, Harriet Ann, 103
Lewis, Harriet Ann 1805, 57, 93,
    107, 112, 123, 127, 132, 144
Lewis, Jemima C., 47
Lewis, Jonathan, 194
Lewis, Lillian, 167
Lewis, No given name, 108
Lewis, Norma Lee 1932, 62
Lewis, Rachel, 42, 52, 80
Lewis, Raymond Carl 1915, 98
Lewis, Russell, 57
Lewis, Russell B., 112
Lewis, Russell V., 112
Lewis, William F. 1852, 197
Lewis, William J., 57, 196
Lewis, Willie, 185
Liddard, John C., 179
Lieurance, John Roscoe, 162
Lilly, George H., 175
Lingle, Leland Lee, 163
Linn, Margaret G. H. 1869, 100
Linster, Margaret, 36
Linthicum, Amanda, 30
Linthicum, Amanda Jean, 126
Linthicum, Ann Marie 1962, 126
Linthicum, Bernard Lee 1934, 126
Linthicum, Beverly Jeanne, 126
Linthicum, Charles, 27
Linthicum, Donna Joan, 126
Linthicum, Eliza, 27
Linthicum, Gassaway Watkins, 27
Linthicum, George Morsell 1926,
    126
Linthicum, George Morsell, Jr.,
    126
Linthicum, Harriet, 27
Linthicum, Irma Jane, 126
Linthicum, James Miel 1952, 126
Linthicum, Jill Suzanne 1962, 126
Linthicum, John Hamilton Smith
    1812, 132
Linthicum, John Monroe 1961, 126
Linthicum, Joseph 1930, 126

Linthicum, Julia Ann 1850, 132,
    137
Linthicum, Lot, 27
Linthicum, Martha Elizabeth 1844,
    150
Linthicum, Mary Martha, 126
Linthicum, Miel E. 1865, 126
Linthicum, Miel Wright, 126
Linthicum, Miel Wright, Jr. 1928,
    126
Linthicum, Robert Earl 1954, 126
Linthicum, Ruth Ann 1822, 27
Linthicum, Slingsby, Reverend, 27
Linthicum, Wesley 1792, 30
Linton, 2
Lloyd, Alice, 2, 9
Lloyd, Edward, Colonel, 2
Lloyd, Elizabeth, 4
Lloyd, Emilie Auge 1978, 118
Lloyd, Erich William 1980, 118
Lloyd, Karin Reine 1982, 118
Lloyd, Martin Webster 1979, 118
Lloyd, Michael Walter 1952, 118
Lockerman, Hester Ann, 4
Loflin, Mary, 194
Long, George, 64
Long, Lawrence L., 193
Long, No given name, 77
Look, Mary, 169
Lopp, Dawn, 68
Lord, John Watkins, 3
Lore, John Hammond, 15
Lorence, No given name, 134
Lovejoy, George W. 1829, 53
Lowe, Beverly 1947, 67
Lowman, Bessie American 1886,
    60
Lowman, Cheri Jean 1959, 72
Lowman, Gina Yvonne 1962, 72
Lowman, Jeffrey Dale 1091, 72
Lowman, Lisa Ann 1958, 72
Lowman, Robert Dale 1954, 72
Lowman, Robert Eugene 1933, 72
Lugenbeel, Hattie BEll 1923, 59
Luhn, Annie Pearl, 59
Luhn, Esther Pearl 1885, 134

Luhn, Myrtle, 59
Luhn, Randolph, 134
Luhn, Sarah Elizabeth, 134
Luhn, Wilbur, 59
Lusby, Susannah, 19
Lydard, Nonie M. 1881, 179
Lyddard, Louisa E. 1858, 182, 183
Lyddard, Matilda 1860, 182
Lyles, Priscilla Bowie, 26
Lyons, Erik Evan 1972, 101
Lyons, Francis Patrick, 101
Lyons, Lisa Ann 1965, 101
Lyons, Robert Ellsworth 1941, 101
Lyshear, Gassaway, 196

—M—

Mack, Mary Elizabeth, 129
MacKenzie, No given name, 50
Maddon, Mary Luella, 163
Maddox, Charles J., 173
Magers, Bryan D., 198
Magers, Deborah Ann, 100
Magers, Howard, 100
Maggard, Betty, 101
Magness, Civita, 169
Magruder, Catherine, 33
Magruder, Mary, 33
Magruder, R. H., 158
Magruder, Robert W., 35
Magruder, Walter M., 180
Maline, Annetta, 132
Manuel, Buck 1930, 130
Manuel, Darin Thomas 1963, 130
Manuel, Donna Lee 1957, 130
Manuel, John Thomas, 130
Manuel, Lovie Lee 1930, 130
Mardirossian, Aris 1951, 68
Mardirossian, Emily Dorcas 1978, 69
Mardirossian, Toni 1980, 69
Mardirossian, Tracy 1984, 69
Markes, Eldon Edward, 163
Marsh, No given name, 134
Martin, Emma 1827, 34
Martin, Melissa 1963, 153

Martz, No given name, 183
Marvel, James J., 194
Marvel, Mary E., 194
Mathews, Florence C., 32
Mathews, Rosa L., 123
Mathews, William, Judge, 32
Mathis, Dexter Gordon, 114
Mathis, Jason Kyle 1987, 114
Mathis, Sarah Diane 1984, 114
Mawdsley, Barbara Ann, 59
Maxedon, Elbert L., 163
Mayer, John Talmadge, 114
Mayer, No given name, 114
McAtee, No given name, 145
McCloughan, David Wesley 1934, 143
McCloughan, Dwight David 1963, 143
McCloughan, Stephen Wayne 1965, 143
McCloughman, Donald C., 143
McClure, Charles T., 87
McComus, Martha, 11
McCormack, Linda, 68
McDavid, C. Scott 1961, 101
McDavid, Charles Clayton, 101
McDonald, Brenda, 154
McElfresh, Anne, 19
McElfresh, Fannie Wagner, 152
McEvoy, No given name, 64
McFadden, Frank, 169
McFarland, Adaline, 25
McFerrin, No given name, 37
McGavern, No given name, 162
McGill, Robert, 6
McGuire, Kathleen 1947, 132
McGuire, Martin Duane, 132
McKee, Mary Ann, 23
McMillan, Peggy, 199
McPherson, Matthew Ronald 1985, 65
McPherson, Ronald Max, 65
McPherson, Ronald Max, Jr. 1959, 65
McPherson, Stephen Duane 1956, 65

McQuay, Jane, 63
McQuay, Jean, 63
McQuay, Kelly, 63
McQuay, Sterling, 63
McQuay, Sterling, Jr., 63
McQuay, Terri Lynn, 63
McVey, George, 162
Mead, Elizabeth, 198
Meads, Amey, 197
Meriweather, Mary, 30
Merson, Ida M., 79, 80
Merson, Lillie L. 1868, 89
Merson, Rosene E., 62
Merson, Sallie 1868, 88
Merson, William C., 79
Merz, Louise Albine 1869, 69
Middle Plantation, 17, 21
Miles, Amon R., 193
Miles, Dorcas 1915, 68, 69
Miles, Eliza A., 195
Miles, Emily Eugenia 1920, 69
Miles, James F. 1853, 68
Miles, Marjorie May, 98
Miles, Roby Byrd 1888, 68
Millan, Dale Alexander 1948, 149
Millan, David Lewis 1942, 149
Millan, James Robert, 148
Millan, Robert Lawrence 1937, 148
Millan, William Bradford 1939, 149
Miller, Beverly Jo 1947, 67
Miller, Bina Sue 1954, 142
Miller, Carl Warren, 59
Miller, David Allen 1982, 67
Miller, Dawn Bliss 1979, 66
Miller, Elsie 1938, 66
Miller, Frederick 1933, 67
Miller, Glenn Michael 1958, 66
Miller, Glenn Scott 1974, 67
Miller, Harriett A. 1855, 105
Miller, Helen G. 1941, 66
Miller, Herbert Allen 1945, 67
Miller, Herbert Gervis 1914, 66
Miller, Jacob 1858, 105
Miller, Jonathan 1857, 105

Miller, Joyce Ann 1937, 66
Miller, Kathleen Michelle 1981, 137
Miller, Margaret, 163
Miller, Martha Maelou, 139
Miller, Mary, 169
Miller, Mary 1943, 67
Miller, Michael Allen 1967, 67
Miller, Patricia Ann 1971, 67
Miller, Rebecca, 195
Miller, Rebecca 1831, 86
Miller, Richard, 142
Miller, Stephen Andrew 1985, 137
Miller, Washington 1849, 105
Miller, William 1830, 105
Miller, William David 1950, 67
Miller, William Gregory, 137
Miller, William P. 1860, 105
Millett, Ada Winifred, 169
Milner, Nancy E., 24
Minksey, Susanna, 199
Minn, Rezin F. 1846, 105
Miracle, Jesse, 162
Miracle, Rachel A., 162
Mitchell, Andrew, 138
Mitchell, Drucilla Iona, 99
Molesworth, Beulah, 60
Molesworth, Eli Thomas, 61
Molesworth, Eli Thomas 1898, 184
Molesworth, Florence Elizabeth, 90
Molesworth, Jennifer, 77
Molesworth, John Raymond 1918, 77
Molesworth, John Raymond, Jr., 77
Molesworth, Loretta Estelle 1926, 61, 184
Molesworth, Olin L. 1920, 184
Montlenone, Dawn Bliss 1979, 66
Montlenone, Michael, 66
Moore, Alfred L., 19
Moore, No given name, 185
Moorland, Doctor, 27
Moran, Dorothea 1931, 120

Morehouses Generosity, 10
Morris, No given name, 82
Mosely, Bertha, 28
Mott, Richard Albert 1917, 99
Mount, Edith P. 1878, 158
Mount, Ethel Hilda 1911, 62
Mount, George W. 1865, 175
Mount, George W. H., 175
Mount, Wilfred Edgar, 63
Mount, William, 158
Moxely, Edgar Maynard 1907, 82
Moxely, Vernie Lansdale 1900, 82
Moxley, Alcinda, 83
Moxley, Ann Wilson 1847, 58, 61,
    67, 70
Moxley, Anna Belle 1863, 82
Moxley, Asbury 1828, 45
Moxley, Asbury 1865, 82
Moxley, Bernice A. 1928, 82
Moxley, Cornelius Edward, 156
Moxley, Cornelius Edward 1861,
    81
Moxley, Della 1902, 82
Moxley, Edna 1904, 82
Moxley, Elsie Leonie 1884, 81
Moxley, Emory Dorsey 1888, 81
Moxley, Ernest M., 89
Moxley, Esther Lee 1898, 65
Moxley, Floyd Keen 1918, 81
Moxley, Floyd Keen Maloy 1926,
    156
Moxley, Floyd Simms 1895, 81
Moxley, Floyd Sims 1895, 156
Moxley, George Clyde, 82
Moxley, George Crawford 1875,
    82
Moxley, George M. 1836, 81
Moxley, Gertrude, 82
Moxley, Glenn Floyd 1953, 81,
    156
Moxley, Golden Jane 1925, 81
Moxley, Hattie Virginia 1872, 89
Moxley, Hilda, 82
Moxley, Ira Dorsey 1876, 82
Moxley, James Golden 1890, 81
Moxley, James Oscar 1868, 82

Moxley, Lucinda 1845, 45
Moxley, Mahlon 1820, 45
Moxley, Mary Edna 1861, 44
Moxley, May, 82
Moxley, Nancy Lee 1957, 81, 156
Moxley, Nellie Estelle 1897, 82
Moxley, No given name, 51, 133
Moxley, Orville 1871, 82
Moxley, Pearl Elizabeth 1912, 82
Moxley, Rachel 1838, 45
Moxley, Risdon 1812, 58
Moxley, Robert Bromwell 1840,
    97
Moxley, Rosa Medora 1865, 97
Moxley, Ruby Lee 1928, 81
Moxley, Thomas, 82
Moxley, Virgie B. 1903, 82
Moxley, William 1794, 45
Moxley, William A. 1823, 45
Moxley, William Cornelius 1903,
    82
Moxley, William Seymour 1866,
    82
Mt. Radnor, 53
Mullen, Timothy 1956, 138
Mullican, Dennis Ray 1965, 186
Mullican, Oscar Ray, 186
Mullican, Oscar Thomas 1886, 48
Mullineaux, Delma Viola 1893, 62
Mullineaux, Eldridge, 62
Mullinix, Alice Flavilla 1867, 125
Mullinix, Angelique 1969, 152
Mullinix, Brooks Grayson 1985,
    153
Mullinix, Cordelia B. 1870, 48
Mullinix, David R., 78
Mullinix, David Ryan 1980, 153
Mullinix, Deborah Mae 1954, 72
Mullinix, Edward L., 78
Mullinix, Edward Warfield 1921,
    152
Mullinix, Eleanor 1821, 58
Mullinix, Estelle W. 1905, 100
Mullinix, Everett Wayne 1946,
    152

Mullinix, Fannie Ernestine 1868, 78
Mullinix, Granville, 125
Mullinix, H. Winford B. 1928, 78
Mullinix, James Albert 1921, 78
Mullinix, James Asbury 1861, 78
Mullinix, James F. 1910, 146
Mullinix, James Herbert 1894, 78
Mullinix, Jason Robert 1977, 153
Mullinix, Jessica Amy 1976, 152
Mullinix, Kevin Patrick 1958, 153
Mullinix, Lindsay Michelle 1984, 153
Mullinix, Margaret E. 1929, 78
Mullinix, Mary, 125
Mullinix, Mary Jane 1937, 146
Mullinix, Megan Ruth 1980, 152
Mullinix, No given name, 49, 55, 78, 81, 82
Mullinix, Noah Warfield 1983, 152
Mullinix, Rhoda Ann 1829, 74
Mullinix, Richard A., 194
Mullinix, Robert B., 78
Mullinix, Robert E., 49
Mullinix, Rose Ethel, 125
Mullinix, Stephen Earl 1952, 153
Mullinix, Thomas William, 152
Mullinix, Urna R., 49
Mullinix, Vertie A. 1873, 132
Mundy, No given name, 97
Murray, Hazel Owings 1905, 100
Murray, Joseph 1865, 100
Musgrove, Hiram Dorsey, 197
Musgrove, Margaret Louise, 124
Musgrove, Nellie, 135
Musgrove, Wampler, 135
Musson, James Edward 1936, 114
Musson, Larry Edward 1966, 114
Myers, Ericka, 64
Myers, Nicole, 64
Myers, No given name, 64
Myers, Tiffany, 64

—N—

Nash, Nancy Jo 1950, 136
Nehouse, Hilton B., 90
Nelson, Beverly Ann, 99
Nelson, William C., 99
Newman, Everett Emory 1919, 90
Newman, Richard Thomas 1943, 89
Newton, William, 161
Nichols, William, 27
Nicholson, Blanche Watkins, 117
Nicholson, Carson, 116
Nicholson, Carson Edward, 127
Nicholson, Clifford Newman 1888, 127
Nicholson, Dorothy Beatrice, 127
Nicholson, Harry L., 121
Nicholson, Jessie Randolph, 127
Nicholson, Reuben M., 127
Nicholson, Walter Wilson, 127
Noble, Elizabeth, 4
Nolte, Elizabeth Watkins, 186
Norson, Sandra 1936, 155
Norton, No given name, 128
Norton, Wayne, 128
Norwood, Alice, 168
Norwood, Arianna, 82
Norwood, Eleanor, 166
Norwood, Joyce Anne 1938, 62
Norwood, Julia, 145
Norwood, Mary Ann, 168
Norwood, Matilda, 165, 166
Norwood, No given name, 147
Norwood, Ralph, 166, 168
Norwood, Ralph, Jr., 168
Norwood, William, 168

—O—

Oakdale, 30
Offenstein, No given name, 134
Ogden, Catherine, 196
Olin, Ruth Irene, 125
Ott, Judith Lynn 1958, 65
Owings, Catherine, 198

229

Owings, Hannah M. 1870, 100
Owings, Henry, Major, 30
Owings, Richard, 30

—P—

Pagano, Rita Ann Elizabeth, 39
Palmer, Amy Nichole 1986, 120
Palmer, Stephen Joseph 1987, 120
Palmer, Steven, 120
Palozi, Margaret, 152
Parker, Barry Ewing, 77
Parker, Charles Carroll 1925, 77
Parker, Golda May, 163
Parker, Hollie, 139
Parker, John S., 199
Parker, Peter Alan, 77
Parker, Randall Charles, 77
Parker, Timothy Lee, 77
Parsons, Elizabeth, 193
Partnership, 22
Patten, David H., 135
Patterson, Sarah Margaretta, 32
Patton, Vina, 78
Pauley, No given name, 48
Pearce, Blanche S. 1882, 85
Pearce, Levi, 85
Pearce, Levi W., 90
Pearce, Mary Catherine 1883, 90
Pearce, No given name, 184
Penn, Francis S. Kent, 38
Penn, John, 13
Penn, Lavenia, 36
Penn, Mary Virginia, 84
Penner, Elizabeth, 86
Pennington, Jesse, 138
Perry, Harriet Catherine Wachter
    1917, 114
Perry, Harry Clay 1806, 135
Perry, James Francis 1921, 135
Perry, Lynn Diane 1944, 135
Peter, George 1894, 168
Peter, George L. 1941, 168
Peterson, Barbara Ann 1964, 156
Peterson, Nadine, 163
Peterson, Roger J., Sr., 156

Phebus, Dora E. 1877, 70
Phelps, Barry, 125
Phelps, Ezekiel, 14, 196
Phelps, Sophronia R. 1846, 123
Phillips, Annie, 130
Phillips, Annie Harriett 1911, 58
Phillips, Ashley Violet 1983, 60
Phillips, Edwin Worthington 1903,
    58
Phillips, Geoffrey Paul 1976, 60
Phillips, Irvin Woodrow 1914, 59
Phillips, Kristen Thersa 1978, 60
Phillips, Linsey Christine 1983, 60
Phillips, Naomi May 1933, 59
Phillips, No given name, 81
Phillips, Noah W. 1874, 58
Phillips, Nowlin S., 59
Phillips, Paul Wesley, 60
Phillips, Paul Wesley 1952, 60
Phillips, R. Wayne 1943, Dr., 59
Phillips, Rebecca Lynne 1968, 59
Phillips, Richard Nowlin 1946, 60
Phillips, Ruth Naomi 1907, 58
Phillips, Ruth Naomi 1941, 59
Phillips, Shannon Dana 1976, 60
Phinnicum, Margaret, 197
Pickett, Bridgett Lynn 1988, 63
Pickett, Bruce, 63
Pickett, Lisa Ann, 153
Pickett, Nathan Robert, 153
Pickett, No given name, 63
Pickett, Rachel Marie, 153
Pickett, Robert Wayne, 153
Pierce, No given name, 162
Pindel, Gassaway, 11
Pindell, Phillip, 21
Pindell, Thomas, 196
Pines, Elizabeth, 194
Pitts, Anna Maria, 19
Pitts, Charles Hall, 19
Pitts, John, 19
Pitts, John Lusby, 19
Pitts, Nicholas Hall, 19
Pitts, Thomas, 19
Pitts, Thomas Griffith, 19
Pitts, William, 19

Plumpton, 20
Polansky, Christina 1962, 66
Poole, Ada Katherine 1952, 140
Poole, Doris, 140
Poole, Florence 1863, 81
Poole, Florence E., 156
Poole, Harry, 140
Poole, Hester 1845, 171
Poole, Philip N., 196
Poole, Sarah A. 1817, 171
Poole, Sarah E. 1855, 171
Popp, James, 125
Price, Daniel, 167
Pugh, Andrew D., 197
Pugh, Mamie, 154, 157
Pugh, Mary Elizabeth, 197
Purdu, Charles W. 1857, 104
Purdum, Cassandra 1804, 148
Purdum, Charles Riggs 1807, 112
Purdum, Eleanor 1784, 104
Purdum, Elizabeth Washington
  1840, 124
Purdum, Emily J. R. 1852, 104
Purdum, Harriett Elizabeth 1854,
  104
Purdum, Henrietta M. 1856, 104
Purdum, Henrietta Maria 1809, 13
Purdum, Henry 1859, 104
Purdum, James M. 1870, 104
Purdum, Jane Dorsey 1840, 112
Purdum, Jemima Elizabeth 1874,
  178
Purdum, John, 13
Purdum, John 1780, 104
Purdum, John 1867, 104
Purdum, John Rufus 1828, 103
Purdum, Luther E. 1865, 104
Purdum, Margaret E. 1858, 104
Purdum, Mary Jane 1882, 120
Purdum, Mary L. 1866, 126
Purdum, Mary Virginia 1919, 136
Purdum, Maurice E., 133
Purdum, Sarah Rebecca 1829, 54
Purdum, William R. K. 1853, 104
Purdy, Deborah, 41
Purdy, Mary, 197

—R—

Rabbit, Emily Catherine 1856, 68
Rabbitt, Eliza Virginia, 129
Rapley, W. H., 36
Rasner, Tamara, 143
Rawles, Carl 1966, 66
Rawles, Cody Allen 1986, 66
Rawles, Jennifer Hope 1981, 66
Rawles, Jessica 1989, 66
Rawles, Marci Ann 1984, 66
Rawles, Robert Cleon 1964, 66
Rawles, Robert Jessie 1935, 66
Rawles, William Douglas 1960, 66
Rawlings, Aaron, 15
Rawlings, Elizabeth, 15
Ray, Andrew Ryan 1978, 118
Ray, Arby Ryan 1957, 118
Ray, Jennifer Marie 1977, 118
Red, Louisa, 12
Redman, Octavia, 183
Reed, Charles Junior 1940, 63
Reed, Fidelia E. 1862, 76
Reed, Rachel A. 1840, 76
Reese, Peggy, 24
Reichard, Gloria Thomisina 1933,
  141
Rench, Ralph, 196
Reynolds, Patricia Ann 1956, 70
Reynolds, Theodore Edward 1919,
  70
Rhodes, No given name, 163
Rice, Olive Elizabeth, 186
Richards, David, 131
Richardson, Joshua 1982, 73
Richardson, Lawrence 1956, 73
Richardson, Rebecca, 26
Richardson, Richard, 26
Richardson, Zachary 1984, 73
Richland, 29
Ridgely, Elizabeth, 22
Ridgely, Emily, 27
Ridgely, Jane, 198
Ridgely, Lloyd 1845, 87
Ridgely, Marie 1949, 61
Ridgeway, Overton, 198

Shaffer, Liana Marie 1977, 71
Shaney, Polly, 195
Sharretts, Samuel, 28
Sharretts, Thaddeus M., 30
Shatard, Joseph C., 173
Shaw, Mary 1803, 112
Sheckles, Elizabeth, 11
Sheckles, John 1822, 43
Sheetenhelm, Clark, 89
Sheffield, Robert Ford, 149
Sherly, Theodore, 196
Sherman, Raymond C., 69
Shields, No given name, 28
Shipley, Addie E. 1887, 95
Shipley, Anne G., 19
Shipley, Elizabeth, 187
Shipley, Elizabeth Hall, 19
Shipley, Louisa Jane, 45
Shipley, Mary, 20
Shipley, Minerva O., 19
Shipley, Nicholas, 19
Shipley, Nimrod O., 19
Shipley, Norman, 64
Shipley, Rachel O., 19
Shipley, Robin, 64
Shipley, Thomas C., 19
Shock, Joseph Francis 1955, 73
Shock, Leslie Winifred 1949, 73
Shock, Stephen Kelly 1952, 73
Shock, William F. 1923, 73
Shock, William Jackson 1986, 73
Shoemaker, No given name, 55
Shriver, Carolyn Ann, 153
Shriver, Glenn Kenneth, III, 153
Shriver, Glenn Kenneth, Jr., 153
Shriver, Sarah Kathryn, 153
Shriver, Susan Lynn, 153
Sibley, Flora Elizabeth 1935, 128, 152
Sibley, Hettie, 128
Sibley, James E. L. 1866, 128
Sibley, Joseph Russell 1901, 128, 152
Sibley, Mary, 128
Sigler, Sallie, 13
Simmons, Archie Douglas, 164

Simmons, Larry 1946, 67
Simms, Nathan, 198
Simonds, Delora, 143
Simpson, Mary, 198
Skiles, Thomas D., 35
Slave, Ann, 172
Slave, Becky, 172
Slave, Charlotte, 172
Slave, Daniel, 172
Slave, Eliza, 172
Slave, Evaline, 172
Slave, Grafton, 53
Slave, Harry, 53
Slave, John, 172
Slave, Lydia Elizabeth, 53
Slave, Margaret, 53
Slave, Medley, 172
Slave, Nelson Hammond, 53
Slave, Perry, 172
Slave, Peter, 172
Slave, Sarah, 53
Slave, William, 172
Smallwood, William, Colonel, 25
Smith, Anthony, 11
Smith, Chad Robert 1987, 72
Smith, Charles G., 170
Smith, Clayton Otis 1913, 62
Smith, Dinah, 22
Smith, Elmer, 58
Smith, Fannie M., 168
Smith, Florence, 170
Smith, Gerald Edward 1947, 62
Smith, Helen, 58
Smith, John, Captain, 2
Smith, Lesley, 170
Smith, Mary, 11
Smith, Oliver, 170
Smith, Patricia Rae, 158
Smith, Philip, 170
Smith, Robert Michael 1956, 72
Smith, Rosie 1895, 67
Smith, Ryan Michael 1985, 72
Smith, Samuel, 9, 14
Smith, Sarah, 13
Smith, Sharon Lee 1851, 62
Smith, Sinclair, 170

Thompson, Marian Phyllis 1923, 146
Thompson, Myrtle Lee 1911, 129
Thompson, Nancy Jeanne 1940, 131
Thompson, Rosa C., 111
Thompson, Sally 1945, 180
Thompson, Sarah Elizabeth 1978, 129
Thompson, Susan, 188
Thompson, William, 180
Thompson, William H., 146
Thrift, Ara Matilda 1857, 121
Tierney, No given name, 123
Tinnon, Susan, 37
Tipton, Sarah Jane 1959, 132
Tipton, Wellstood White, 132
Tittsworth, No given name, 82
Todd, Loren, 161
Tregoning, John M., 133
Tregoning, Robert, 133
Tschiffely, Frederick L., 109
Tucker, Joseph Lester, 49
Tucker, Shirley 1952, 49
Turner, Jane E., 199
Turner, Maggie, 37
Turpin, Laura, 143
Tydings, Elizabeth Belt, 14, 17
Tydings, Margaret, 195

—U—

Ulmer, Louis S., 97
Umberger, No given name, 149
Unglesbee, Rebecca 1859, 192
Uplands, 10

—V—

Van Glabeke, Eric Leopold 1924, 62
Vandorf, Kathryn Ann 1951, 118
Vedder, Annie E., 35
Venable, McDowell R., 36
Venable, Susan 1824, 34
Venable, William H., 34

Vickroy, Donna Lynn 1958, 128, 152
Vickroy, No given name, 128, 152

—W—

Wade, Caroline, 36
Wade, Mary Ann, 37
Wade, Walter, 37
Wagner, Clark Matthew 1961, 131
Wagner, James Francis, 131
Wagner, Matthew 1995, 131
Wagner, Shannon 1993, 131
Waldron, Dora, 161
Walker, Elizabeth m/1786, 196
Walker, Eugene V., 194
Walker, John, 198
Walker, John Wesley 1849, 148
Walker, Lula B. 1870, 148
Walker, Mark Lawrence, 196
Walker, McKendree 1870, 115
Walker, William Ralph, 196
Walker, William Ralph 1905, 115
Wallach, Bessie T. 1892, 134
Walnut Grove, 26, 30
Walter, Agnes Jeanette 1930, 117
Wandishin, John, 137
Ward, Albertis 1883, 121
Ward, Augusta 1888, 121, 122
Ward, Carleton Wendell 1935, 155
Ward, Carrie B. 1873, 175
Ward, David Irvin 1907, 154
Ward, David Lloyd 1957, 155
Ward, Harrison Gilmore 1853, 121
Ward, J. Garnet, 121
Ward, Jennifer 1986, 155
Ward, Lloyd Irvin 1931, 154
Ward, Mary Sybil 1880, 52, 180
Ward, Robert Christopher 1983, 155
Ward, Steven Craig 1967, 155
Ward, Thomas Carleton 1958, 155
Ward, William English, 175
Warfield's Range, 38
Warfield, Alice, 28
Warfield, Albert Gallatin 1817, 30

Warfield, Albert Gallatin, III, 30
Warfield, Albert Gallatin, Jr. 1843, 30
Warfield, Alberta Clay, 28
Warfield, Alexander, 4
Warfield, Alice, 31
Warfield, Alverta, 28
Warfield, Basil T. 1859, 125
Warfield, Beale, 27
Warfield, Beale A., 28
Warfield, Bowie Clagett, 28
Warfield, Camsadel, 28
Warfield, Catherine, 27, 31
Warfield, Diane Louise 1948, 140
Warfield, Donald Elisha 1918, 139
Warfield, Dorothy, 126
Warfield, Edwin, 26, 30, 31
Warfield, Eleanor Amelia, 27
Warfield, Elisha S., 139
Warfield, Elizabeth A. 1841, 46
Warfield, Elizabeth Ann, 32
Warfield, Ellis, 126
Warfield, Emma, 28
Warfield, Ethel P. V., 139
Warfield, Frances, 31
Warfield, Gassaway Watkins, 28
Warfield, Gassaway Watkins 1846, 31
Warfield, Georgietta, 28
Warfield, James Harvey 1947, 139
Warfield, James Paul, 111
Warfield, Jason Edward 1979, 62
Warfield, Jennifer Lynn 1987, 140
Warfield, John, 26, 31
Warfield, Joshua, 30
Warfield, Joshua Nicholas 1845, 31
Warfield, Joshua Nicholas, Jr., 31
Warfield, Kristin Leeann 1984, 62
Warfield, Margaret, 31
Warfield, Margaret G., 31
Warfield, Marshall T., 31
Warfield, Mary, 22
Warfield, Merhle Wayne 1950, 62
Warfield, Norman, 31
Warfield, Rachel, 31

Warfield, Raymond Lafayette, 125
Warfield, Raymond Lafayette, Jr., 126
Warfield, Richard, 188
Warfield, Roderick, 7, 38
Warfield, Rosalba, 28
Warfield, Sarah Elizabeth 1981, 140
Warfield, William Ridgely, 27
Warfield, William Ridgely, Jr., 28
Warhime, Roxanne Marie 1962, 69
Warman, Frances Hanstep, 198
Warman, Mary, 9
Warman, Stephen, 9
Warnick, Gail, 63
Warnick, No given name, 63
Warnick, Susan, 63
Warren, Basil, 18
Warrenfelz, Connie L., 70
Waskey, Melvin T., 59
Waters, Franklin, 127
Waters, William, 105
Watkins Hope, 2
Watkins, A. Broadhurst 1906, 193
Watkins, A. Guy 1897, 176
Watkins, A. H., 193, 194
Watkins, Abraham 1793, 25
Watkins, Ada E. 1880, 80
Watkins, Ada Frances 1911, 51
Watkins, Ada Weisenfels 1852, 187
Watkins, Addie 1902, 63
Watkins, Addie Sophronia 1875, 127
Watkins, Agnes, 133
Watkins, Agnes E. 1862, 57, 93
Watkins, Agnes S. 1919, 114
Watkins, Airy C. 1853, 84
Watkins, Albert B. 1906, 193
Watkins, Albert Dewey 1899, 55
Watkins, Albert G., 24
Watkins, Albert James 1892, 39
Watkins, Albert Lewellys 1922, 61, 184
Watkins, Albina, 31

Watkins, Alburn H. 1862, 94
Watkins, Aleatha 1800, 45
Watkins, Alexander F. 1906, 182
Watkins, Alexandria Florida 1906, 182
Watkins, Alfred 1856, 191
Watkins, Alfred C. 1862, 165
Watkins, Alfred W. 1864, 44
Watkins, Alfred Woodfield 1906, 117
Watkins, Alice B. 1860, 78
Watkins, Alice Johnston 1849, 36
Watkins, Alice M. 1866, 44
Watkins, Alice Olivia, 158
Watkins, Alice V. m/1886, 193
Watkins, Allen H. 1862, 94
Watkins, Alma O., 184
Watkins, Alonzo 1896, 56
Watkins, Alonzo Claggett 1867, 124
Watkins, Alpha 1803, 57, 91, 93, 103, 107, 112, 123, 127, 132, 144
Watkins, Alpha 1900, 109
Watkins, Alta Viola 1907, 178
Watkins, Alton L., 193
Watkins, Alton L., Jr., 193
Watkins, Alverta, 106
Watkins, Alvin Rudell 1921, 67
Watkins, Alvin Rudell, Jr. 1946, 67
Watkins, Amanda, 29, 30
Watkins, Amanda 1841, 47, 147
Watkins, Amanda C. 1871, 56
Watkins, Amanda E. 1836, 86
Watkins, Amanda J. m/1912, 193
Watkins, Amanda m/1835, 198
Watkins, Amanda Zerah 1893, 77
Watkins, Amelia May 1903, 182
Watkins, Amos F. 1890, 77
Watkins, Amy C. 1844, 147
Watkins, Andrew, 24
Watkins, Andrew A. 1882, 193
Watkins, Angie I. 1890, 108
Watkins, Ann, 3
Watkins, Ann 1720, 10

Watkins, Ann 1730, 21
Watkins, Ann 1737, 3
Watkins, Ann 1778, 41
Watkins, Ann 1822, 85
Watkins, Ann 1878, 35
Watkins, Ann D. 1895, 94
Watkins, Ann Dorcas 1862, 149
Watkins, Ann Elizabeth, 12, 27
Watkins, Ann M., 9, 15
Watkins, Ann Rebecca 1884, 39
Watkins, Anna Louise 1903, 55
Watkins, Anna May 1891, 110
Watkins, Anna Reba 1908, 64
Watkins, Anna S. 1876, 191
Watkins, Anne 1719, 15
Watkins, Anne 1795, 6
Watkins, Annie C. 1899, 192
Watkins, Annie D. 1864, 49
Watkins, Annie E. 1872, 56
Watkins, Annie E. 1876, 80
Watkins, Annie E. m/1895, 193
Watkins, Annie L. 1863, 165
Watkins, Annie Loree 1906, 126
Watkins, Annie S. 1847, 191, 193
Watkins, Anny d/1808, 193
Watkins, Antonia C. 1860, 149
Watkins, Ara A. 1790, 42
Watkins, Ara Ann 1814, 53, 56, 92, 104
Watkins, Archer Brett 1895, 110
Watkins, Archibald Brett 1895, 110
Watkins, Archibald m/1799, 193
Watkins, Archibald Washington, 32
Watkins, Arey, 195
Watkins, Arey m/1855, 193
Watkins, Ariana 1799, 25
Watkins, Arthur 1876, 177
Watkins, Arthur Leonard, Jr. 1912, 178
Watkins, Arthur Leroy 1945, 186
Watkins, Arthur Linthicum 1885, 134
Watkins, Arthur Linthicum, Jr. 1912, 135

Watkins, Arthur Reese, 97
Watkins, Asa Hull, 98
Watkins, Audrey Jean 1927, 77
Watkins, Augustus 1850, 76
Watkins, Avie C., 111
Watkins, Barbara, 111
Watkins, Barbara Ann, 176
Watkins, Barbara Ann 1938, 63
Watkins, Barry Kenneth 1952, 193
Watkins, Basil 1701, 198
Watkins, Basil Gaither 1804, 25
Watkins, Bates Ewing 1894, 77
Watkins, Belle P. 1896, 114
Watkins, Benjamin, 188
Watkins, Benjamin 1759, 11
Watkins, Benjamin 1762, 14
Watkins, Benjamin 1802, 193
Watkins, Benjamin B. 1788, 12
Watkins, Benjamin Franklin 1844,
    106, 127
Watkins, Benjamin, Dr., 190
Watkins, Benjamin, III 1877, 190
Watkins, Benjamin, IV 1903, 190
Watkins, Benjamin, Jr. m/1870,
    190
Watkins, Bernard Lee 1887, 88
Watkins, Bernard Lee 1960, 67
Watkins, Bertha 1889, 85
Watkins, Bertha Catherine 1900,
    56
Watkins, Bertha E. 1872, 194
Watkins, Bessie 1880, 134
Watkins, Bessie 1923, 108
Watkins, Bessie K. 1899, 115
Watkins, Bessie May 1884, 83
Watkins, Bessie Myrtle 1888, 130
Watkins, Bettie M. 1866, 106
Watkins, Betty Jane, 176
Watkins, Betty Lee 1924, 62
Watkins, Beverly Elizabeth 1956,
    155
Watkins, Blanche, 116, 117
Watkins, Blanche Sheridan 1893,
    44
Watkins, Bonaparte, 26
Watkins, Bradford Lee 1955, 111

Watkins, Bradley 1870, 150, 156
Watkins, Bradley Ellsworth 1947,
    99
Watkins, Bradley G. 1877, 128
Watkins, Bradley Mitchell 1974,
    99
Watkins, Bradley Parker 1931, 158
Watkins, Brenda Lee 1952, 61
Watkins, Bruce Allen 1948, 111
Watkins, Bruce Edward 1957, 62
Watkins, Burton 1851, 168
Watkins, Caleb, 53
Watkins, Caleb 1818, 57
Watkins, Caleb H. 1816, 53, 54
Watkins, Calvin Samuel 1905, 50,
    70
Watkins, Camsadel, 27
Watkins, Carlton T. 1914, 155
Watkins, Carol Lee 1953, 114
Watkins, Caroline, 30
Watkins, Caroline 1804, 27, 172
Watkins, Caroline Clark 1870, 51
Watkins, Caroline E. 1869, 88
Watkins, Carrie, 185
Watkins, Carrie E. m/1894, 193
Watkins, Carrie G. 1873, 177
Watkins, Carrie G. m/1889, 193
Watkins, Carrie L. 1892, 192
Watkins, Cary G., 177
Watkins, Catharine M. 1870, 95
Watkins, Catharine P. 1857, 198
Watkins, Catherine, 94, 189
Watkins, Catherine E. 1847, 35
Watkins, Catherine J. m/1861, 193
Watkins, Catherine Jemima 1891,
    48
Watkins, Catherine Marie 1963,
    50
Watkins, Cecil V. 1884, 193
Watkins, Celeste P., 115
Watkins, Charity A. 1838, 57, 92
Watkins, Charles A. 1849, 167
Watkins, Charles A. 1874, 191
Watkins, Charles Edward 1914,
    113

Watkins, Edgar M. 1869, 106
Watkins, Edgar P. 1853, 36
Watkins, Edith M. 1875, 177
Watkins, Edith M. m/1890, 194
Watkins, Edith Maude 1882, 167
Watkins, Edith Pearl 1912, 159
Watkins, Edmund 1845, 46
Watkins, Edna C. 1897, 184
Watkins, Edna V., 158
Watkins, Edna Vernonice 1916, 77
Watkins, Edward, 3
Watkins, Edward 1867, 58, 194
Watkins, Edward E., 177
Watkins, Edward E. 1861, 48
Watkins, Edward Evan 1906, 162
Watkins, Edward G. d/1941, 189
Watkins, Edward King 1837, 105,
  123
Watkins, Edward Levi 1911, 90
Watkins, Edward Taylor, 161, 163
Watkins, Elbert L. 1888, 44
Watkins, Eleanor, 27
Watkins, Eleanor 1800, 11
Watkins, Eleanor 1853, 168
Watkins, Eleanor Elizabeth 1769,
  12
Watkins, Eleanor Jane 1887, 110
Watkins, Eleanor Rebecca 1919,
  77
Watkins, Eleanora Evans 1873,
  190
Watkins, Eli, 189
Watkins, Elizabeth, 30, 181, 186,
  189
Watkins, Elizabeth 1693, 9, 14
Watkins, Elizabeth 1715, 10
Watkins, Elizabeth 1727, 17
Watkins, Elizabeth 1748, 23
Watkins, Elizabeth 1760, 14
Watkins, Elizabeth 1780, 41
Watkins, Elizabeth 1801, 15, 21
Watkins, Elizabeth A. 1805, 91, 92
Watkins, Elizabeth A. 1841, 106
Watkins, Elizabeth B. 1848, 171
Watkins, Elizabeth Gaither 1802,
  25

Watkins, Elizabeth Hall 1811, 47,
  80, 81
Watkins, Elizabeth Hope, 185
Watkins, Elizabeth J. 1880, 178
Watkins, Elizabeth L. m/1846, 199
Watkins, Elizabeth m/1795, 197
Watkins, Elizabeth m/1807, 194
Watkins, Elizabeth m/1866, 194
Watkins, Elizabeth Sellman 1808,
  12
Watkins, Ella M. 1858, 78
Watkins, Ella May, 167
Watkins, Ella May 1879, 167
Watkins, Ella May m/1896, 194
Watkins, Ella May m/1899, 194
Watkins, Ellen 1818, 166
Watkins, Ellen Elizabeth, 29
Watkins, Ellen J. 1887, 110
Watkins, Ellen L. 1852, 43
Watkins, Ellen M. 1858, 78
Watkins, Ellen R. 1867, 107
Watkins, Ellen V. 1870, 109
Watkins, Elmon Everett 1863, 54
Watkins, Elmore Everett 1863, 54
Watkins, Eloise Nadine 1925, 49
Watkins, Elsie M. 1869, 57, 93
Watkins, Elsie N. 1869, 105
Watkins, Elvirah Ann, 188
Watkins, Emily Catherine 1903,
  70
Watkins, Emily Dawn 1981, 61
Watkins, Emily J. 1841, 83
Watkins, Emma Lee 1890, 90
Watkins, Emory Thomas 1879,
  183
Watkins, Emory William 1911,
  183
Watkins, Enoch S. 1870, 44
Watkins, Erma Sophronia 1903,
  126
Watkins, Ernest, 162
Watkins, Ernest C. 1885, 184
Watkins, Ernest C. 1927, 134
Watkins, Ernest E., 49
Watkins, Esther Blanche 1883,
  106

Watkins, Ethel, 90
Watkins, Ethel Maude 1886, 135
Watkins, Etta May 1883, 108
Watkins, Etta Viola 1910, 60
Watkins, Eugenia Elizabeth 1843, 166
Watkins, Eva Louise 1894, 110
Watkins, Evan R., 163
Watkins, Eveline K. 1846, 57, 93
Watkins, Evelyn Eader 1924, 194
Watkins, Fannie E. 1913, 115
Watkins, Fannie Frank 1869, 127
Watkins, Fannie G. 1868, 78
Watkins, Fannie H. 1848, 165
Watkins, Fannie Z. m/1889, 194
Watkins, Faye Huntington 1894, 124
Watkins, Fayette, 25
Watkins, Fillmore C. 1852, 182
Watkins, Flora Elizabeth 1900, 128, 152
Watkins, Florence C. 1886, 191
Watkins, Florence Edward 1870, 127
Watkins, Florida B. 1877, 87
Watkins, Flossie I. 1892, 94
Watkins, Flossie Ivoy 1892, 194
Watkins, Foster, 106
Watkins, Frances, 2, 161
Watkins, Frances 1723, 10
Watkins, Frances E. 1870, 127
Watkins, Frances Marian 1895, 135
Watkins, Frances V. 1858, 94
Watkins, Frances Virginia 1858, 94
Watkins, Francis, 1, 2, 3, 189, 194
Watkins, Francis 1741, 194
Watkins, Francis 1857, 168
Watkins, Francis Dungar 1847, 33
Watkins, Francis m/1769, 194
Watkins, Francis T. 1854, 88
Watkins, Francis Thomas 1854, 88
Watkins, Francis Washington 1858, 95
Watkins, Frank F. 1900, 191

Watkins, Franklin Wilbur 1959, 118
Watkins, Franklin Wilbur, Jr. 1978, 119
Watkins, Frederick B. 1884, 110
Watkins, Gail M. 1951, 146
Watkins, Garrett Webster 1872, 132
Watkins, Gassaway, 24, 172
Watkins, Gassaway 1695, 9, 15, 21
Watkins, Gassaway 1723, 15
Watkins, Gassaway 1731, 21
Watkins, Gassaway 1752, Colonel, 7, 25, 38, 172
Watkins, Gassaway 1771, 22
Watkins, Gassaway 1772, 41, 82, 188
Watkins, Gassaway 1781, 33
Watkins, Gassaway 1789, 42
Watkins, Gassaway 1807, 171
Watkins, Gassaway d/1737, 194
Watkins, Gassaway m/1784, 194
Watkins, Gassaway m/1826, 194
Watkins, Gassaway, Lieutenant, 26
Watkins, George 1868, 173
Watkins, George E. 1848, 43
Watkins, George Lacy 1922, 111
Watkins, George Nevlon 1946, 61
Watkins, George Orlando 1864, 123
Watkins, George Rust 1840, 32
Watkins, George Simpson 1868, 173
Watkins, George Victor 1904, 161
Watkins, George W. 1851, 165
Watkins, George W. 1864, 194
Watkins, George W. 1879, 191
Watkins, George Washington 1835, 32
Watkins, George Washington 1869, 161
Watkins, Georgia A. 1892, 192
Watkins, Georgia May 1957, 118
Watkins, Georgianna 1856, 44
Watkins, Georgianna 1873, 192
Watkins, Gerald W., 185

Watkins, Gerrianne 1961, 119
Watkins, Gertie 1873, 191
Watkins, Gertrude, 114
Watkins, Gladys, 176
Watkins, Gladys 1899, 56
Watkins, Gladys D. 1894, 114
Watkins, Gladys Irene 1916, 90
Watkins, Glenda Eileen 1950, 67
Watkins, Gloria Jean 1944, 194
Watkins, Grace, 133
Watkins, Grace Alice 1907, 154
Watkins, Grace Louise 1891, 135
Watkins, Grace Olive 1907, 154
Watkins, Grafton, 53
Watkins, Grafton 1823, 74, 79
Watkins, Granville W. 1906, 133
Watkins, Greenberry 1827, 188
Watkins, Greenbury 1853, 87
Watkins, Greenbury M. 1808, 33
Watkins, Grover Cleveland 1886,
   106
Watkins, Grover Sim 1892, 54
Watkins, Guy D. 1908, 115, 117
Watkins, Guy Hansen, 176
Watkins, Hamilton 1847, 162
Watkins, Hannah, 100
Watkins, Harold, 162
Watkins, Harold Hall 1901, 116
Watkins, Harold Willard 1919,
   155
Watkins, Harriet, 26, 27
Watkins, Harriet 1844, 106
Watkins, Harriet 1874, 163
Watkins, Harriet Roberta 1872,
   127
Watkins, Harriett A. 1857, 149
Watkins, Harry 1858, 36
Watkins, Harry 1874, 163
Watkins, Harry B. 1888, 184
Watkins, Harry Everett 1910, 194
Watkins, Harry G. 1874, 88
Watkins, Harry L. 1872, 116
Watkins, Harry W., 29
Watkins, Harry W. 1888, 191
Watkins, Harvey C. 1881, 129

Watkins, Harvey Lansdale 1888,
   89
Watkins, Harwood, 29
Watkins, Hattie 1873, 162
Watkins, Hattie G. 1882, 52
Watkins, Helen, 186, 190
Watkins, Helen 1873, 35
Watkins, Helen Elizabeth 1917, 66
Watkins, Helen Maria 1844, 32
Watkins, Helen R. 1881, 106
Watkins, Henrietta m/1799, 194
Watkins, Henrietta V. 1849, 177
Watkins, Henry, 29
Watkins, Henry 1843, 189
Watkins, Henry Clay, 194
Watkins, Henry Clay 1898, 176
Watkins, Henry Hall Howard
   Middleton 1799, 11
Watkins, Henry L. 1872, 116
Watkins, Henry Thomas 1845, 187
Watkins, Hepsie P. 1863, 78
Watkins, Herbert A. d/1957, 185
Watkins, Herbert Hamilton 1876,
   133
Watkins, Herbert Taylor 1910, 161
Watkins, Herbert W., 134
Watkins, Herman 1895, 90
Watkins, Hester 1729, 11
Watkins, Hester Blanche 1883,
   106
Watkins, Hester m/1805, 195
Watkins, Hezekiah c/1862, 48
Watkins, Hilda Estell 1911, 184
Watkins, Hilda W. 1892, 184
Watkins, Howard H. 1884, 13
Watkins, Howard K. m/1916, 185
Watkins, Howard R. d/1960, 185
Watkins, Howard Raymond 1903,
   157
Watkins, Humphrey 1867, 192
Watkins, I. E., 77
Watkins, Ida Belle m/1894, 195
Watkins, Ida C. 1872, 107, 109
Watkins, Ida Louise 1925, 119
Watkins, Ida M. m/1884, 195
Watkins, Ida P. 1873, 95

Watkins, Ignatius m/1793, 195
Watkins, India Marie 1921, 185
Watkins, Inza Isidore, 163
Watkins, Ira D. 1885, 177
Watkins, Ira Dorsey, 90
Watkins, Ira Dorsey 1883, 97
Watkins, Ira H. 1878, 88
Watkins, Irene, 183
Watkins, Iris Rebecca 1914, 178
Watkins, Irma 1903, 126
Watkins, Irvin B. 1912, 195
Watkins, Irving Bromwell 1913, 56
Watkins, Isaac, 25
Watkins, Isaac Jones 1788, 24
Watkins, Isabella Virginia 1848, 147
Watkins, Isaiah W. 1831, 195
Watkins, Israel, 189
Watkins, Iva May 1897, 151
Watkins, Ivy May 1897, 151
Watkins, J. Anita, 184
Watkins, J. L., 51
Watkins, J. W., 43
Watkins, Jack, 134, 162
Watkins, James, 1, 2
Watkins, James 1783, 187
Watkins, James 1829, 188
Watkins, James 1884, 192
Watkins, James Alan 1946, 163
Watkins, James Barnes 1814, 187
Watkins, James d/1842, 46
Watkins, James Edgar 1847, 187
Watkins, James Edward 1842, 166
Watkins, James Edward 1925, 111
Watkins, James Elwood, 37
Watkins, James G., 197
Watkins, James Gilford, 110
Watkins, James H., 188
Watkins, James H. 1869, 55
Watkins, James Haller 1888, 145
Watkins, James m/1757, 195
Watkins, James m/1788, 195
Watkins, James Norman 1885, 110
Watkins, James Oliver 1921, 95
Watkins, James Russell 1908, 56

Watkins, James W. 1864, 95
Watkins, James Willard 1848, 107, 144
Watkins, Jan Parker 1960, 158
Watkins, Jane 1732, 11
Watkins, Jane 1743, 189
Watkins, Jane A., 114
Watkins, Jane D. 1731, 15
Watkins, Jane m/1714, 195
Watkins, Jane m/1766, 195
Watkins, Janet, 134
Watkins, Janice Pearl 1917, 98
Watkins, Jason P. 1852, 165
Watkins, Jay Bradley, 158
Watkins, Jean, 189
Watkins, Jeanette Alvene 1942, 163
Watkins, Jeannie, 176
Watkins, Jennie, 117
Watkins, Jennie E. 1864, 194
Watkins, Jennie E. 1867, 115
Watkins, Jepe 1821, 161
Watkins, Jerauld Alva 1940, 163
Watkins, Jeremiah 1743, 22, 41, 42, 82, 91, 93
Watkins, Jeremiah 1787, 42, 52, 74
Watkins, Jeremiah 1814, 171
Watkins, Jeremiah Columbus 1841, 54, 57, 61, 67, 70
Watkins, Jeremiah M. 1881, 60
Watkins, Jeremiah m/1842, 195
Watkins, Jeremiah m/1855, 193, 195
Watkins, Jeremiah, Jr. 1765, 41
Watkins, Jesse 1872, 162
Watkins, Jesse H.1893, 108
Watkins, Jessica, 190
Watkins, Jessie 1874, 56
Watkins, Jessie Nadine 1921, 99
Watkins, Jessie P., 145
Watkins, Jetson, 14
Watkins, Joan Marie 1943, 139
Watkins, Joan Marie 1949, 117
Watkins, Joanna 1848, 54
Watkins, Joanne, 176

245

Watkins, Julia Ann 1850, 43
Watkins, Julia Anna 1794, 15, 21
Watkins, Julia Elizabeth, 133
Watkins, Julia M. 1888, 192
Watkins, Juliann 1850, 43
Watkins, Julianna m/1811, 195
Watkins, Julie, 185
Watkins, Juliet 1802, 172
Watkins, Julius, 149
Watkins, Julius 1802, 27, 172
Watkins, Julius 1833, 46, 47
Watkins, Julius Monroe 1876, 51
Watkins, June Marie, 56
Watkins, Karen, 134
Watkins, Kate, 29
Watkins, Kate Cochran 1853, 33
Watkins, Katherine Welsh 1871, 190
Watkins, Kathryn Marie 1978, 61
Watkins, Kelsey Lynn 1992, 178
Watkins, Kenneth, 125, 161, 162
Watkins, Kenneth Leroy 1950, 118
Watkins, Kezia, 189
Watkins, Kim Allen 1955, 163
Watkins, Kristina Marie 1973, 118
Watkins, L. Elizabeth, 134
Watkins, Laura, 29
Watkins, Laura Blanche 1884, 162
Watkins, Laura C. 1877, 191
Watkins, Laura Dorcas 1858, 149
Watkins, Laura G. 1877, 13
Watkins, Laura G. m/1903, 195
Watkins, Laura Louise 1812, 29
Watkins, Laura V., 167
Watkins, Laura V. 1847, 167
Watkins, Laura V. 1857, 109
Watkins, Laura V. 1859, 57, 93, 105
Watkins, Laura V. 1884, 168
Watkins, Laura V. m/1875, 195
Watkins, Laura Victoria 1848, 13
Watkins, Lavander W. 1852, 195
Watkins, Lavinia 1857, 78
Watkins, Lawrence 1893, 162
Watkins, Lawrence Clark, 24
Watkins, Lawson Clark, 24

Watkins, Leah Jane 1874, 133
Watkins, Lelia Edward 1907, 89
Watkins, Lena 1892, 166
Watkins, Lena Elizabeth 1898, 156
Watkins, Leonard, Major, 193
Watkins, Leonard, Sergeant, 12
Watkins, Leroy Alva 1916, 163
Watkins, Lester Basil 1910, 64
Watkins, Lester Edsel 1927, 49
Watkins, Lester Steele 1895, 49
Watkins, Levi Lewis 1839, 105
Watkins, Levin Belt 1806, 46, 47
Watkins, Lewis Jones, 29
Watkins, Lewis Jones 1803, 196
Watkins, Leyton m/1841, 196
Watkins, Lillian May 1875, 128
Watkins, Lillian Maybelle 1922, 135
Watkins, Lillie B. 1874, 87
Watkins, Lillie May 1886, 89
Watkins, Linda, 134
Watkins, Linda Diane 1950, 61
Watkins, Linda L., 133
Watkins, Lisa Diane 1983, 61
Watkins, Lizzie J. 1867, 115
Watkins, Lodge d/1973, 111
Watkins, Lois, 133
Watkins, Lois Allene 1915, 161
Watkins, Lois Evelyn 1931, 65
Watkins, Lois Virginia 1914, 98
Watkins, Lola Leanna 1897, 84
Watkins, Lorenzo 1878, 191
Watkins, Lorenzo Dallas 1835, 105, 112, 116, 119
Watkins, Lorenzo Dow 1807, 53, 56, 92, 104
Watkins, Lorraine, 196
Watkins, Lorraine E. 1906, 115
Watkins, Lorraine Virginia 1912, 89
Watkins, Lottie F. 1898, 78
Watkins, Louis 1880, 174
Watkins, Louis Fillmore 1879, 183
Watkins, Louis Fillmore, Jr., 184
Watkins, Louis J. m/1879, 196
Watkins, Louisa 1886, 193

Watkins, Louisa Agnes 1874, 58
Watkins, Louisa H. 1896, 197
Watkins, Louise 1899, 184
Watkins, Louise L. 1879, 48
Watkins, Louise Stewart, 185
Watkins, Lucian Barnes 1859, 188
Watkins, Lucille 1899, 184
Watkins, Lucinda 1844, 83
Watkins, Lucinda 1845, 189
Watkins, Lucinda 1875, 58
Watkins, Lucinda 1899, 184
Watkins, Lucinda A. 1842, 179
Watkins, Lucretia A. 1829, 43
Watkins, Lucy 1866, 173
Watkins, Lucy B. m/1817, 196
Watkins, Lucy Marian 1914, 65
Watkins, Lucy S. 1823, 171
Watkins, Lula Mae, 126
Watkins, Luther 1845, 166
Watkins, Luther L., 166
Watkins, Luther M. 1831, 57, 93, 104
Watkins, Luther M. 1845, 166
Watkins, Lyde A. 1849, 86
Watkins, Lydia A. 1870, 191
Watkins, Lydia Isabella 1843, 13
Watkins, Lydia m/1698, 198
Watkins, M. C., 197
Watkins, Mabel A. 1909, 133
Watkins, Madeline, 184
Watkins, Maggie, 36
Watkins, Maggie L. 1867, 106
Watkins, Maggie m/1917, 196
Watkins, Malcolm 1900, 191
Watkins, Malissa J. 1878, 106
Watkins, Mamie Alice 1886, 84
Watkins, Mamie Cleveland 1884, 47
Watkins, Manelia E. m/1864, 196
Watkins, Manona E. 1873, 144
Watkins, Marcella K. 1907, 196
Watkins, Marcellous 1886, 60
Watkins, Margaret, 53, 57, 188
Watkins, Margaret 1722, 15
Watkins, Margaret 1744, 22
Watkins, Margaret 1765, 37

Watkins, Margaret 1767, 14
Watkins, Margaret 1770, 41
Watkins, Margaret 1776, 41
Watkins, Margaret 1798, 45
Watkins, Margaret 1805, 33
Watkins, Margaret 1824, 24
Watkins, Margaret 1842, 187
Watkins, Margaret 1857, 87
Watkins, Margaret A. 1841, 95
Watkins, Margaret E. 1917, 114
Watkins, Margaret E. m/1937, 196
Watkins, Margaret Elizabeth 1911, 150
Watkins, Margaret Ellen 1917, 114
Watkins, Margaret Florence 1862, 112, 119
Watkins, Margaret Gassaway, 30
Watkins, Margaret Gassaway 1765, 22
Watkins, Margaret Gassaway 1767, 23
Watkins, Margaret J. 1893, 114
Watkins, Margaret Jones m/1817, 24
Watkins, Margaret L. 1844, 147
Watkins, Margaret L. m/1878, 196
Watkins, Margaret L. V. m/1878, 196
Watkins, Margaret m/1755, 196
Watkins, Margaret m/1789, 196
Watkins, Margaret m/1794, 196
Watkins, Margaret m/1795, 196
Watkins, Margaret R. 1870, 192
Watkins, Margaret Rae 1919, 98
Watkins, Margaret W., 24
Watkins, Maria L. A. 1875, 174
Watkins, Maria m/1820, 196
Watkins, Marie Columbia, 124
Watkins, Marion Edmonston Berry 1906, 190
Watkins, Marjorie Ann, 157
Watkins, Marjorie B. 1904, 111
Watkins, Marjorie Nell 1922, 161
Watkins, Marsh 1869, 78
Watkins, Marsha Ann, 163

Watkins, Marsha Lynn 1958, 111
Watkins, Marshall Crittenden
  1857, 177
Watkins, Marshall J. 1900, 94
Watkins, Marshall T. 1886, 177
Watkins, Martha 1771, 37
Watkins, Martha 1838, 36
Watkins, Martha 1847, 76
Watkins, Martha 1872, 191
Watkins, Martha A. 1878, 51
Watkins, Martha E. 1847, 43
Watkins, Martha Elizabeth 1838,
  189
Watkins, Martha Joanne 1947, 155
Watkins, Martha L. 1832, 13
Watkins, Martha m/1737, 196
Watkins, Martha P. 1858, 94
Watkins, Martha P. 1867, 95
Watkins, Martha P. 1868, 95
Watkins, Martha T. 1839, 57, 93,
  104
Watkins, Martha Virginia 1859, 96
Watkins, Martin Spaulding 1856,
  188
Watkins, Mary, 181
Watkins, Mary 1725, 11
Watkins, Mary 1727, 15
Watkins, Mary 1761, 11
Watkins, Mary 1783, 171
Watkins, Mary 1793, 37
Watkins, Mary 1830, 162
Watkins, Mary 1840, 36
Watkins, Mary 1842, 192
Watkins, Mary 1877, 86
Watkins, Mary 1882, 193
Watkins, Mary A. 1898, 192
Watkins, Mary Ann 1756, 14
Watkins, Mary Ann 1820, 33
Watkins, Mary Avondale 1878,
  133, 137
Watkins, Mary B., 25
Watkins, Mary B. 1861, 112
Watkins, Mary C. 1848, 57, 93
Watkins, Mary Clare, 188
Watkins, Mary d/1906, 37
Watkins, Mary E., 115, 176, 178

Watkins, Mary E. 1837, 83
Watkins, Mary E. 1846, 85
Watkins, Mary E. 1865, 165
Watkins, Mary E. 1871, 106
Watkins, Mary Elizabeth, 97, 183
Watkins, Mary Elizabeth 1867,
  115
Watkins, Mary Ellen 1829, 13
Watkins, Mary Francis 1873, 51
Watkins, Mary J. m/1890, 196
Watkins, Mary Jean 1931, 63
Watkins, Mary Jo, 114
Watkins, Mary Julia 1872, 173
Watkins, Mary L., 177
Watkins, Mary Laura, 181
Watkins, Mary Lee, 185
Watkins, Mary Louise 1850, 33
Watkins, Mary Louise Brocchus,
  29
Watkins, Mary Luana 1870, 124
Watkins, Mary M. 1854, 43
Watkins, Mary m/1780, 196
Watkins, Mary m/1786, 196
Watkins, Mary m/1792, 196
Watkins, Mary m/1794, 196
Watkins, Mary m/1797, 196
Watkins, Mary R. 1868, 95
Watkins, Mary Rebecca 1905, 154
Watkins, Mary S. 1829, 103
Watkins, Mary Virginia 1927, 49
Watkins, Mary Winifred 1876, 162
Watkins, Matilda, 168
Watkins, Matilda 1820, 161
Watkins, Matilda m/1809, 196
Watkins, Matilda R. 1838, 147
Watkins, Maude, 29
Watkins, Maude Ethel 1886, 135
Watkins, Maude G. 1890, 166
Watkins, Maurice 1867, 128, 150
Watkins, May, 117
Watkins, May B. 1873, 106
Watkins, May Belle m/1882, 196
Watkins, May Grace, 111
Watkins, Maybelle Geraldine
  1903, 100
Watkins, Maynard 1890, 110

Watkins, Maynard D. 1891, 145
Watkins, Maynard D., Jr. 1928,
146
Watkins, Maynard Wilson 1894,
48
Watkins, Mazie Marie 1891, 110
Watkins, Mazie Noreen 1899, 158
Watkins, McKendree 1833, 162
Watkins, McKinley H. 1896, 108
Watkins, Melia May 1903, 182
Watkins, Melvin E. 1879, 108
Watkins, Merhle 1896, 162
Watkins, Michael Craig 1964, 178
Watkins, Michael James 1962, 164
Watkins, Mildred Colleen 1933,
65
Watkins, Mildred Eveline 1914,
159
Watkins, Mildred Lolita 1917, 163
Watkins, Mildred M., 48
Watkins, Mildred M. m/1943, 196
Watkins, Mildred V. 1913, 195
Watkins, Millard Fillmore 1856,
32, 39
Watkins, Milton 1873, 58, 70
Watkins, Milton B. 1845, 162
Watkins, Minnie E. 1878, 182
Watkins, Minnie Hazel 1900, 115
Watkins, Miranda 1828, 162
Watkins, Missouri E., 78
Watkins, Mordecai 1851, 87
Watkins, Morgan H. 1874, 51
Watkins, Morgan Herbert 1882,
83, 90
Watkins, Morris 1886, 60
Watkins, Mosehel 1886, 196
Watkins, Myra Lavinia 1896, 55
Watkins, N. B., 193
Watkins, N. Evelyn 1912, 135
Watkins, Nancy Elizabeth 1848,
24
Watkins, Nancy J. 1794, 25
Watkins, Nancy Lee, 50
Watkins, Nancy Louise 1952, 118
Watkins, Nancy m/1797, 196
Watkins, Nancy Raye, 196

Watkins, Nannie G. 1886, 108
Watkins, Naomi m/1806, 196
Watkins, Nathan B. 1826, 165
Watkins, Nathan B., Jr. 1857, 165
Watkins, Nathaniel m/1788, 196
Watkins, Nellie 1878, 127
Watkins, Nellie Irene 1901, 50
Watkins, Nellie Mae 1897, 55
Watkins, Nellie O., 190
Watkins, Nelly, 184
Watkins, Nettie B. 1869, 94
Watkins, Nevlon Marcellous 1917,
60
Watkins, Nicholas, 53
Watkins, Nicholas 1731, 15
Watkins, Nicholas 1737, 12
Watkins, Nicholas 1758, 11
Watkins, Nicholas 1763, 32, 41,
42, 52, 80
Watkins, Nicholas 1771, 23
Watkins, Nicholas 1802, 45
Watkins, Nicholas 1848, 46
Watkins, Nicholas 3rd, Sergeant
1751, 25
Watkins, Nicholas Beall, 23
Watkins, Nicholas d/1794, Major,
196
Watkins, Nicholas Edwin m/1834,
196
Watkins, Nicholas G. m/1798, 197
Watkins, Nicholas I. m/1801, 197
Watkins, Nicholas J., Jr. 1812, 187
Watkins, Nicholas J., Reverend
1784, 187
Watkins, Nicholas m/1782, 187,
196
Watkins, Nicholas m/1786, 196
Watkins, Nicholas m/1801, 197
Watkins, Nicholas m/1806, 196
Watkins, Nicholas O'Bryan 1979,
119
Watkins, Nicholas of Thomas
d/1826, 196
Watkins, Nicholas T., 197
Watkins, Nicholas, Jr. 1722, 17,
22

Watkins, Reuben E. 1864, 175
Watkins, Reuben E. 1865, 44
Watkins, Rezba m/1822, 197
Watkins, Rezin m/1798, 197
Watkins, Rhinaldo 1850, 84
Watkins, Rhoda A. 1829, 74
Watkins, Rhoda J. 1888, 177
Watkins, Richard, 53, 134
Watkins, Richard 1766, 41
Watkins, Richard 1784, 38
Watkins, Richard 1795, 45
Watkins, Richard 1797, 37
Watkins, Richard 1812, 174
Watkins, Richard 1816, 166
Watkins, Richard 1821, 188
Watkins, Richard 1875, 86
Watkins, Richard A. 1866, 181
Watkins, Richard d/1837, 25
Watkins, Richard d/1842, 27, 172
Watkins, Richard G. m/1824, 197
Watkins, Richard Gassaway, 172
Watkins, Richard Gassaway 1794,
    26
Watkins, Richard Jefferson, 181
Watkins, Richard M. 1881, 192
Watkins, Richard m/1695, 197
Watkins, Richard m/1778, 197
Watkins, Richard m/1800, 197
Watkins, Richard m/1813, 197
Watkins, Richard Morgan 1944, 91
Watkins, Richard, Captain, 27, 52
Watkins, Rizpah Norwood 1802,
    168
Watkins, Robert, 66, 197
Watkins, Robert 1882, 86
Watkins, Robert Bart 1859, 88
Watkins, Robert Emory 1842, 32
Watkins, Robert Eugene 1958, 164
Watkins, Robert Lee 1910, 89
Watkins, Robert Lee 1932, 154
Watkins, Robert Lincoln, Dr., 190
Watkins, Robert m/1736, 197
Watkins, Robert Malcolm 1901,
    100
Watkins, Robert Malcolm, Jr.
    1932, 100

Watkins, Robert W. 1837, 35
Watkins, Roberta Eveline 1901,
    157
Watkins, Robin Leigh 1960, 154
Watkins, Roby Selman 1899, 50
Watkins, Rodolphus Grafton 1846,
    44, 175
Watkins, Roland Eugene 1917,
    181
Watkins, Ronald Eugene 1947, 61
Watkins, Ronald L., 97
Watkins, Rose A. 1857, 197
Watkins, Rose Eveline 1915, 98
Watkins, Rosetta 1888, 192
Watkins, Rosetta F. 1849, 177
Watkins, Rosetta May 1879, 51
Watkins, Rosie Elaine 1939, 51,
    70
Watkins, Rosie J. 1900, 194
Watkins, Rosie M. 1898, 49
Watkins, Roy W. 1897, 133
Watkins, Royal P., 190
Watkins, Royce Maynard 1923, 48
Watkins, Royce Maynard, Jr., 49
Watkins, Royce T. 1918, 114
Watkins, Ruby G., 97
Watkins, Rudell Edward 1932, 62
Watkins, Rudolph 1844, 172
Watkins, Rudolph Lewis, Jr. 1874,
    173
Watkins, Rudy Edward 1898, 62
Watkins, Russell, 47
Watkins, Russell C. 1886, 48
Watkins, Russell C. 1912, 97
Watkins, Ruth, 181
Watkins, Ruth 1836, 42
Watkins, Ruth A. 1841, 45
Watkins, Ruth Elizabeth m/1936,
    197
Watkins, Ruth Estelle 1919, 95
Watkins, Ruth Evelyn 1926, 153
Watkins, S. G., 194
Watkins, Sallie B. 1895, 115
Watkins, Sallie V. m/1925, 197
Watkins, Sally, 134
Watkins, Sally Ann, 188

251

Watkins, Sally Disney, 188
Watkins, Sally Fay 1939, 99
Watkins, Sally Virginia, 158
Watkins, Samuel, 189
Watkins, Samuel 1827, 188
Watkins, Samuel 1849, 190
Watkins, Samuel 1877, 127
Watkins, Samuel B. 1807, 147, 149
Watkins, Samuel Brewer 1813, 36
Watkins, Samuel C. 1868, 50, 70
Watkins, Samuel Calvin 1905, 50
Watkins, Samuel m/1757, 197
Watkins, Samuel m/1896, 197
Watkins, Sarah, 2, 25, 188
Watkins, Sarah 1718, 10
Watkins, Sarah 1815, 33
Watkins, Sarah A. 1842, 85
Watkins, Sarah C. 1845, 54
Watkins, Sarah C. 1862, 44
Watkins, Sarah E. 1814, 82, 83
Watkins, Sarah E. 1859, 94
Watkins, Sarah E. 1870, 191
Watkins, Sarah Elizabeth, 188
Watkins, Sarah Elizabeth 1871, 50, 58, 67
Watkins, Sarah Harwood 1771, 12
Watkins, Sarah J. 1819, 147
Watkins, Sarah J. 1869, 94
Watkins, Sarah Louise 1856, 24
Watkins, Sarah R. m/1834, 197
Watkins, Shannon 1966, 100
Watkins, Shannon Marie 1974, 61
Watkins, Sharon Lynn 1958, 154
Watkins, Sheila Marie, 164
Watkins, Shirley, 145
Watkins, Shirley Lee 1933, 63
Watkins, Silas B. 1814, 82, 188
Watkins, Silas Franklin 1853, 177
Watkins, Solomon m/1749, 198
Watkins, Sophia 1792, 37
Watkins, Sophia 1799, 6, 38
Watkins, Sophia m/1827, 198
Watkins, Sophia m/1875, 198
Watkins, Spencer 1844, 35

Watkins, Spencer J. 1864, 57, 93, 105
Watkins, Stacy Elizabeth 1964, 111
Watkins, Stanley, 106
Watkins, Stella A. m/1897, 198
Watkins, Stella Florence 1872, 161
Watkins, Stephanie Ann 1971, 118
Watkins, Stephen 1735, 11
Watkins, Stephen 1758, 14
Watkins, Stephen 1763, 11
Watkins, Stephen 1793, 45
Watkins, Stephen 1824, 42
Watkins, Stephen Edward 1964, 90
Watkins, Stephen Eugene 1947, 198
Watkins, Stephen m/1784, 198
Watkins, Stephen m/1793, 198
Watkins, Stephen R. 1878, 192
Watkins, Steven Edsel 1952, 49
Watkins, Sue Ann 1955, 118
Watkins, Survila Catherine 1839, 175
Watkins, Survila Washington 1841, 175
Watkins, Susan 1800, 53
Watkins, Susan E. 1855, 78
Watkins, Susan G. 1855, 167
Watkins, Susan R. 1845, 83
Watkins, Susanna Ashton 1870, 173
Watkins, Susanna m/1708, 198
Watkins, Susannah, 198
Watkins, Susannah Margaret 1843, 175
Watkins, Susie A. 1881, 184
Watkins, Sylvester 1869, 58, 61
Watkins, T. C. 1859, 198
Watkins, Talmadge Lodge 1891, 113
Watkins, Tammy Sue 1967, 186
Watkins, Thelma, 184
Watkins, Theopholis 1880, 86
Watkins, Thomas, 27, 29, 30, 36, 90, 103, 189, 198

Watkins, Thomas 1736, 22
Watkins, Thomas 1746, 23
Watkins, Thomas 1767, 12
Watkins, Thomas 1769, 171
Watkins, Thomas 1774, 41, 57, 91, 92
Watkins, Thomas 1779, 198
Watkins, Thomas 1798, 13
Watkins, Thomas Andrew 1970, 61
Watkins, Thomas Bascom 1824, 32
Watkins, Thomas Coke 1800, 32
Watkins, Thomas d/1814, 189
Watkins, Thomas Ellsworth 1862, 96, 97
Watkins, Thomas Ellsworth 1922, 98
Watkins, Thomas F. 1854, 88
Watkins, Thomas G., Doctor d/1830, 24, 25
Watkins, Thomas Gassaway, 29
Watkins, Thomas Gassaway 1729, 15, 21
Watkins, Thomas H. 1838, 189
Watkins, Thomas Hunter 1882, 174
Watkins, Thomas J. 1868, 191
Watkins, Thomas Jones 1773, 23
Watkins, Thomas m/1698, 198
Watkins, Thomas m/1738, 198
Watkins, Thomas m/1779, 198
Watkins, Thomas m/1797, 198
Watkins, Thomas m/1799, 198
Watkins, Thomas m/1825, 198
Watkins, Thomas of Thomas 1807, 198
Watkins, Thomas Spencer, 36
Watkins, Thomas Spencer 1769, 33
Watkins, Thomas Spencer d/1897, 37
Watkins, Thomas W. 1823, 198
Watkins, Thomas W. 1834, 36
Watkins, Thomas Worthington 1818, 188

Watkins, Thomas, III 1699, 198
Watkins, Thomas, Jr., 27
Watkins, Thomas, Jr. c.1670, 198
Watkins, Thomas, Jr. m/1835, 198
Watkins, Thompsy, 25
Watkins, Thomsey 1829, 24
Watkins, Timothy Lee 1972, 186
Watkins, Tobias C. 1859, 47
Watkins, Tobias Calvin 1865, 54
Watkins, Tobias of Thomas 1780, 198
Watkins, Townsend, 12
Watkins, Turenne, 7, 27, 38
Watkins, Ulysses G. 1868, 92, 93
Watkins, Unice 1884, 60
Watkins, Uriah Thomas 1851, 177
Watkins, Velma Winifred 1906, 72
Watkins, Vernon Dorsey 1865, 96
Watkins, Vernon Edward 1898, 164
Watkins, Vernon T. 1871, 150, 158
Watkins, Vernon U. S. 1856, 88
Watkins, Vernon W. 1860, 192
Watkins, Vertie, 51
Watkins, Vilora Washington 1841, 175
Watkins, Violett m/1696, 198
Watkins, Virgie I. 1899, 55
Watkins, Virgie Lee 1882, 129, 130
Watkins, Virgil Lloyd 1895, 164
Watkins, Virginia, 94, 134
Watkins, Virginia M., 134
Watkins, Vivy Myrtle 1894, 48
Watkins, W. Maurice m/1887, 198
Watkins, Walter Howard 1879, 128
Watkins, Walter Lee, 125
Watkins, Walter Wilson 1866, 123
Watkins, Wanda Jean 1952, 164
Watkins, Wannie Blanche 1879, 162
Watkins, Watkins 1410, 1
Watkins, Wayne Sellman 1938, 50
Watkins, Wayne Stuart 1968, 91

Watkins, Wendy, 177
Watkins, Wesley W. 1871, 128
Watkins, Wesley Willard 1984, 156
Watkins, White, 36
Watkins, Whitney d/1989, 185
Watkins, Wilbur D., 116
Watkins, Wilbur Day 1900, 117
Watkins, Wilbur Day, Jr. 1923, 117
Watkins, Wilbur E. 1885, 88
Watkins, Wilbur Fiske 1836, 32
Watkins, Wilbur Noah 1900, 133
Watkins, Wilen m/1860, 198
Watkins, Wilfred Morgan 1914, 90
Watkins, Willard R. m/1940, 198
Watkins, William, 11, 30, 133, 188
Watkins, William 1792, 12
Watkins, William 1817, 85
Watkins, William 1832, 105
Watkins, William 1834, 188
Watkins, William 1841, 46
Watkins, William 2nd, 1
Watkins, William A. 1844, 193
Watkins, William A. 1847, 83
Watkins, William A. 1879, 145
Watkins, William A. 1893, 192
Watkins, William Brazelton 1850, 24
Watkins, William C., 176
Watkins, William C. 1870, 175
Watkins, William C. 1878, 80
Watkins, William Clarence 1873, 128
Watkins, William Crawford 1909, 184
Watkins, William D. 1914, 145
Watkins, William d/1539, 1
Watkins, William E., 133
Watkins, William E. 1859, 165
Watkins, William Edward, 89
Watkins, William Edward 1855, 83, 90
Watkins, William Edward 1916, 161

Watkins, William Eldridge 1867, 55
Watkins, William Ernest 1881, 150
Watkins, William Ernest, Jr. 1909, 150
Watkins, William F. 1879, 13
Watkins, William F. 1894, 192
Watkins, William Francis Asbury 1816, 32
Watkins, William H. 1843, 191
Watkins, William H. 1845, 85
Watkins, William H. 1876, 106
Watkins, William Henry 1867, 161, 163
Watkins, William Howard 1918, 185
Watkins, William L. 1918, 85
Watkins, William L. m/1878, 199
Watkins, William Lewis, 164
Watkins, William Lewis 1931, 164
Watkins, William m/1741, 198
Watkins, William m/1779, 198
Watkins, William m/1791, 198
Watkins, William m/1792, 199
Watkins, William m/1799, 199
Watkins, William m/1805, 199
Watkins, William m/1822, 199
Watkins, William Mansfield 1835, 35
Watkins, William Maurice 1902, 152
Watkins, William McKendree 1828, 32, 39
Watkins, William McKendree 1886, 39
Watkins, William O. 1934, 199
Watkins, William Pitt, 25
Watkins, William S. 1878, 85
Watkins, William T. 1863, 163
Watkins, William Thomas 1837, 147, 149, 150, 156, 158
Watkins, William Thomas 1900, 158
Watkins, William W. m/1826, 199